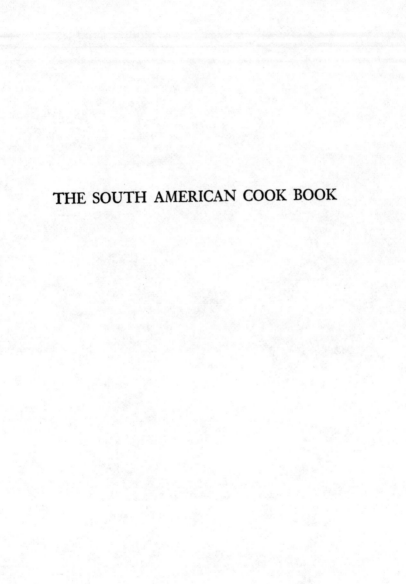

THE SOUTH AMERICAN COOK BOOK

THE SOUTH AMERICAN COOK BOOK

INCLUDING CENTRAL AMERICA, MEXICO AND THE WEST INDIES ☆

BY *Cora, Rose and Bob Brown*

DOVER PUBLICATIONS, INC.
NEW YORK

This Dover edition, first published in 1971, is an
unabridged and unaltered republication of the work
originally published by Doubleday, Doran & Company, Inc., in 1939.

International Standard Book Number: 0-486-20190-2
Library of Congress Catalog Card Number: 72-166427

Manufactured in the United States of America
Dover Publications, Inc.
180 Varick Street
New York, N.Y. 10014

For Bill and Marie,
with *saudades* for a quarter century's
feasting—from Mexican *molé*, to *vatapá*
and flying fish in Bahia.
CoRoBo.

NOTE

Since Portuguese is the language of Brazil, whose population equals that of all the other South American republics put together, many of our recipe titles are given in Portuguese, which should not be mistaken for misspelled Spanish on account of the similarity of some words.

CONTENTS

SOUPS

CUBAN TURTLE SOUP

3 cups turtle meat
6 peppercorns
Salt
1 garlic clove, minced
1 green pepper, chopped
1 teaspoon parsley, chopped
½ teaspoon mint, chopped
1 hard-boiled egg, chopped
1 cup white wine

Cook turtle with garlic, peppercorns and salt in 1½ quarts of water until meat is half done. This takes quite a time, because the older the turtle, the tougher the meat.

Take out the meat; cut in small pieces. Skim and strain its broth; put them back into the pot together and cook until tender. Add green pepper, and 5 minutes later the wine, parsley, mint and egg. Bring to boiling point and serve at once, with croutons.

Sherry and Madeira are the wines considered most appropriate for turtle soup. However, the white wine in this recipe from Havana allows the full rich turtle flavor to dominate the finished soup, as would be preferred by many devotees to this dish. (From *The Wine Cookbook*, by the Browns.)

In Rio de Janeiro, where turtle soup is quite as popular as in Havana, you will often see a huge hump-backed sea monster weighing around 500 pounds tied outside a Portuguese restaurant with this inviting sign whitewashed on his shell: MEET ME IN THE SOUP TOMORROW.

With the sea cow, which is sold in West Indian food markets, turtle shares the distinction of having many kinds of different-tasting meat in one body. Some say there are seven, such as chicken, veal, pork, beef, etc., and certainly there are several, all of whose savors mingle to make the world's superb soup.

ECUADORIAN FISH SOUP
Potaje de Pescado

Allow 1 quart water to each pound of fish. Add onion, cut fine, and dried or fresh herbs according to fancy. When fish is well cooked strain off the broth and return to heat with butter, salt, pepper, Spanish paprika and chopped parsley to taste.

Serve with diced bread fried in oil, thin slices of onion and grated hard-cooked egg floating on top.

VENEZUELAN FISH BROTH
Caldo de Pescado

1 large onion, chopped fine	1 cup white wine
3 tablespoons olive oil	1 tablespoon Madeira
4 tomatoes, quartered	2–3 pints fish stock
1 garlic clove	Salt
1 tablespoon parsley, chopped	4 slices thin toast

Fry onions golden in oil; add tomatoes, garlic, parsley and wines. Stir until wine reduces, then pour fish stock over. Season; add toast and simmer 20 minutes.

CUBAN MUSSELS SOUP
Sopa de Almejas

Wash mussels, let lie in fresh water to discharge any sand, scrub shells and pull off hanging tendrils. Prepare a sauce by gently frying a minced onion, a chopped green pepper and a little minced parsley in 1 tablespoon oil or butter until soft and golden. Season with 2 cloves, a few gratings of nutmeg and a teaspoon of lemon juice. Put mussels into a kettle, add 2 cups boiling water to sauce and pour it over them. Cover kettle closely. Let mussels steam 20 minutes and take from heat. Take out mussels and remove shells. Drain mussel meats and strain with broth. Thicken with flour of maize or banana and simmer

5 minutes. Add mussel meats; simmer 5 minutes more. Add 1 cup white wine and serve poured over little square croutons and minced hard-cooked egg.

Rice or vermicelli may be used for thickening in place of corn or banana flour by adding them to the sauce and cooking the necessary time.

Mussels are plentiful in North America and should be more commonly used, for even oysters and clams have a hard time competing with them in flavor. And another good thing about mussels is that they're still cheap; you can buy a whole basket of them for the price of a dozen blue points.

URUGUAYAN FROG SOUP

12 large frogs	1 sprig basil
3 tablespoons olive oil	Celery leaves
1 garlic clove, minced	1 tomato, chopped
1 small onion, minced	2 mushrooms, chopped
1 small carrot, minced	Salt and pepper
1 sprig parsley	2 tablespoons bread crumbs

Toast fingers

Remove frogs' hind legs and reserve. Chop together all other meat left on the carcass, including livers. Slightly color in smoking-hot olive oil the garlic, onion, carrot, parsley, basil and celery leaves. Then add tomato and mushrooms with the chopped frog meat and 3 pints water. Bring slowly to boiling point and simmer until meat falls from bones. Strain and season. Finally put in hind legs and simmer until tender; add crumbs and serve with toast fingers.

Both Uruguay and Argentina are addicted to frogs and do not like to waste any of the animal as we do, following the French fashion of using only the hind legs. Gigantic frogs are as much in demand in the markets of Montevideo and Buenos Aires as turkeys or sirloins.

LATIN-AMERICAN EGG SOUPS

Beat 2 raw egg yolks slightly. Pour over them 1 quart boiling hot consommé, stirring vigorously. Serve in hot soup plates.

Or, fill hot cups with boiling hot consommé. Carefully slide 1 unbroken raw egg yolk into each cup and serve. Each person stirs the egg yolk into the consommé before eating.

COLOMBIAN CONSOMMÉ OF PIGEONS
Consommé de Pichones

Singe, clean and joint pigeons. Grind or pound them to paste with their bones. Cover well with cold water. Add a bay leaf, a little sage, thyme, mashed garlic and any other seasoning, except salt. Let lie 1 hour to soak, then cover and put over slow heat to cook gently 2 hours. Now salt to taste. Remove from heat and strain through cloth. Add a little white wine or mashed capers and serve.

DUTCH GUIANA PEA SOUP
Potaje de Guisantes

2 cups split peas	2 garlic cloves
2 onions	2 sprigs parsley
1 carrot, sliced	1 tablespoon mixed herbs
1 pound salt codfish	2 tomatoes, chopped
1 bay leaf	Salt
2 pounds spinach	Pepper
1 tablespoon fat	1 hard-cooked egg

Soak peas overnight. Drain; cover with plenty of cold water and bring gently to boiling point. Add 1 onion, sliced, carrot, codfish and bay leaf. Simmer until peas are tender. In the meantime wash and cook spinach separately; chop fine and add to soup pot. Heat fat in frying pan. Chop second onion, garlic and parsley. Fry in fat until soft; add tomatoes and herbs. Cook until smooth and bubbling, then add 1 cup broth from soup pot. Season to taste and let simmer 30 minutes. When peas and codfish have cooked tender mash through strainer. Add contents of frying pan to soup. Season; stir well. Garnish with chopped egg and serve.

The rich cuisine of the Dutch has had its effect along the little strip of Atlantic coast between Venezuela and Brazil.

COLOMBIAN LENTIL SOUP
Sopa de Lentejas

Soak lentils overnight. In morning put over heat in plenty unsalted water. When lentils are partly done add ¼ pound salt pork, diced, and a little Colombian Seasoning Sauce (see recipe). When pork is cooked add salt, if necessary, and slices of hard-cooked egg.

PURÉE OF CHICK–PEAS
Puré de Garbanzos

1 cup chick-peas	½ teaspoon pepper
3 pints cold water	2 tablespoons flour
1 teaspoon salt	4 tablespoons butter
	1 cup cream

Soak garbanzos overnight in water to cover. Next morning boil 10 minutes and remove skins. Add water; cook until soft and rub through purée sieve. Return to saucepan; reheat. Add salt and pepper, and flour mixed to a paste, with ½ of butter. Stir until smooth and cook slowly 15 minutes. Add cream and remaining butter in small pieces.

An excellent garbanzo purée is made by substituting 2 quarts of a highly seasoned broth for the 3 pints of cold water and omitting cream.

Chick-peas are to Latin America as navy beans are to Boston.

CANJA

1 fat hen, jointed	1 garlic clove, minced
Salt and pepper	½ cup uncooked rice
1 medium onion, sliced	¼ pound ham, diced
2 tablespoons fat	1 herb bouquet

Salt and pepper chicken and let stand 30 minutes. Meanwhile slowly fry onion in fat. Add garlic and continue slow frying until onion is golden. Add chicken. Cover pan closely and let chicken smother and fry until lightly browned on one side, then turn and brown lightly on other side. Wash rice through many waters. Drain and add rice and ham; cover pan and continue slow frying, shaking pan occasionally to prevent sticking. Add 2 quarts boiling water and an herb bouquet consisting of 1 bay leaf, 2 parsley sprigs and 1 sprig marjoram or thyme. Simmer until chicken is tender and broth is slightly thickened. Take out chicken, remove bones. Cut meat into convenient pieces and return it to broth. Serve very hot.

This national chicken and rice soup of Brazil bears a mouth-watering name, for "Canja" translates "Rice Cream." And Brazilians esteem it as highly as we do our ice cream. They have a saying, "E canja!" meaning, "That's easy!" or, "Pretty soft!"

When Teddy Roosevelt was looking around down there for the River of Doubt he became so enamored with this cream of chicken and rice that he told reporters on his return home, "Canja is the finest soup in the world."

AROMATIC SOUP
Sopa Aromatizada

Put several thin slices of bread or toast into a casserole. Pour boiling broth over and let simmer 5 minutes, then sprinkle with dry powdered *herba buena* or mint (½ teaspoon to 1 quart broth). Put on cover. Let simmer 2 minutes and take to the table. Do not remove cover until the moment of serving.

CUBAN SOUP
Sopa Cubana

The rich meaty broth of the *puchero* is the usual foundation of this soup. Slices of onions, plenty of garlic cloves, a few carrots, celery stalks, green peas or beans are first fried in a little butter or lard and then added to the broth to simmer until tender. It is served poured over thin slices of toasted bread.

HAVANA SOUP
Sopa a la Habanera

Cover bottom of a large soup tureen with thin slices of bread freshly toasted. Over toast spread a thin layer of finely chopped onions, mixed with 1 teaspoon minced parsley. Sprinkle a layer of grated cheese over onions. Have enough stock heating to fill tureen to top, add a few spoonfuls of it to ½ cup almonds or filberts (toasted and ground) and mix to a paste. When stock boils add paste and stir until well blended. Drop in a few tiny sticks of cinnamon and pour over contents of tureen.

BREAD SOUP, CUBAN STYLE
Sopa de Pan al Cubana

Slices of bread are laid in a casserole and the broth from a *cocido* poured over. When bread is well soaked the dish is brought to boiling point, then cooked vegetables are laid on top, and your Cuban Bread Soup is ready.

CUBAN OKRA POTTAGE
Quimbombó

Select tender pods of okra, wash. Cut off stems; if large cut in pieces, if small leave whole. Put into saucepan with several small pieces of jerked pork (*tasajo*) which has first been parboiled and drained. Cover with cold water and cook until pork is tender. Mash and pound 2 or 3 sliced onions with a couple of bay leaves and a few sesame seeds. Gently fry in 1 tablespoon oil or butter until soft and golden and stir in a little okra broth until seasonings are diluted and bubbling. Stir this into the pottage and keep stirring until well blended. When meat is tender add little balls of avocado. Sprinkle with lemon juice and serve.

The Cuban usually mashes and pounds his seasonings in a mortar, fries or "smothers" them in a very little fat and adds a bit of broth to dilute them before adding to the cooking food. This he calls *sofrito*—slightly fried.

CUBAN GREEN SOUP
Sopa Verde

2 leeks	1 tablespoon lard
2 green onions	1 quart boiling water
1 head lettuce	Salt and pepper
2 sprigs parsley	2 egg yolks, beaten
Croutons	

Grind together leeks, onions, lettuce and parsley. Fry in lard until soft and pour boiling water over. Season to taste and let simmer 30 minutes, then stir in beaten egg yolks and remove from heat. Serve with small thin squares of bread freshly fried in lard.

COLOMBIAN ONION SOUP
Sopa de Cebollas

1 pound white onions	2 tablespoons flour
Juice of ½ lemon	Stock
2 tablespoons butter	1 cup milk
1 teaspoon salt	Pepper
1 tablespoon sugar	

Peel and slice onions. Cover with cold water and lemon juice and let soak 1 hour. Drain and fry light yellow in butter. Add salt and flour. Stir until blended but not browned. Heat stock; add onion mixture, milk, a little pepper and sugar. Cover and cook slowly until onions are very soft. Remove from heat. Whip in 1 cup wine beaten with 2 egg yolks and serve.

COLOMBIAN PEARL ONION SOUP
Sopa de Cebollitas

Fry 1 sliced onion golden in 2 tablespoons butter. Color with caramel (burnt sugar dissolved in water) and *achiote* (native yellowish-red coloring prepared from pulp surrounding seed of the annatto tree). Chop 1 pound any animal's backbone with meat on it (chine) into small pieces. Put in with onion and move it around until well seasoned and colored all over. Then pour pan contents into soup kettle with plenty of cold water and let stand 1 hour. Season with salt and put to simmer over slow heat. When meat is nearly tender add 1 bottle of pickled pearl onions, draining off their liquid, and 3 tablespoons or more tapioca. When tapioca is done put 1 cup wine in which 1 egg yolk has been beaten in the bottom of a large soup tureen and pour soup over.

Latin Americans know their onions and have separate names for the many different kinds—*cebolla*, ordinary onion; *cebolleta*, a tender onion; *cebollino*, a young onion; *cebollón*, a large onion; and last, as well as least in size, *cebollitas*, tiny pickled onions that certainly put piquance in this soup.

GARLIC SOUP
Sopa de Ajos

Heat 2 tablespoons olive oil in a deep saucepan and slowly fry 12–18 garlic cloves until soft but not browned. Cover with 2–3 cups boiling water, season with salt and pepper. Lay in several squares of toasted bread and let boil 10–12 minutes. When done break in an egg for each person. Cover to let eggs poach lightly. Remove from heat and serve.

Interestingly, when garlic cloves are fried, as above, all their fire is painlessly removed and none of their original odor is left. They hop around in the pan like Mexican jumping beans (which, by the way, are not edible).

COLOMBIAN COCONUT SOUP
Sopa de Coco

Peel and grate 2 fresh coconuts. Scald 1 cup milk in double boiler. Stir in grated coconut. Let stand until cool and wring out juice through a napkin. Add juice to any good clear stock, from which grease has been removed, and bring to boiling point. Have 2 egg yolks beaten in tureen. Pour soup over; drop in a few freshly roasted almonds, whole or crushed, and serve hot.

BRAZILIAN PLUM SOUP
Sopa de Ameixas

Cover plums with cold water. Add a few slivers of lemon peel. Bring slowly to boiling point. Simmer until plums are tender, and put through sieve. Sweeten to taste and pour over toasted bread.

BRAZILIAN MULBERRY SOUP
Sopa de Amoras

Wash fruit thoroughly and cook in white wine. Season with sugar and cinnamon. When fruit falls to pieces pour it over strips of toasted bread and serve.

BRAZILIAN QUINCE SOUP
Sopa de Marmelos

Peel, core and cut quinces in pieces. Cover with cold water. Add slices of lemon, a little sugar and cinnamon. Bring to boiling point and add a few tablespoons rice. Cook until rice and fruit are tender, and pass through sieve.

VENEZUELAN CASHEW SOUP
Sopa de Caju

Cut cashew fruits in pieces and cook until tender in a little water seasoned with lemon peel and sugar. Then strain. Add an equal amount of white wine and a few pieces of toasted bread. Chill before serving.

A popular summer soup made of the same fruit that produces the cashew nut.

ECUADORIAN ORANGE SOUP
Sopa de Naranjas

Remove skins from a dozen oranges. Cover with 3 pints water, slightly sweetened. Bring slowly to boiling point. Simmer 20 minutes and strain into a tureen over bits of toasted bread and slices of lemon.

COLOMBIAN LEMON SOUP
Sopa de Limón

Crush a small dry bread roll (or twist) and cook it in a little lard until softened. Then press it through a sieve. Add 1 cup of red or white wine, a little sugar and some slices of lemon. Heat to boiling point and serve.

ARGENTINE APPLE SOUP
Sopa de Manzanas

Cut up 4 large green apples. Cover well with cold water. Add a few slivers of lemon peel. Sugar to taste and cook until apples fall to pieces. Put through sieve. Add a few soaked and seeded raisins. Whip in an egg yolk and serve.

Argentina has a climate cold enough to raise apples, which is exceptional in South America. The commonest variety is big and green.

FISH AND SEA FOOD

PERUVIAN SEVICHE

Lay thin fillets of any very delicate fish on a platter side by side. Cover with juice of freshly squeezed limes, being careful to remove all lime pits. Let stand away from dust at least 6–7 hours until lime juice has completely tendered fish.

When fish is ready peel 1 large, firm ripe tomato. Split crosswise and flick out seeds, then chop rather fine with very sharp knife. Remove seeds and veins from 1 green pepper and chop. Remove seeds and veins from 1 red sweet pepper and chop (or substitute 1 canned pimiento). Mix tomato and peppers, adding ¾ cup chopped white onion, 1 teaspoon minced parsley, 1 well-crushed garlic clove (which may be removed afterward) and 1 well-minced chili pepper (or 1–2 dashes Tabasco). Add vinegar until mixture is semiliquid. Season with salt, pepper and a very little sugar. Drain fish fillets thoroughly. Put them on platter and spread mixture over them.

Served as a first course for luncheon, this freshly and delicately pickled fish is much better than any you'll find in the delicatessen store.

On the differences between Chilean and Peruvian cooking, we quote from Dr William Lytle Schurz, author of that fascinating book, *The Manila Galleon,* and a scholarly article, "Latin America at Table," published in the *Pan American Magazine:*

"When diplomatic relations were finally renewed between Chile and Peru the new Peruvian ambassador took with him his private chef, that he might have on his table the dishes of his native Lima. On his arrival in Santiago his Chilean colleagues honored the Peruvian chef with a banquet. Wrote one lyric Chilean in the *Mercurio* of Santiago, apropos the new culinary rapprochement between the long-estranged neighbors: 'The *seviche,* the piquant eggs and the yellow potatoes of up yonder would meet at the same fraternal table with our stews, our meat pies, our lemon fritters, and our conger, the blessed conger that wears around it the golden halo of the saints.' "

PERUVIAN PICANTE

Divide 1 large or several small fish into convenient serving pieces. Cover thickly on all sides with coarse kitchen salt and let stand 1 hour or more. Place in a saucepan 1 minced garlic clove, 1 chopped yellow pepper (a green one would do) and the juice of 2 sour oranges (or juice of 1 sweet orange and 1 lemon). Cover with just enough water to cook fish and bring to boiling point. Wash salt from pieces of fish. Lay in pan. Bring rapidly to boiling point. Cover tightly and simmer until fish is done.

BAKED TUNA, PUERTO RICAN STYLE

Clean tuna fish and remove skin.

Put the cleaned fish in a tightly covered roasting pan in a little boiling salted water. Boil and steam about 10 minutes (for a 6–7 pound fish).

Remove most of the water. Sprinkle salt, pepper and wild marjoram over the fish. Cover with sliced onions and tomatoes. Pour over the fish 1 teaspoon vinegar, 1 teaspoon olive oil and the juice of 1 lime. Bake in a moderate oven for an hour or until done.

If desired add mayonnaise to the sauce left in the pan after the baked fish is removed and cover the fish with the mixture, or use:

PUERTO RICAN FISH SAUCE

1 tablespoon tomato catsup	4 tablespoons mayonnaise
1 tablespoon olives, chopped	1 teaspoon green peppers, chopped
1 tablespoon sweet pickles, chopped	A little onion, chopped

Juice of ½ lime

COLOMBIAN CATFISH WITH RAISIN SAUCE
Bagre en Salsa de Pasas

First catch your Colombian (or any other) catfish, wash it well and skin it easily by splitting lengthwise and laying it skin side down in a dry hot frying pan for a minute. Then take it up and leave all the skin sticking to the pan. Put fish on a greased fish pan. Sprinkle with salt; brush with melted butter and lay thin slices of tomato over. Bake in quick oven and serve with:

RAISIN SAUCE

To 1 cup well-seasoned beef stock add 1 cup chopped, seeded raisins and simmer until soft. Then add 1 tablespoon butter, 1 cup wine and thicken with 1 tablespoon cornstarch dissolved in a little cold water. Cook, stirring constantly until smooth. Add a little cold water to 2 beaten egg yolks and stir slowly into sauce. Remove from heat. Add juice of 1 lemon and a little chopped parsley.

CORBINA BAKED WITH EGG SAUCE
Corbina Asada con Salsa de Huevo

Cut a *corbina*, or croaker, in portions to be served and arrange in baking dish. Put a piece of raw onion or carrot on each portion. Squeeze the juice of 1 lemon over and sprinkle with salt and pepper. Also pour on ½ cup olive oil. Put in oven and bake. When done pour off gravy. Strain into a small saucepan. Add 2 egg yolks and stir slowly over heat until sauce thickens. Serve hot with the fish.

Corbina is a common but popular fish on both the Atlantic and Pacific coasts of South America. The French fancy it, too, and call it *corbine*. Our name for the same fish is croaker, and it has many devotees who like a soft-fleshed sea fish.

HAVANA RED SNAPPER

Lay fillets of red snapper in buttered baking dish. Season with plenty of pepper and salt. Cover with tomato sauce and grated cheese and bake brown in oven.

VERA CRUZ RED SNAPPER
Huauhchinango

Fry minced onion, parsley and olives in olive oil and add canned tomato liberally to make a thin sauce in which to cook a whole red snapper without any water. Cook fish in sauce until done and toss in a palmful of capers.

CHILEAN CONGER EEL IN CASSEROLE
Congrio en Fuente a la Chilena

Cut into individual portions 2½ pounds conger eel. Season with salt and pepper and brown lightly in a little oil or butter. Heat 2 tablespoons each of butter and lard in a saucepan, add 2 chopped onions, 2 minced garlic cloves, a little dry marjoram and ground cumin. Fry gently until onions are soft, then add 4 peeled and thinly sliced tomatoes, 4 peeled and not too thinly sliced potatoes and the kernels and cream grated from 2 fresh ears of corn. Stir; cover. Cook until potatoes are done, then season to taste. At this point cooked peas or limas may be added for a fuller dish. Place half of the vegetables and sauce in a casserole. Lay fish over this and cover with remaining sauce. Put in slow oven and cook covered until fish is done. Garnish with croutons and sprigs of parsley. Serve hot.

A chef at the Hotel Crillon in Santiago de Chile who wrote down this—his own recipe—for us says conger eel is the best-liked fish dish in all Chile, and since this sister republic has a seacoast about as extensive as California's, it is interesting that an eel should head the list of fish delicacies. But these marine monsters that run as long as eight feet are certainly fine in flavor and as meaty as capon. Even if you don't care for fresh water eels you should go for fat congers.

CHILEAN CALDILLO DE PESCADO

1 large fish	2 tomatoes
2 onions	8 potatoes
Oil, salt and pepper	⅓ cup rice

Clean the fish and cut into individual portions. Pour a little olive oil into an earthenware dish. Add a layer of thinly sliced onions and one of potatoes cut into slices. On this lay your pieces of fish, then more potatoes, onions, rice and tomatoes cut in slices. Season well and put on the stove 5 minutes, then pour boiling water over and allow to cook slowly, well covered. Serve hot in the same dish.

Although *caldillo* is a light broth or gravy in Spain here it becomes a fish stew and is at its best in Chile when made with conger eel, the favorite "fish" of the prolific coast that stretches more than half the length of South America.

COLOMBIAN FISH ROLL
Rollo de Pescado

Put sufficient water in a kettle with a little milk, to cover 2-pound fish. Season with a bay leaf, a bit of sage and a slice of onion. Bring to boiling point and drop in cleaned fish. Simmer till meat will leave bones. Take out; remove meat and flake. Beat 2 eggs with 1 tablespoon cornstarch. Mix it with fish and spread out on a napkin, previously well powdered with bread crumbs. Pile on this cooked kidney beans, sprigs of parsley and tender carrots cut in strings. Envelop all in napkin in shape of a roll and secure with string. Cook 30 minutes in salted boiling water, then take out. Remove from napkin and place in hot serving dish. Pour on hot Colombian Yellow Sauce. (See recipe.) Garnish with slices of lemon.

STUFFED FISH, BRAZILIAN STYLE
Peixe Recheado

1 fish, weight 3 pounds	6 peppercorns
24 shrimps	1 tablespoon parsley,
18 oysters	chopped
1 teaspoon cornstarch	1 bay leaf
1 chopped onion	2 tablespoons butter
1 onion, sliced in rings	1 scant cup bread crumbs
Salt	1½ cups white wine

Pepper

Select bluefish, sheepshead, grouper or any good baking fish. Leave the head on. Dry well. Place in baking pan the chopped onion, peppercorns, parsley, bay leaf and butter.

Scald shrimps, remove shells and turn them over in butter in a frying pan over a slow fire until golden brown. Add bread crumbs, salt and pepper and a teaspoon of the mixture waiting in the roasting pan. Pour in the liquor from the oysters until the mixture is the right consistency for stuffing—not too wet.

Stuff the fish. Sew it up. Place it in the pan and decorate with onion rings. Pour in 1 cup wine. Place in oven, and when hot begin to baste. As it dries add the last ½ cup wine, a little at a time.

When fish begins to brown it is time to put the oysters in a covered pan over a slow fire and heat until they curl. Turn them into the baking pan. Stir in a teaspoon of cornstarch already melted in a little cold water and cook a few more minutes. If there is not enough liquid left in pan boiling water can be added.

Place fish on platter and surround with oyster sauce and strained broth. (From *The Wine Cookbook*, by the Browns.)

One thing we should learn from our Southern neighbors is to leave heads on fish, no matter how they are cooked. In cutting off the head some of the shoulder meat is wasted and there are nuggets such as the fat cheeks to be picked out of the head itself, in the same way that French gourmets delve into the head of even a small bird to capture the luscious brains and tongue. And besides, a fish looks much more natural and appetizing on a platter if it isn't beheaded.

ESCABECHE

Any meat or fish may be *escabeche*-ed, or treated with a sour sauce, in the Spanish manner that is popular all over Latin America. But this method of dressing is most commonly applied to good firm sea fish, as follows:

ESCABECHE OF FRIED FISH
Escabeche de Pescado Frito

Slice fish. Rub with salt and let stand ½ hour. Meanwhile slowly fry 1 sliced onion in plenty of olive oil until tender but not browned. Add 1 minced garlic clove and fry golden. Remove onion and garlic and reserve. Wipe fish dry. Dip in beaten egg and then in crumbs or meal (cassava or corn meal) and fry in onion-garlic flavored oil until nicely browned on both sides. Meanwhile boil fried onion and garlic in ½ cup water with 1 small bay leaf, 6–8 whole peppers and a few toasted coriander seeds or a tiny bit of stick cinnamon or root ginger. Add ½ cup red wine vinegar and stir in several tablespoons olive oil. Lay fish in a hot platter and pour vinegar sauce over, arranging onion rings and specks of garlic on top of slices. Sprinkle with freshly chopped onion and garnish with olives.

May be eaten hot or cold as a first course, and any left over makes a fine snack. In some localities *pescado en escabeche* is made by the keg and sold in delicatessen shops. The very best fish for the purpose is pompano.

CUBAN CODFISH

1½ pounds salt codfish, soaked	1 teaspoon parsley, minced
1 tomato, chopped	¼ teaspoon cinnamon
1 onion, minced	½ cup sherry
	Cayenne

Either buy salt codfish already soaked in a Spanish or Italian store, or soak it yourself overnight in cold water, changing water occasionally. Remove bones and cut in 2½-inch squares. Put in saucepan with a little water. Add onion, tomato, parsley and cinnamon. Cover and simmer 10 minutes or so before pouring on the sherry. Then simmer until fish is tender and sauce is greatly reduced. Season with cayenne and serve.

One of the distinctive sights throughout Latin America is the flat slab of dried salt codfish hanging like a sail in nearly every kitchen, ready for cutting off portions. In hot weather it is apt to get rather high in smell, and you have to hurry by the food stores where it's stacked up by the bale. Most of the salt cod is imported from Portugal, and as a service to customers shopkeepers soak the huge slabs overnight in zinc-lined tanks to be ready for the morning rush—especially on Fridays.

AKEE AND CODFISH

The *akee* is a fruit that grows on a tree. It is oblong in shape, ribbed, and a dull orange in color. The top, the part used, is creamy white and so delicate it has to be cooked in a muslin bag. This takes 10–15 minutes. The codfish is cooked and flaked. Sliced onions are sautéed in a little fresh pork fat for a sauce, seasoned with salt and colored with *annatto*. The *akee* and codfish are then well mixed with the sauce and served.

This is a favorite Jamaican dish usually eaten with roasted breadfruit.

Annatto is a West India spice used mostly for color. It, too, grows on a tree, is shaken off and dried in the sun. Husks are removed, and the bright red seeds are used for coloring and seasoning. It is used much the same as paprika.

BRAZILIAN FISH AND SEA FOOD

The Portuguese who settled Brazil could not live without their salt codfish (*bacalhao*), their shrimps, both fresh and dried, and their sardines fresh out of the nets into the baskets of the fishwives or into the baskets of the mules bound for the canning factories all along the coast of Portugal.

So Portuguese navigators took their dried and canned fish, together with their recipes, wherever they sailed. In Japan one finds that shrimp fried in batter still bears its Portuguese name, *tempura*, and Chinese cooks make the same dish in kitchens far from modern foreign influences.

It was natural that Brazil's early colonists, accustomed to getting their living out of the sea, should carry the habit to the new world where the treasures of the tropical waters were so much richer. Thus we find *tempura* shrimp prominent among Brazilian sea foods and a rich list of recipes for preparing the many varieties of fresh fish and salt codfish, and for combining vegetables and rice with crabs, octopus, squid, rayfish, eels and shellfish.

Saint Anthony, who presides over fishermen and cooks alike, usually is represented in the Brazilian kitchen by a small painted wooden statue that looks down from his little shelf with especial benignity when *roballo* (a sea pike) or pompano is ceremoniously laid out on the board and the dressing of it begun, while the tail is being wrapped in a bit of oiled paper to keep it intact and the head perhaps is being tied with string to keep the jaws from sagging open in cooking. For no Latin would spoil the looks of a roast fish by cutting off its most decorative features. Saint Anthony watches over it from the laying of the onion rings in a pattern on the silvery side to the placing of a slice of raw carrot or a sprig of green over the eye when it is done and has been laid on a bed of parsley and covered with its own flavorsome sauce. But after all this tender

care if the dish has not turned out well, the cook is apt to yank
the saint down from his perch and hang him head down in the
well for punishment, or otherwise disgrace him, for it is invariably his fault, not hers.

MARIA'S BOUQUET DO MAR
A Bouquet from the Sea

2 cups fish broth	2 tablespoons cooked celery,
1 cup white wine	minced
6–8 shrimps, raw	2 tablespoons onion juice
6–8 scallops	1 teaspoon parsley, minced
¼ cup crab meat	6–8 oysters
¼ cup lobster meat	Salt

Pepper

Put broth and wine in saucepan over slow heat. Shell shrimps
and cut in small pieces. Cut scallops in quarters and add with
crab and lobster meat. Add celery, onion juice and parsley and
simmer 12 minutes. Then put the oysters in, cut in quarters;
season. Simmer 3 more minutes and serve in soup plates.

Maria was a Portuguese cook who came to our Rio de
Janeiro house to stay, and her *Bouquet do Mar* was indeed a
nosegay from the sea that made us all look forward to Friday.
It had the tang of seaweed and made you think of mermaids.

BRAZILIAN FISH WITH SEA–FOOD SAUCE
Peixe com Molho do Mar

2–3 pounds fish	1 onion, sliced
½ pound small fish	2 tablespoons olive oil
1 dozen large shrimps	1 garlic clove, minced
Herb bouquet (parsley,	Flour
celery leaves, bay leaf)	Salt and pepper
1 dozen clams or oysters	1 teaspoon parsley, minced

Select a fish with solid flesh, such as sheepshead, bluefish, sea
bass, striped bass, etc. In Brazil a favorite variety for this dish

is robalo. As for the small fish, any sort will serve since they are to be used only for the sauce.

Cook shrimps 10 minutes in a little boiling water with herb bouquet. Take them out and shell them, reserving cooking water. Have clams or oysters open and ready, being sure to save their juice.

Fry onion slowly in olive oil, adding garlic clove when onion begins to get tender. Salt and pepper small fish and dredge with flour. Lay them in pan with onions and garlic and brown nicely. Place them in long earthenware or glass baking dish. Salt and pepper big fish. Dredge with flour and lay it on top of them. Add 1 cup shrimp water. Cover and set over asbestos ring to cook slowly. Let simmer until underside of fish is becoming tender. If necessary add a little more shrimp water. The big fish must not be allowed to stick. Carefully turn it over without breaking cooked part, pushing little fish to one side. Add more shrimp water. Take out bones and heads of little fish, leaving only their meat in dish. Lay clams (or oysters) and shrimps around fish and add clam juice. Add more shrimp juice. Cover closely and let steam. At no time must liquid in which fish lies cover more than lower half of it.

When fish is done sprinkle chopped parsley over top and carefully thicken gravy with 1 tablespoon flour worked smooth in a little cold water and slipped into sauce here and there, a little at a time, shaking dish gently. Let thicken and serve in baking dish with plain boiled rice in separate tureen.

This is much better than baked fish because all the flavors are thoroughly cooked into it.

SALT CODFISH IN SAUCE, BRAZILIAN STYLE
Bacalhao em Molho

1 pound salt cod	2 tomatoes, chopped
1 large onion, chopped fine	1 onion, sliced thin
2 garlic cloves, minced	1 sprig parsley
2 tablespoons olive oil	1 sprig celery
Cayenne	2 egg yolks, beaten

Soak codfish 24 hours, changing water frequently. Parboil 10–15 minutes, remove and cut into convenient pieces, taking out all visible bones. Fry onion and garlic in oil until light brown and tender. Add cayenne and tomatoes, onion, parsley and celery. Pour in 1½ cups boiling water and simmer for a few minutes. Lay in the pieces of fish, baste and simmer. When tender take from the fire and slip in, here and there, the beaten egg yolks. Shake the pan gently to mix, and serve, sliding the contents of the pan carefully into a deep hot platter.

There are forty Portuguese recipes for cooking salt cod, and most of them are popular in Brazil.

BRAZILIAN BAKED CODFISH
Bacalhao Assado

1½ pound salt cod	Olive oil
Cayenne	Onion rings
1 egg, beaten	Garlic cloves, halved
Bread crumbs	Red wine vinegar
Parsley for garnishing	

Choose a thick slice of salt cod. Soak in cold water 24 hours, changing as often as convenient. Parboil 10–15 minutes over hot fire. Drain and wipe dry. Dash it with cayenne; dip in beaten egg and then in crumbs. Sprinkle with olive oil. Lay in a buttered baking dish and brown in oven. Lay on a hot platter. Decorate with onion rings and garlic halves. Sprinkle generously with olive oil and vinegar. Garnish with parsley and serve at once. If there is to be any delay in serving, the oil and vinegar should be added at the table, since the crispness of the fish will be spoiled if it stands with the vinegar soaking into it. A sprig of parsley is served with each portion, to be nibbled while eating the fish.

FISH AND SEA FOOD
Brazilian Shrimp Dishes

SHRIMP CROQUETTES
Croquettes de Camarões

1 onion, sliced
1 garlic clove, minced
1 tablespoon butter
1 teaspoon parsley, chopped
1 slice dry bread
1 tablespoon milk

2 eggs
12 large shrimps, chopped
Salt and pepper
Flour
Bread crumbs
Deep fat for frying

Fry onion and garlic in butter until light brown and tender. Add parsley, moistened bread, milk, 1 beaten egg, shrimp, seasonings and enough flour to bind. Mold into oval shapes and allow to cool thoroughly. Dip in beaten egg, then in crumbs and fry in deep fat.

This is one of the dishes taken by Portuguese traders centuries ago to Japan, where with slight modifications it is made to this day under the name *tempura*, which identifies the frying in batter, rather than the shrimp, for lobsters and other delicacies of the sea are cooked by the same recipe.

SHRIMPS FRIED IN BATTER
Camarões Fritos em Massa de Vinhee

1 pound raw shrimps
Salt and pepper
2 tablespoons lemon juice
2½ tablespoons olive oil
1 cup flour

1 egg white, beaten
1 egg yolk, beaten
Deep fat for frying
Minced parsley
Quartered lemons

Shell shrimps. Mix salt, pepper, lemon juice and all but 1 teaspoon of olive oil. Beat and mix with the shrimps. Marinate ½ hour; drain. Make a batter with flour, egg white and yolk,

1 teaspoon olive oil and enough tepid water to thin. Run tooth-picks through the shrimp so they are skewered together in groups of four or five. Dip the groups of shrimps into batter until completely covered. Fry in deep fat. Drain on absorbent paper. Sprinkle with parsley and serve with quartered lemons.

BROWNED SHRIMPS
Camarões Torados

Choose large fresh shrimps. Wash well, letting them lie in cold water until free of all sand. Dry well in a linen towel. Have ready enough hot olive oil in a pan to make a depth of half the thickness of a shrimp. Heat to smoking point. Drop in shrimps one by one, turning them often until they are done. Lay on brown paper in a hot place to drain. Sprinkle with salt and pepper. Serve on a hot platter. They are shelled at the table.

The larger the shrimps are, the better.

In Brazil, when gourmets gorge on Camaroes Torados em Casca, the best local shrimps, browned in their shells, are bigger than our biggest jumbos. So don't try this dish with ordinary run-of-the-tide shrimps or you'll be vexed.

SHRIMPS AND OYSTERS WITH MACARONI
Camarão Ostras com Macarrão

1 dozen large shrimps	⅛ pound butter
1½ dozen oysters	2 slices bacon, minced
1 pound macaroni	1 large tomato, chopped
Salt	Pepper
3 small onions	Juice ½ lemon
1 garlic clove, minced	1 teaspoon parsley, minced

Shell the shrimps. Make sure there are no pieces of shell clinging to the oysters. Cook shrimps 15 minutes in salted water. Meanwhile break macaroni in short lengths and drop into rapidly boiling salted water. Cook 15 minutes. Drain and douse with 1 cup of cold water. Poach oysters in own liquor until they crinkle. Slice onions and cut slices in two. Fry with garlic in butter until they begin to be tender. Add bacon and fry. Add tomato and seasonings, 1 cup of the shrimp water and ½ cup of the oyster liquor. Simmer until well blended. Add lemon juice and parsley. Mix oysters, shrimp, the well-drained macaroni and the sauce together. Heat until the flavors are well mingled.

Save the heads and shells of the shrimps. Grind; press them through a sieve and add them to the sauce.

SHRIMP AND FLOUNDER MAYONNAISE
Mayonnaise de Camarão e Linguado

1 pound fillet of flounder	1 head lettuce
Salt and pepper	1½ cups mayonnaise
¼ cup butter, melted	2 dozen olives, stoned
Juice of 3 lemons	Mixed pickles
2 dozen shrimps	6 slices pickled beets
½ teaspoon burnet, minced	3 hard-boiled eggs, halved
1 teaspoon parsley, minced	6 anchovy fillets
6 capers	

Put fillets in a buttered baking dish. Sprinkle with salt and pepper and pour on melted butter and ½ the lemon juice. Place in a moderate oven, 350°, and baste. Cover after 10 minutes so they will not brown. Cook shrimps 20 minutes and cool. Combine lemon juice, burnet, parsley and season both fish and shrimp with the mixture. Chill. When ready to serve chop least attractive shrimps and slice fine an equal quantity of lettuce leaves. Mix together with a little of the mayonnaise. Cut fillets in service portions and lay on a chilled platter. Put some of shrimp-lettuce mixture on each portion. Mask with mayonnaise. Decorate platter with remaining materials, putting a bit of mayonnaise on each egg half and 1 caper within a curled fillet of anchovy on the mayonnaise.

Save shrimp liquor and pan gravy from fish for cooking eggs in *Ovos com Molho de Peixe*. (From the Portuguese section of *The European Cookbook*, by the Browns.)

BRAZILIAN BOILED SHRIMPS
Camarões

Choose 2 dozen big shrimps, the larger the tastier. Make a bouillon as follows:

Into a pot put 1 quart water and 1 tablespoon salt. Prepare herb bouquet of sprigs of celery with leaves, 2 bay leaves, 3 sprigs parsley, a bit of thyme and 1 red pepper pod, tying them with a string. Throw in ½ dozen peppercorns, 1 clove and ½ dozen allspice. Bring mixture to boiling point and allow to cook until flavor is extracted. Strain; put back into pot and bring to boiling point again.

Add shrimps and boil 20 minutes. Take from heat and let shrimps cool in liquid. When cold take them out and carefully remove shells. Serve very cold. If preferred, they can be laid on cracked ice and garnished with parsley or piled in a pyramid around a cone of ice, like crayfish.

Everything grows big in Brazil. In Pernambuco there's a kind of edible frog that's bigger than a baby and quite as tender. The oysters from old Bahian beds are often a foot long and have to be eaten individually with knife and fork, like a steak. But the biggest sea food, in comparison to ours, is shrimp. The giant kinds are netted at the full of the moon when they occur as big as baby lobsters and make little English prawns look like mosquitoes.

SHRIMPS BAHIA STYLE
Camarões Bahiana

Wash 1 dozen large shrimps thoroughly. Put into saucepan with 2 dried sprigs of celery leaves, 2 fresh parsley sprigs and 1 slice onion. Cover with salted boiling water and boil 15 minutes. Remove shrimps, make sure there is no sand in bottom of saucepan and add 2 cups of sliced okra to cooking water. Cook okra until tender, meanwhile shelling the shrimps. Add 2 tablespoons coconut milk (see p. 272) and return shelled shrimps to pan. Heat to just below boiling point. Thicken sauce with toasted *farinha de mandioca* (cassava meal) and serve at once.

BRAZILIAN OKRA WITH SHRIMPS AND MANDIOCA MEAL
Quiabos com Camarões e Farinha

Remove shells from 1 pound uncooked shrimps and clean well. Slowly fry 1 sliced onion and 1 minced garlic clove in olive oil until tender and brown. Season with salt and freshly ground pepper and add shrimps early to frying mixture so they will brown at same time, but will not be thoroughly cooked. Add ½ pound sliced okra and enough boiling water to cook it. Cover and boil gently. When done slowly sprinkle in 1 cup toasted *farinha de mandioca* (cassava meal). Let cook for a moment. The dish should be the consistency of thick mush.

The same recipe is made by using cooked rice instead of manioc; and the vegetables are varied also, diced squash or carrots being favorite substitutes for okra.

BRAZILIAN VATAPÁ

The secret of this delectable Afro-Brazilian dish is shrimps, both fresh and dried, and the milk of freshly grated coconut. It is a specialty of Bahia, where Negro slave cooking was brought to high perfection. Eaten in its native habitat, stinging hot with crushed chilies, it is a unique experience not to be matched in any other country. There are many variations, since the meat ingredient may be fish, chicken or even lean pork; the nuts which enrich and flavor it may be peanuts, cashew nuts or almonds, and the thickening agent may be rice flour, corn meal, or a mixture of corn meal with cassava meal.

But no matter what it's made of, all *vatapás* are made in the same fashion, of which the following recipe is a good example:

1 coconut	1 bay leaf
1 cup roasted peanuts, or ½ cup blanched almonds	1 tablespoon olive oil
	7 cups water
	Salt
½ pound dried shrimps	1 pound fresh firm fish
1 onion, sliced	1 pound fresh shrimps
1 garlic clove	Yellow corn meal
1–4 crushed fresh chilies	2 tablespoons oil

Grate coconut. Spread gratings in dripping pan. Sprinkle with a little hot water and set into open oven to warm slightly. Lay gratings in a strong cloth. Squeeze out all coconut milk, reserving both milk and gratings. Grind nuts fine. Shell, toast and grind dried shrimps very fine. Cook onion, garlic, bay leaf, chilies and olive oil a few minutes in 2 cups water. Season with salt and add sliced fish and shelled fresh shrimps. Cover and simmer until fish is done, about 15 minutes. Lift out fish slices and shrimps. Remove skin and bones from fish; strain broth and set all aside. Add 5 cups water to coconut gratings. Bring to boiling point. Simmer a few minutes. Strain, pressing out and reserving all liquid, but throwing gratings away. To this coconut broth add ground nuts and ground dried shrimps. Bring to boiling point and cook until nut and shrimp flavor have been extracted. Add strained broth from fish. Heat together and strain. Bring strained liquid to boiling point. Season with salt and stir in sufficient corn meal to make a smooth, thick mush. Cook 30 minutes, stirring frequently to prevent scorching. Add cooked fish, cooked shrimps and coconut milk, then add 2 tablespoons oil. (Brazilians use dende oil for this purpose, but olive oil will do.) Serve in soup plates. The consistency of the dish should be that of thick cream, with shrimps and bits of fish scattered through.

Ordinarily only half the coconut milk is added to the *vatapá*. The other half is thickened with rice flour or cornstarch seasoned only with salt, cooked to blancmange thickness, and set away in a mold to cool and solidify. A thick slice of this delicately flavored and cooling unsweetened pudding is set in the center of each plate of *vatapá*, and a bit of the pudding nicked off with each peppery and steaming hot soupspoonful of the stew tempers it and furnishes a delightful contrast.

Although Bahianos claim the only place to get a real *vatapá* is in their colorful coast city we used to have our fill of it in Rio de Janeiro every Friday, made to perfection at the old Villa Barcellos or the Rio Minho. The synthetic kinds palmed off to tourists at the hotels are pretty pallid in comparison to the ones you'll get along the water front around the lush market.

Nevertheless, Bahia should have full credit for this dish of dishes and no visitor there should miss it, or the famous flying fish which is served fried, broiled and stewed just like any more prosaic fish. These two dishes, indeed, have helped the fame of Bahian cuisine on both sides of the Atlantic.

CHUPE—PERU'S NATIONAL CHOWDER

½ pound fresh shrimps
3 pints water
Salt and pepper
3 celery stalks, chopped fine
1 green pepper, chopped
    fine

2 onions, chopped fine
1 bay leaf
A pinch allspice
1 tablespoon rice
2 cups milk
Chopped parsley

Boil shrimps in water 7 minutes. Strain and keep liquor. Shell shrimps. Return them to the strained liquor and season. Simmer vegetables and spices separately in 1 cup water 5 minutes. Add rice. Boil 15 minutes, adding milk 2 minutes before removing from heat. Sprinkle a little chopped parsley in each bowl.

This chowder is also made with any whitefish, or shrimps and whitefish together and, instead of rice, it is sometimes thickened with grated Parmesan or any aged hard cheese. Chupe is delicate but very tasty, and to make it richer a lightly poached egg is dropped into each bowl to be stirred in by the soup eater himself.

CHILEAN CLAM "FUTTES"
"Futtes" de Almejas

Use large freshly opened clams. Prepare a mixture of toasted crackers or bread crumbs and flour in equal quantities. Dip clams in milk and then in flour and crumbs. Fry in boiling lard about 5 minutes. Serve with butter sauce.

Chile and the Argentine are the very best places in all South America to get good fresh butter, because of the cooler climate and the fine cattle. Down around the equator butter has to be imported in tins, as in Spain.

The name "futtes" may be phonetic Spanish for "fritters," or it may be a playful allusion to "feet," the word "foot" being Spanishized in many funny ways, such as "futte-ball" for "football." The idea that clams have no feet, but after they're prepared in this fashion they resemble little brown feet, may have struck some Chilean cook's funny bone. And this doesn't seem so farfetched when we recall that Dr Samuel Johnson refused to eat fried oysters because to him they looked like "babies dropped in sawdust."

(For another good clam dish see Brazilian Rice with Clams.)

BRAZILIAN CRABS
Caranguejos

Drop live hard-shelled crabs into salted boiling water with 2 sprigs each of parsley, fresh tarragon and celery leaves, salt and 8–10 peppercorns. Cover and boil 15 minutes. Serve hot with a dish of French dressing at side of each plate in which to dip bits of meat as taken out of shells. Shells are cracked with nutcrackers at the table.

BRAZILIAN STUFFED CRABS
Carangueijos Recheados

Prepare crabs as above. Let them cool and take out meat from body and claws, keeping shells intact. Mix meat with mashed hard-cooked egg yolks and chopped olives. Stuff back in the shells. Scatter over the top finely chopped egg white and fine bread crumbs. Dot with butter. Sprinkle with chopped parsley and brown in quick oven.

STUFFED SQUIDS
Caranguejos Recheados

4 squids
2 thin slices cooked ham, chopped
1 teaspoon minced parsley
Salt
Pepper
Juice of ½ lemon
1 green pepper, chopped

⅓ cup fine bread crumbs
Flour
3 tablespoons olive oil
¼ cup white wine
¼ cup oyster liquor or fish broth
1 onion, chopped

Remove the ink or sepia sacks from squids, then take out the cartilage. Cut off octopuslike tentacles. Chop them. Mix with chopped ham, bread crumbs, parsley and lemon juice. Season with salt and pepper and stuff the squid bodies with this mixture. The prepared squid bodies are natural pockets for filling.

Roll in flour and fry in hot olive oil. Place close together in a baking pan with broth and wine. Season with salt and pepper and place in oven, basting occasionally. Keep closely covered. Fry onion in oil left in frying pan. Add green pepper. When squids are done turn the liquid in which they have baked into the frying pan. Lay the squids on a hot platter and pour contents of frying pan over.

Chile's long coast line also yields the similar octopus and the salty little sea anemone, both of which have millions of fans.

SQUIDS IN THEIR OWN INK
Calamares en su Tinta

The "ink" of squids, from which sepia coloring is made, is relished as a natural sauce for this fish in the same way that ducks and chickens are cooked in their own blood in creole recipes and in Brazil's favorite *gallinha ao molho pardo*. But since North Americans are squeamish about cooking with blood, the same rich dark color may be simulated by cooking squids with chocolate, as Mexicans do. Dashes of orange flower water also add piquance to this dish.

Squids are as succulent as octopuses, of which Argentinians are specially fond, and sell cheaply in many of our coastal markets. They are also cooked and canned in the West Indies for export to Latin-American residents in New York and other melting pots.

WEST INDIAN TURTLE IN ITS SHELL

Open turtle, reserving top shell. Remove edible portions. Scald legs and feet. Skin and trim off toenails. Remove bones and cut all meat in small pieces. Fry 1 small onion in 1 tablespoon butter. Add 1 large chopped tomato and fry until tomato thickens. Add 1 teaspoon minced parsley, ¼ teaspoon minced marjoram, ¼ teaspoon pepper, 1 teaspoon salt, 1 dash nutmeg, 1 dash cinnamon, 1 cup diced salt pork, ¼ cup melted butter, ¼ cup lime juice and ¼ cup sherry. Mix all with turtle meat. Clean turtle shell thoroughly. Place mixture inside. Cover with bread crumbs. Dot with butter and bake in the oven.

EGGS

EGGS GOYA STYLE
Ovos Goyadense

In a buttered baking dish place a layer of freshly cooked hot rice. Dot with butter, then cover with hot green peas and dot with butter again. Break required number of eggs on top. Put into slow oven and bake until eggs are set but still soft. Dash paprika over them, and serve with white sauce.

All Latins like eggs, but Spaniards have a real passion for them, cooked in a myriad of styles, ranging from plain boiled, *ovos pasada por agua* (eggs put through water) to fancy dishes like the above, named after national heroes, places of origin, etc. Cubans say that to order food in a foreign country it's not necessary to learn a new language, all you have to do is draw an oval on a piece of paper, hand it to the waiter and he'll bring what every hungry Habanero's heart desires.

BRAZILIAN SCRAMBLED EGGS
Ovos Mexidos

Break required number of eggs in a bowl. Season with salt and paprika. Add 1½ tablespoons orange juice for each egg and beat only until mixed but not light. Pour into well-buttered hot frying pan and scramble, lowering heat to keep mixture soft. Serve with buttered toast and orange marmalade.

SCRAMBLED EGGS A LA HAVANA

2 tablespoons butter	1 tablespoon onion, chopped
4 tablespoons sausage meat	4 eggs
1 tablespoon parsley, chopped	½ teaspoon salt
	Pepper

Heat butter in omelet pan. Put in sausage meat, parsley and onion. Cook until onion and parsley brown and sausage is done. Beat eggs slightly. Season and pour into pan with sausage. Cook slowly, stirring constantly until eggs begin to set. Take up on toast.

MEXICAN SCRAMBLED EGGS

6 sweet peppers	1 cup cold water
1 tablespoon olive oil	1 teaspoon salt
½ onion, minced	¼ cup butter
1 garlic clove, minced	6 eggs, slightly beaten
1 cup rice	Pepper and salt

Remove seeds from peppers. Parboil 2 minutes. Drain and chop fine. Heat olive oil in omelet pan. Put in peppers, onions and minced garlic. Cook until lightly browned, then add rice and water. Cover and cook slowly until rice is tender and most of liquid absorbed. Season with 1 teaspoon salt. Add butter and pour in eggs. Scramble until all is a creamy mixture. Sprinkle with pepper and a little more salt.

BRAZILIAN SWEET SCRAMBLED EGGS

½ cup sugar	1 tablespoon orange flower
¼ cup lemon juice	water
¼ teaspoon salt	4 eggs, slightly beaten
1 tablespoon butter	

Mix together sugar, lemon juice, salt and orange flower water. Add mixture to the slightly beaten eggs and turn into a buttered pan with 1 extra tablespoon butter. Cook slowly, stirring constantly until eggs are firm but still tender.

FRIED EGGS, SPANISH STYLE, I

Fry 2 eggs in 1 tablespoon olive oil, on 1 side only. Season and remove to hot plate. Then throw into the hot oil 1 minced garlic clove, 1 whole black pepper, freshly ground, 1 teaspoon vinegar, 1 teaspoon hot water. Mix well together and pour over eggs.

FRIED EGGS, SPANISH STYLE, II

Put a little bacon into pan just for its fat. When crisp remove, mix a tablespoon of honey with the fat and break in a half-dozen eggs to fry slowly. When done take up with skimmer. Lay on serving plate and nearly smother eggs with sliced green and red pickled peppers.

This dish is highly esteemed by Spanish-American lovers of sour-sweet dishes and has a name that translates "The Grace of God."

DRUNKEN EGGS
Huevos Borrachos

2 cups fresh Lima beans	6 eggs
Salt and pepper	3 tablespoons melted butter
6 bacon slices	¼ cup claret

Cook Limas in as little water as possible. Season with salt and pepper. Drain; press through colander and cover bottom of buttered baking dish with the purée. Fry bacon and lay on top of purée. Break in eggs on top and season with salt and pepper. Beat melted butter and wine together and sprinkle over eggs. Bake in moderate oven until eggs set.

This is only one of many Spanish dishes called "drunken" because of the slight alcoholic content which in this case mostly cooks away and leaves but a ghost of its potence. The English, too, have playful names for such spiked dishes—Typsy Parson, for instance.

MEXICAN EGGS

Wash and dry 6 tablespoons rice and finely chop 1 large onion. Melt 2 tablespoons butter in saucepan and brown rice and onion in it. Add ½ cup meat broth (can be made with meat cube), ½ teaspoon salt and ½ teaspoon chili powder. Mix well. Turn into a buttered casserole. Cover and bake about 40 minutes in moderate oven. Uncover; make half a dozen hollows in rice and break 1 egg into each. Sprinkle with 3 tablespoons grated cheese and return to oven for 8–10 minutes to let eggs set and cheese melt. (From *10,000 Snacks*, by the Browns.)

CARACAS (VENEZUELA) EGGS

2 ounces dried beef	¼ pound grated mild cheese
2 tablespoons butter	1 cup tomatoes
1 teaspoon chili powder	3 eggs, beaten

Shred dried or chipped beef quite fine and cook it crisp and brown in butter. Add chili powder, cheese and tomatoes. When the dish is simmering stir in beaten eggs and treat as you would scrambled eggs, stirring until eggs are lightly cooked. Serve piping hot.

Sundried beef is as popular throughout South America as Texas "jerky" is along our Mexican border. And Texas chili powder, notably Gebhardt's, is as fine a product as any to be had in Venezuela, Mexico or elsewhere, so this dish is easy to duplicate in any American kitchen.

MOORISH EGGS

4 tablespoons olive oil	¼ teaspoon saffron
2 garlic cloves	½ teaspoon cumin seed
12 blanched almonds	A few gratings of nutmeg
1 small slice bread	Salt and pepper

Eggs

Put olive oil in small frying pan and fry garlic, almonds and bread until lightly browned. Remove and grind to a paste. Add saffron, cumin and nutmeg pounded together. Salt and pepper the oil in which garlic and almonds were fried. Add a little boiling water and mix with the paste. Stir everything smooth and put in baking dish. Break required number of eggs carefully over the sauce and put in quick oven to set.

Since both Spain and Portugal adopted many Moorish dishes after their conquest centuries ago, such oriental dishes as Moorish Eggs spring up unexpectedly throughout Latin America.

BRAZILIAN POACHED EGGS WITH FAROFA

Slice 1 onion very thin, cover with plenty of cold water, season with salt and pepper, and simmer about 10 minutes until tender. Break required number of eggs, slide them into the pan and poach with the onion. Take up eggs separately on warm plate and keep them hot. Thicken pan liquor and onion slices with toasted *farinha de mandioca* (cassava meal) until as thick as mashed potatoes. Arrange on a hot dish and place poached eggs on top.

FAROFA

Cassava, *manico*, manioc, or whatever local name it goes by, is the poisonous root of a plant whose foliage resembles that of the castor bean, and it supplies the base of innumerable dishes throughout tropical America. Spanish and Portuguese settlers early learned to make cassava meal from the Indians, who grate the raw root, hang it in a flexible basket from a crude frame, apply weights until all possible juice is squeezed out, then heat the fine gratings until the poisonous element is chemically changed and the resulting meal is a sustaining and useful food, known in Brazil as *farinha de mandioca*. It is prepared commercially and is not only on every Brazilian table in a wooden bowl furnished with a special wooden spoon for sprinkling it over almost every dish, but it is continually dipped into the kitchen as a handy thickening agent for sauces and a nourishing but bland addition to meat and vegetable dishes. Cassava meal, and sometimes cassava flour (*fuba*), can be purchased in Spanish stores in many American cities.

Farofa is a dish in which cassava meal is a chief ingredient, as in the preceding recipe for Brazilian Poached Eggs.

Directions for making other *farofa*-egg dishes:

(1) Spread cassava meal in bottom of a shallow pan and toast slightly in oven until dry and crisp. Butter a second pan and break into it required number of eggs. Season and set in oven until eggs are set but yolks still soft. Stir into eggs as much toasted cassava meal as they will take without becoming too dry.

(2) Drop eggs into hot butter in frying pan. Season and scramble with sufficient toasted cassava meal to thicken slightly without being too dry.

(3) Mince required number of hard-cooked eggs. Heat butter in frying pan in proportion of 1 teaspoon to each egg. Add minced eggs, seasonings and toasted cassava meal to make a dry crumbly mixture. When flavored with chopped onion, minced garlic and chopped parsley this is a favorite stuffing for chicken, turkey and suckling pig.

(4) A second-day dish is often made of leftover roast pork by reheating its leftover gravy, dropping in 1–2 well-beaten eggs and then thickening with toasted cassava meal to get an effect like Yorkshire pudding. Slices of roast pork, heated separately in a little broth or gravy, are laid on top of this *farofa* specialty.

MEXICAN HUASVULCLI
A Holy Week Egg Dish

Fry 3 peeled and chopped tomatoes in a pan with 2 tablespoons butter and seasonings. Break 3 eggs into pan and stir a little. Season, then add 3 tablespoons grated cheese. (Seasoning may include a generous dash of chili powder.)

MEXICAN OMELET
Tortilla de Huevos

Make Mexican Red Sauce (see recipe). Break 4 eggs into a
bowl. Add 2 tablespoons cold water, salt and pepper and beat
only until well mixed. Melt 2 tablespoons butter in frying pan
over moderate heat. Add eggs and make omelet in French
fashion; that is, lift film as it forms on bottom and let liquid
egg run under until almost no liquid remains. Lay part of
sauce across center and fold. Increase heat 1 minute to brown
the bottom, then invert over hot platter. Cover with remaining sauce.

MEXICAN STUFFED EGGS
Huevos Rellenos

Split 4 hard-cooked eggs lengthwise. Remove yolks and mash
with ½ minced onion, ½ minced green pepper, ¼ teaspoon
salt, several dashes Tabasco, 1 teaspoon minced parsley, 2 teaspoons lemon juice and 1 tablespoon olive oil. Refill and place
a pitted or stuffed olive on top. Garnish platter with half slices
of avocado and whole slices of tomato.

If this dish is desired hot arrange egg halves in a buttered
baking dish. Pour around them ½ cup Mexican Red Sauce and
heat in oven.

BRAZILIAN STUFFED EGGS
Ovos Recheados

6 hard-cooked eggs	1 tablespoon grated cheese
½ cup soft bread crumbs	1 teaspoon parsley, minced
Milk	1 teaspoon onion juice
2 tablespoons butter, melted	Salt and pepper
Tomato sauce	

Split eggs lengthwise. Soak crumbs in milk and press dry.
Mash yolks, mix smooth with crumbs, butter, cheese, parsley,

onion juice and seasonings. Stuff into split egg whites. Reheat in covered baking dish or over steam, and serve hot with tomato sauce.

BRAZILIAN EGGS IN FISH SAUCE
Ovos com Molho do Peixe

Split hard-cooked eggs lengthwise and arrange halves in buttered baking dishes, cut sides up. Thicken Brazilian Fish Sauce (see recipe) with toasted cassava meal and pour over. Dot with butter. Press 1–2 hard-cooked egg yolks through sieve and scatter over top. Heat in covered dish in oven or over steam.

PERUVIAN PIQUANT EGGS
Huevos Picantes

6 hard-cooked eggs	A little tomato sauce
1 small tin of sardines	A little cream or mayonnaise

Cut a little from top and bottom of hard-cooked eggs to make them stand nicely. Cut in halves and take out yolks. Skin and bone sardines and mash fine with tomato sauce. Season to taste. Moisten with a little cream or mayonnaise dressing and add ½ the egg yolks. Fill cavities in egg whites with the mixture; place a strip of red pepper across top and serve on lettuce leaf with mayonnaise.

PARAGUAYAN EGGS WITH TOMATO SAUCE
Huevos con Salsa de Tomate

Devil eggs by removing yolks from hard-cooked eggs. Mix with a little salt, onion and melted butter, then replace in the whites. Put on platter in slow oven for 8 minutes and then pour over them a rich tomato sauce made by boiling tomatoes, salt, pepper, onion and a taste of vinegar until thick.

CUBAN RUM OMELET
Omelette al Ron

5 eggs
5 tablespoons cold water
½ teaspoon salt
1 tablespoon sugar

3 tablespoons butter
1 cup mixed canned fruit
1 teaspoon powdered sugar
½ cup rum

Beat eggs slightly with water, salt and sugar. Melt 2 table-spoons butter in a very smooth thick frying pan over moderate heat. Add eggs, and as film forms on bottom of pan lift with spatula to let eggs run underneath, adding bits of remaining butter around edge of pan when it seems to be needed. When eggs are nearly all coagulated lay chopped canned fruit across center and fold. Increase heat for a moment and invert into a hot platter. Sprinkle with powdered sugar. Pour rum over and light. Let burn until flame dies down.

To give the proper touch, there should be at least one tropical fruit in the canned fruit mixture, such as figs which are always easy to obtain. And the omelet must be taken up while still very moist, since the burning rum will finish cooking it.

LITTLE MEAT PIES

EMPADAS, EMPADINHAS, EMPANADAS, EMPANADITAS AND EMPANADILLAS

The difference between *empadas*, *empadinhas*, *empanadas*, *empanaditas* and *empanadillas* is largely in the degree of affection. Theoretically *empadas* are grown-up Portuguese meat pies while *empadinhas* are little ones. Likewise *empanadas* are regulation-size Spanish ones, with *empanaditas* and *empanadillas* representing their offspring. But as a matter of fact they're all about equally small and the words are as interchangeable as the fillings.

BRAZILIAN EMPADAS, OR EMPANADAS

Empadas are the Brazilian-Portuguese equivalent of the *empanadas* and *empanadillas* of Spanish-speaking countries and are like them also in that they are served at the beginning of a meal, as well as for a quick snack at any hour. In the late afternoon pastry shops are crowded with customers who buy them out of heated glass cases and stand about consuming them on the spot, a smart and sociable custom in fashionable shopping districts.

PASTRY FOR EMPADAS
Masa para Empadas

1½ cups flour	1 egg white
½ teaspoon salt	2 egg yolks
¼ pound butter	Hot water

Mix flour and salt. Cut in butter as for pie crust. Slightly beat egg white with egg yolks and add gradually to flour mixture with just enough hot water to make a stiff dough. Separate dough into portions and roll out in rounds the size of a saucer or smaller. Fill with any of the following:

FILLINGS FOR EMPADAS

Almost everything good goes into these delicious tidbits in turn, for fillings are legion, including shrimps, oysters, fish, the finer meats such as veal, chicken and game—venison, rabbit, armadillo, partridge, *jacu*, etc. The filling must have sufficient gravy to moisten thoroughly without its running all over the fingers or plates.

SQUAB FILLING

Fry seasoned squabs until done, in butter or fat with a chopped onion, a teaspoon or more of minced parsley and a slice or more of chopped bacon. Cut meat in small pieces. Chop 2–3 hard-cooked eggs. Mix together, adding frying pan remains and 1 cup or less white wine to moisten well. Simmer together until well mixed, adding additional seasonings if necessary, and let cool. Lay a portion on one half of each pastry round made as above. Fold other half over and crimp or pinch edges together. Bake in oven like pies.

SHRIMP FILLING

Mix cut-up cooked shrimps with an equal amount of flaked cooked fish. Add ¼ the quantity of chopped mushrooms, 1 small minced onion, 1 teaspoon minced parsley and 1–2 slices cooked palm heart for each *empada*. Add 1 cup wine and simmer until mushrooms and onion are tender. Make *empadas* as above, putting 1 pitted olive and 1 bit of hard-cooked egg in each. Bake in oven.

Fillings for *empadas* and *empanadas* are interchangeable of course.

ARGENTINE EMPANADAS A LA CRIOLLA
Meat Pies Creole Style

Pastry:

1 teaspoon salt	1 cup shortening
½ cup boiling water	3 cups flour
	1 teaspoon baking powder

Add salt to water. Put shortening in a bowl and pour salted water over. Stir until creamy and add flour sifted with baking powder. Mix to smooth dough and put in cool place to chill. In the meantime prepare the following:

Filling:

3 onions	½ teaspoon chili pepper
1 garlic clove	sauce
2 green pimientos	6 ground peppercorns
1 tomato	1 teaspoon salt
Olive oil	1 teaspoon sugar
½ pound well-chopped	1 tablespoon flour
meat	1 hard-cooked egg, sliced

Olives

Chop vegetables very fine and fry in olive oil until all are well cooked. Add seasonings and flour. Stir and cook 15 minutes. The filling should be moist and quite hot with chili pepper.

Cut chilled pastry dough into pieces about the size of small biscuit and roll out into thin rounds, trimming with knife if necessary. Place a large spoonful of stuffing on each round with an egg slice and 1 olive. Fold over and press edges together. Brush with egg, beaten with a little cold water, and bake to a rich brown in a hot oven.

In Latin America these individual meat pies of Spanish origin are as handy for snacks as are sandwiches here or *piroshnis* in Russia. *Empanadas* are made of plain or puff paste and filled with many different mixtures usually containing meat and always juicy with good gravy. Their distinguishing characteristic, however, is the slice of cooked egg and the olive. Any kind of an olive will do, but a plain green one is most piquant and for tang, chili pepper sauce, almost as hot as Tabasco, which should not be confused with our mild chili sauce relish.

As with our sweet American pies, *empanadas* are made in two styles: open face and hunting case (covered with a top crust). They're also baked within one crust, like the great individual meat pies of old England.

In bars, quick lunches and bakery shops throughout Latin America you will find little square glass steam boxes standing on the counter displaying a toothsome variety of these pastries, and all you have to do is lift the lid and help yourself at a few pennies per pie. For unlike the cold English pork and lark pies, *empanadas* are at their very best when eaten piping hot.

The *empanadas* of Latin America are as varied as the *vol au vents* of France. Although basically much the same, their composition varies somewhat in Argentine, Mexico, Chile, etc.

PUERTO RICAN EMPANADILLAS
Little Meat Pies

Crust:

2 cups flour	2 tablespoons Crisco
1 teaspoon baking powder	1 egg
½ teaspoon salt	½ cup cold water

Sift flour, baking powder and salt together. Add Crisco by cutting in with two knives. Add egg and mix well. Add cold water to form a firm dough. Place in icebox for about 1 hour.

Filling:

2 tablespoons lard	½ teaspoon garlic, finely minced
3 tablespoons minced onions	
2 tablespoons sweet green peppers, minced	1 hard-cooked egg, chopped fine
⅓ cup tomato sauce	1 tablespoon capers
1 cup cooked meat, ground	2 tablespoons seedless raisins
½ teaspoon salt	2 tablespoons olives, minced

Fry onion and garlic in the fat for a minute. Add chopped peppers and tomato sauce and fry another minute. Add meat and salt and fry until the liquid has evaporated, then add remaining ingredients.

Roll the crust pastry very thin. Cut in circular pieces about 5 inches in diameter. Put 1 tablespoon of the filling in the center of each circular piece of pastry. Moisten edges and double over until they meet. Press edges together with a fork to make a crimpy pattern. Fry in deep fat for about 3 minutes.

This Puerto Rican recipe makes 16 small *empanadas*, or meat pies. The difference between *empanadas* and *empanadillas* is in size only.

It's interesting to note that Crisco is called for in making the crust while the filling specifies lard. For as a matter of fact in many Latin-American countries influenced by American advertising the two are synonymous, and although Crisco is a vegetable fat it means pork lard to most of our neighbors. So when you find Crisco in a Latin-American recipe it means plain lard. Likewise Royal means baking powder of any brand, and is often spelled without the capital letter, showing that the publicity of Royal Baking Powder has put a new word into the Spanish language. Also, Maizena, an American brand name for cornstarch, is the word generally used for any fine white corn flour. It would be hard to find more convincing proof of the effect of Yankee advertising, in spite of the fact that local substitutes usually are used in place of the ballyhooed article.

CHILEAN FRIED MEAT PIES
Empanaditas Fritas

Dough:

3 cups flour	3 tablespoons melted lard
3 tablespoons tepid water	

Mix well. Divide dough in 2 equal parts and roll out as thin as possible. Put spoonfuls of meat filling at regular intervals on 1 piece of dough and moisten around filling. Cover with the other strip of dough and stamp out *empanaditas* with a cutter around the fillings, pressing moistened edges so they will stick.

Meat Filling:

Put 5 tablespoons melted butter, highly seasoned with Spanish paprika, into a saucepan over low heat. Fry in it 1 chopped onion until soft, then add some minced cold meat, sprinkled with a little flour and seasoned with salt, pepper and cumin seed. Stir until lightly browned. Soften with a little boiling water and set aside to cool. When cold add chopped hard-cooked egg and minced parsley.

In place of the butter and Spanish paprika given above Chileans use a prepared cooking fat highly colored with red peppers. Its kitchen name is "color," meaning just the same as in English, and it is used for giving an attractive rosy hue to countless dishes.

The process of preparing *empanaditas* is close to that of making ravioli, except much more filling is used for *empanaditas* and the filling may be varied, of course, in the same way. Chileans are fond of chopped giblets, such as chicken livers, in their *empanaditas*.

ECUADORIAN CHEESE PIES
Empanadas de Queso

2 cups flour	3 tablespoons chopped and
4 tablespoons butter	seeded raisins
¼ teaspoon salt	2 hard-cooked eggs, sliced
1 beaten egg	1 teaspoon sugar
Cold water	2 ounces fresh white cheese

Make first 5 ingredients into firm dough and roll out thin. Put raisins, hard-cooked eggs, sugar and cheese in bowl. Chop fine. Mix to a paste and arrange in small heaps over dough. Cut into 4–5 inch squares including 1 heap of filling in each square. Double corners to form a triangle and flute edges with a fork. Fry in deep fat. Drain; sprinkle with sugar and eat hot.

NATIONAL STEWS

SPANISH–AMERICAN STEW
Olla Podrida or Cocido Espanol

3 pints chick-peas
  (garbanzos)
¼ pound each: salt beef,
  bacon, salt pork and
  salty sausage
1 large chicken, jointed
3 small birds (or 1 pigeon)
1 pig's tail, ear or snout
Salt
1 onion
1 clove
2 garlic cloves
6 peppercorns

Thick flour paste
1 pint fresh Lima beans
1 small cabbage
6 small beets
6 small carrots
½ pound pork sausage,
  sliced
¾ pound blood sausage,
  sliced
¼ pound cooked veal
¼ pound ham, cooked
2 eggs
Bread crumbs

12 small potatoes, peeled

Soak garbanzos (chick-peas), salt beef, salt pork and salty sausage (chorizo) overnight. Drain meat and put into a deep kettle with chicken and, if possible, 3 small birds, or a pigeon, certainly a pig's tail, ear or snout. Cover deep with cold water. Put over the fire and bring to boiling point. Then lower the flame and cook slowly. Parboil chick-peas (garbanzos). Drain, and add them to the stewpot gradually, taking care that the boiling does not cease or the peas will harden. Salt to taste and skim. Add an onion, pierced with a clove. Add garlic and peppercorns. Cover and seal kettle lid with flour paste. Simmer without stirring, 5 hours. The pot can be shaken occasionally, but the skin of the peas must not be broken or they will not color well and besides the stew will become mushy.

At the end of the fourth hour place in another large kettle

with plenty of water the fresh Lima beans, cabbage, beets, carrots, sliced pork sausage, blood sausage and meat balls made of minced cooked veal, minced ham, eggs and enough sifted bread crumbs to hold them in shape. Twenty minutes later remove some of the broth from the kettle and cook potatoes in it.

Just before serving the *cocido*, season with teaspoon of cinnamon and another of saffron to give the *cocido* the rich color that stamps it perfect to the Spanish eye. Pile the garbanzos, well drained, in the center of a large deep platter. Circle with the potatoes and place the meats around them. In another plate serve the other vegetables. Serve both dishes at the same time with the following sauce:

SAUCE FOR THE COCIDO
Salsa para el Cocido

1 clove garlic, minced	1 large potato, cooked
1 sweet pepper, minced	1 tablespoon parsley,
1 teaspoon saffron	chopped
3 tomatoes, cooked	2 tablespoons vinegar
Salt	¼ cup *cocido* broth

Mix garlic, pepper and saffron in a bowl. Add strained pulp of tomatoes and the potato. Mash all together thoroughly. Add parsley, vinegar and *cocido* broth. Salt to taste and serve hot.

In another bowl serve a cold pepper sauce.

Strain the broth in the two cooking pots and use as soup course.

A salad and an iced melon, or a compote of fruit, finishes this meal most satisfactorily.

The *cocido*, literally a stew cooked in an olla, a big round earthen pot with a small opening at the top, resembling the bean pot of Boston, is the classic dish of Spain and a four-course dinner in itself. There are forty-nine provinces in Spain, and regionalism is so strong it is said there are forty-nine national *cocidos*, every one of which has found its way to one part of Latin America or another.

There is no cut-and-dried rule for what goes into the olla. That detail is more or less left to the resources of the kitchen larder and the genius of the cook, so it varies a good deal in such places as Buenos Aires, Lima and Mexico City, yet it's on tap everywhere in one form or another.

It is not only a dish of delicious savor, but it is really most economical. Its rich broth furnishes the basis of various soups and sauces for other meals, and the selection of its ingredients allows a variation to fit the changing seasons and locality of production.

Cervantes' Don Quixote says of the olla grande, the "grand dish" to which game birds are added, "It is eaten only by canons and bishops."

Olla pudrida translates literally "putrid pot," but this is only a quirk of Spanish humor and is really an affectionate pet name for the national dish. The Germans, however, add insult to the injurious name by transferring it into their language as *stink-topf*, stinkpot. The dish indeed is as "high" as an Englishman's grouse, which is ready for the grill only when the leg bones have turned powdery and green and the bird is ready to drop off them. The reason for suspecting the olla at all is merely that the earthenware pot from which its name derives is never entirely emptied and washed out for a fresh beginning. It is like the old-fashioned soup pot, sitting unchanged on the back of the stove, ready to receive any enriching tidbit to revivify the brew. Furthermore, Spanish bacon, one of the olla's main ingredients, which has its counterparts throughout Latin America is often greasy and rancid, and since its strong savor persists in the pot in some out-of-the-way *posadas*, where refreshment is had for man and beast, this international *cocido* does live up to its name.

An olla is also the porous clay waterpot, painted with fruits and flowers, which stands on every Spanish and Latin-American table, cooling the drinking water by evaporation. Where ice is scarce there is no better way to keep water sweet and potable. And nothing makes a more stunning table piece than a colorful olla from Peru, Bolivia or Mexico. (From the Spanish section of *The European Cookbook*, by the Browns.)

CUBAN OLLA OR COCIDO

2 pounds beef or veal	4 tender carrots
1 pound fresh pork	1 young eggplant
6 slices bacon	½ cabbage
½ pound *tasajo* (jerked meat)	1 pint string beans
	6 potatoes
½ pound *carne salada* (salt meat)	2 onions
	1 young turnip
1 pork sausage	4 tomatoes
1 pint soaked garbanzos (chick-peas)	3 garlic cloves
	Chili
2 plantains, or bananas	Cumin
2 ears green corn	Coriander
1 young squash	½ teaspoon saffron

A good sized kettle is needed for this generous recipe in order to allow for plenty of broth. Half fill it with water. Put in meat and garbanzos. Cover and set over medium heat to cook slowly. Skim during first hour of cooking and add salt, if needed. At the end of 1½ hours add bananas in their skins, cut in several chunks, and the ears of corn, also cut in 3 or 4 pieces. Peel remaining vegetables, but put them in whole and continue cooking. Mash garlic cloves with a bit of hot pepper, a few crushed cumin and coriander seeds and pound to a paste. Work in a little of the stew broth to thin it and stir into contents of kettle. When ready to take up dissolve saffron in a little of the broth, stir in and let simmer until thoroughly blended.

The Cuban olla or *cocido* is served with very little of its broth, for this rich essence usually is reserved as the foundation for the fine soups of Cuba.

In Cuba several other vegetables, such as yuca and chayote,

go into this great stew, so if you can find them in your market put them in, too, to give the proper native touch. And if you can't locate the real Cuban *tasajo* and the *carne salada* that Cuba chiefly imports from Argentina and Uruguay you'll have to get by with dried beef and salt pork.

BRAZILIAN COZIDO
Boiled Dinner

A Brazilian boiled dinner or *cozido* is quite different from the usual Spanish-American *cocido*. It begins with counting noses and portioning out the ingredients accordingly, for a confusing number of meats go into it, not to mention vegetables, and each person must get a taste of everything. With the exception of the sausages which are cooked whole and cut up after the dish is done, all other ingredients are divided into the exact number of portions. Everything comes ready for cooking except the jerked beef, which must be soaked in cold water at least 3 hours. And all the meats can usually be bought in Spanish stores or foreign markets in any big American city. This recipe serves 6.

1 tablespoon butter or fat	3 slices salt pork
1 onion, chopped	½ pound beef brisket
1 garlic clove, minced	Back and less desirable parts
Herb bouquet	of 1 chicken
8 whole peppers	¼ pound jerked beef
1 small red chili	½ pound smoked pork
Salt	sausage
¼ pound raw ham, sliced	½ pound smoked beef
thin	sausage

3 pints boiling water

Heat fat. Add onion and slowly fry until golden. Add garlic and continue slow frying until lightly browned. Add herb bouquet consisting of bay leaf, parsley sprigs and 1 sprig celery leaves. Add whole peppers, chili and boiling water. Be sparing with salt, remembering that nearly all the meats are already too salty. Bring liquid to boiling point. Add cut-up meats and whole sausages and simmer until all are becoming tender. Then add the following vegetables in the order of their cooking time:

6 small onions	6 pieces yellow squash
1 small cabbage, cut in	3 grated carrots
sixths	6 3-inch pieces green corn
6 portions cassava root	

The vegetables are varied at will, turnips, cauliflower, collards and whole carrots sometimes being included, and white potatoes in place of cassava root. Sometimes, too, sweet potatoes or plantains are cooked separately and added to the platter after taking up.

When all are done take up meats in center of platter, arrange vegetables around them and pour broth into a tureen.

Dish out at the table into soup plates and pour over each serving a generous ladle of the broth. Have a dish of Brazilian Pepper Sauce (see recipe) within reach of everyone. Eat with knife, fork and soup spoon.

Needless to say, this is a complete dinner if followed by fruit for dessert, and then black coffee.

ARGENTINE PUCHERO

The *puchero*, a version of the Spanish *cocido* and the national Argentine noontime stand-by of rich and poor alike, is as simple or complicated as the occasion requires, like our boiled dinner. It has long been the custom to make a specialty of this dish in such places as the old Petit Salon which catered to early Buenos Aires night-club trade. At about three o'clock in the morning a *puchero* is ready in enormous pots and the service thereof is unique in the realms of heavy eating. One portion is arranged on a turkey platter, with a grinning half of a calf's head in the center—ears, teeth and all—surrounded by legs, wings and breast of chicken, boiled sausages, slices of boiled beef and an assortment of vegetables, including ears of green corn, an astonishing and formidable array of food sufficient for six people. We have seen one lone man consume it all.

A simple recipe for *puchero* runs as follows:

2 pounds boiling beef	2 turnips
2–3 smoked sausages	1 onion, sliced
1 thin slice raw ham	½ small cabbage
2 carrots	2–3 ears corn
3–4 potatoes	Salt and pepper

Cook meats in boiling water until beef is beginning to be tender. Add vegetables in order of cooking time. Season and boil until all are done. Arrange meats and vegetables on a platter and serve soup in a tureen. Place a bit of each ingredient in a soup plate and pour over a ladle of soup. Eat with knife, fork and spoon. (The sausages are of the well-smoked and dried variety that may be purchased in Italian groceries or Spanish.)

PEPPER POT

The essential ingredient for the true pepper pot as made in the West Indies and the Guianas is cassareep, a dark brown syrupy liquid, looking something like caramel, made by boiling down the juice expressed from grated cassava root (mandioca) in the process of making cassava meal. Except in some districts the dish is not highly spiced, nor is cassareep peppery, but it has a flavor all its own, and furthermore it has the property, like that of the papayo fruit and leaves, of tendering the toughest meats. Like the custom of the *Olla Podrida* in Spain, leftover pepper pot is used in starting the pot the following day. Thus some of the best pepper pots have been going for years, perhaps for generations, until their distinctive taste cannot be imitated by mere parvenus. West Indians in New York City must have their pepper pots always simmering, and since cassareep is not sold in local stores, even those that handle other tropical products for this trade, they have discovered that a similar flavor is imparted by the commercial sauce, Kitchen Bouquet. A number of similar sauces, including Worcestershire, are said to contain this concentrated extract of cassava.

Here is a recipe from Trinidad:

TRINIDAD PEPPER POT

1 small chicken, or	¼ pound salt pork
½ large chicken	1 onion, sliced
1–1½ pounds beef	1 garlic clove, minced
1 pound lean pork	Salt and pepper

3 tablespoons cassareep (or Kitchen Bouquet)

Start meats cooking with onion and garlic over very low fire with very little water, and when they have been bubbling gently but constantly for ½ hour or more add the cassareep, remembering that too much cassareep makes the stew too dark, according to Trinidad standards. After a while add salt and pepper to taste, using not only black pepper but also a whole chili or several dashes of pepper sauce, since this particular dish is hotter than those of some other localities. Let simmer until meats are very tender.

In some places onion, garlic and pepper are never put in until the moment of serving.

Boiled okra is often eaten with this dish.

There is another kind of pepper pot common in the West Indies that takes its name from the amount of peppers that go into it, and that contains no cassareep. It is made as follows:

JAMAICAN PEPPER POT

½ pound salt pork	1 pound cut-up okra
1 pound pickled spareribs	1–2 green plantains
1 pound jerked beef, or	1 portion cassava root
corned beef	1–2 yautias (dasheens)
3 pounds chopped spinach	Salt

Plenty of pepper and pepper sauce

(If plantains, cassava root [yucca] and yautias cannot be obtained in local market, substitute 4–5 white potatoes and 2 sweet potatoes.)

Soak meats overnight in plenty of cold water to remove part of their salt, then wash in fresh water. Cover with sufficient cold water to cook vegetables and simmer until meats are becoming tender, then add spinach, okra, peeled plantains and peeled roots with salt to taste, if needed, and pepper until mixture stings the tongue. Cook until vegetables are done, stirring with a wooden spoon occasionally to prevent scorching. The finished dish should be quite thick.

CHILEAN CARBONADA

1 pound beef, diced
1 onion, chopped
Butter
Spanish paprika
2–3 potatoes, diced

3 tablespoons rice
3 tablespoons peas
A piece of pumpkin, diced
½ cup corn
Salt and pepper

1 egg yolk, beaten

In a casserole fry meat with onion in butter highly colored with Spanish paprika. Cook about 20 minutes until well browned, then add potatoes and cook another 10 minutes, giving an occasional stir. Cover with boiling water. Add rice, peas, pumpkin (a piece about 4 inches square, diced) and corn, preferably cut from fresh cob. Season well and simmer 1 hour. Put beaten egg in bottom of soup tureen. Pour the soupy stew over. Stir and serve.

This is more like a thick soup or beef stew than a Spanish *carbonada*, but that's the name it goes by in both Chile and the Argentine. (See note under Argentine Beef Stew with Noodles.)

ARGENTINE LAMB STEW
Cazuela de Cordero

3 pounds lamb	1 cup green peas
3 quarts boiling water	2 cups green beans, cut fine
1 tablespoon salt	1 ear green corn
2 tablespoons butter	6 cubes of squash
1 onion, chopped	Salt and pepper to taste
1 carrot, sliced	6 small potatoes
1 celery heart, minced	1½ tablespoons rice
1 garlic clove, minced	1 egg yolk
½ teaspoon marjoram (dry)	4 tablespoons milk
A tiny pinch cumin seeds	1 teaspoon parsley, minced

Cut lamb into 6 portions. Cover with water. Add salt and let cook gently. Melt butter in frying pan and fry in it onion, carrot, celery, garlic and herbs slowly. When onion is soft turn mixture into the lamb stew. Add peas, beans, squash cubes and ear of corn cut into 6 pieces. When meat is nearly done, about 25 minutes before serving, add potatoes. Season to taste and add rice. When all are done beat egg yolk with milk. Remove stew from heat. Stir in egg mixture. Add parsley and serve at once in deep bowls, portioning each with meat and vegetables.

The original recipe calls for goat's milk, but since so little is used in it, cow's milk will do as well.

ARGENTINE BEEF STEW WITH NOODLES
Carbonada con Refalosas

Chop very fine 2 large onions, 2 garlic cloves, 1 sprig parsley and 1 red pepper, peeled and partly seeded. Fry in 2 tablespoons oil or lard. Add 4 peeled and sliced tomatoes, and when smooth and bubbling stir in ½ pound chopped veal and same amount of potatoes, cut in eighths. Add 1 cut-up turnip, 2 minced carrots and a few fresh peas or corn cut from cob. Pour boiling water over to more than cover. Stir until thoroughly mixed and add enough tomato paste to give a rich color. Cover and cook until tender over slow fire.

For noodles: mix 1 cup flour to a firm dough with a little salted warm water. Roll this out thin. Cut into short narrow strips. Shape into circles and drop into stew 10 minutes before taking up.

In the rich agricultural section around Mendoza Italian farmers have popularized the making of tomato paste so that in season there are trays of seeded tomatoes laid out everywhere, being sun-cooked into paste. And another specialty of this rich Argentine province is dried squash which goes into all sorts of *carbonadas* and *locros* (see directions for making it, under *Argentine Chichoca de Zapallo*).

Both Argentina and Chile enjoy hearty stews like this under the name of *carbonada,* although the original Spanish *carbonada* consists of nothing but meat, fish or fowl, well scored and grilled over charcoal, carbon, whence the name. But they're good ragouts or stews in spite of their somewhat misleading name.

ARGENTINE JERKED BEEF STEW
Charquican

In the Argentine portions of beef, pork, emu and guanaco are cut into steaks, put through a drying process and chipped or pounded into flakes when used. Such dried meats are called charqui, and *charquican* is almost any stew of them. Beef charqui is imported here, but Texas jerked beef (not dried beef) will do just as well in this tasty stew.

Fry a red pepper in 2 tablespoons oil or lard and remove it. Fry a good-sized chopped onion until soft in the same seasoned fat. Add 3 sliced tomatoes, and when the sauce is smooth and bubbling add ½ pound jerked beef, previously put through chopper, and 1½ cups water. Season to taste with salt, pepper and marjoram. Cut in 2 or 3 potatoes. Add 1 cup fresh peas or Limas and 2 tablespoons washed rice. Cover close and cook over low heat until everything is tender.

CHARQUI (JERKED BEEF) AS MADE IN MENDOZA, ARGENTINA

Select tender parts of beef, pork, guanaco or rhea. Cut out as large a piece of meat as possible. Slice into thin steaks and put under a press to extract excess juice. Rub coarse salt into meat on each side and stack pieces on top of each other without pressing. Let stand 24 hours. Then drain and expose to air, protected with a wire screen and a cover on top to avoid dew. After 4 or 5 days put steaks on a table and pound them with a wooden mallet. This operation should be repeated 2 or 3 times in order to obtain a *parejo charqui*, tender and fibrous. They must be kept in dry, fresh air. You will find various recipes in this book that specify *charqui*—meaning beef charqui which is the common commercial kind.

The rhea is South America's ostrich that still runs wild on the pampas. (See Argentine Ostrich.)

The guanaco, too, travels the plains in herds. It's supposed to be the great grandpappy of both the llama and the alpaca and has served Indians and plainsmen with meat in the same abundance as did our almost extinct bison. It also inspired an early North American poet to song:

> *O, give me a ship with sail and with wheel,*
> *And let me be off to happy Brazil!*
> *I long to rest 'neath the broad spreading palm,*
> *To gaze at her rivers so placid and calm—*
> *Pluck her gold fruits so delicious and sweet,*
> *And try a taste of her guanaco meat!*

Young guanaco is such good eating that many far-southern South Americans prefer it to veal, but the older animal yields a tough, strong-tasting meat that becomes all the more individualistic when made into *charqui* and allowed to get a little rancid.

Charqui is known in Brazil as *xarque*, in the Spanish West Indies as *tasajo* and in French Haiti as *boucan*, the latter giving the name to the buccaneers who early settled that island and subsisted almost entirely on this jerked beef.

CHILEAN CHARQUICAN

4 medium potatoes	2 tablespoons fat
Salt	1 teaspoon paprika
½ cup green peas	1 medium onion, chopped
½ cup string beans	1 tomato, sliced
4 cubes yellow squash	1 cup grated green corn
½ red chili	¼ pound charqui or dried
(or 2–3 dashes cayenne)	beef
1 teaspoon minced parsley	

Peel potatoes and start cooking in just enough salted boiling water to cover. Cover pan, and after 15–20 minutes add peas, sliced beans and squash. Fry chili in fat and remove. Add paprika and onion to fat and slowly fry until tender. Add tomato and stir and fry until tomato thickens. Add corn and continue slow frying 5 minutes. If charqui is used have it soaked overnight in plenty of cold water. Grind or pound charqui or smoked beef rather fine and add to onion-corn mixture, then add drained vegetables with sufficient of their cooking liquor to form a sauce.

Charqui (jerked beef) can be purchased in Spanish or specialty stores.

Canned vegetables, well drained, may be substituted for fresh peas, string beans, tomato and corn, which makes this a handy dish for quick preparation.

FEIJOADA, OR FEIJOADA COMPLETA
The National Dish of Brazil

¾ pound jerked beef	¼ pound bacon
½ pound smoked sausage	1 pig's foot
½ pound smoked pork	1 pig's ear
¼ pound smoked tongue	1 pig's tail
3 cups black beans	

Soak jerked beef in plenty of water overnight. Drain; cover with cold water. Bring to boiling point. Boil 5 minutes. Drain again and cool. Place all meats in a saucepan. Cover with tepid water. Bring slowly to boiling point and simmer until nearly tender. Meanwhile in a separate saucepan cook the beans, and they must be black. Start them in cold water with no seasonings and cook gently until nearly tender. (Beans and meats will take approximately the same length of time.) Put contents of the 2 saucepans together and simmer until meats are very tender and beans are soft enough to mash easily. One half hour before they are done make the following sauce:

1 green onion, chopped	1 garlic clove, minced
1 onion, chopped	2–3 chilies, or
1 piece fresh sausage	dashes of cayenne

Slowly fry onions with mashed sausage until they begin to color, then add garlic and chopped chilies from which seeds have been removed. Stir and fry until lightly browned. Add 1 cup beans from saucepan and partially mash them with a wooden spoon. Add a little of the bean liquid and stir and simmer until a sauce is formed. Add this sauce to beans and meat and simmer until well blended. Slice meats so each person can have at least 1 small piece of each kind, down to the pig's tail, and arrange them on a large platter with the tongue in the center, according to long-established custom, and all the other sliced meats surrounding it artistically. Moisten them all with some of the soupy beans. The remaining crushed beans are served separately in a hot tureen. And there must be another big dishful of plain boiled or Spanish-style rice to accompany the feast.

The eating of this great dish that looks like a black man cut to bits, sluiced with gravy and sprinkled with snowy *farinha*, is quite as conventional and ceremonious as the laying out of the many meats on the platter. A personal selection of meats is first spread out on the diner's plate with a steaming heap of rice alongside, then the ebony beans and their rich sauce are ladled over, to be mixed with mouthfuls as desired. The finishing touch is a tablespoon or more of plain or toasted cassava meal (*farinha* or *farinha de mandioca*) dusted all over the meats with a wooden spoon dipped into the attractive little hardwood *farinha* bowl that is as necessary as a salt shaker on every Brazilian table. Also a small spoonful of hot freshly made Brazilian Pepper Sauce (see recipe) should be sprinkled on. Serve cut-up oranges in small separate dishes, and set a cordial glass of white rum (*cachaca*) at each place to be drunk as a digestive while consuming this rich food.

Feijoada is the best bean dish of all time, and is the daily midday fare of every Brazilian family, the number of meat ingredients varying to suit the means of the household. A plain *feijoada* may have but 1 or 2 kinds of meat, but a *feijoada completa* (complete) has everything. For special occasions a pint of orange juice is included in the liquid that cooks the meat, and needless to say adds much to the flavor.

So necessary are beans and rice to the sustenance of the Brazilian nation that a man is said to earn his *feijao e arroz* instead of his bread and butter.

DOMINICAN SANCOCHO

Have 2 pounds lean pork cut into convenient serving pieces and stew with 1 sliced onion, 1 garlic clove, 1 bay leaf, several parsley sprigs, salt and 6–8 whole peppers. When nearly done add peeled and cut-up yucca tubers (also called yautia and sold in New York markets under the name of *leren*, dasheen, and eddo—a brown potatolike root marked with growth rings). Then add cubes of hard yellow squash (*aujama*), and not long before taking up add a sufficient number of 2-inch lengths of peeled plantain (or banana). When all are tender serve as a stew with broth poured over.

Plantain is a big green starchy cooking banana, not to be confused with our roadside weed of the same name.

Sancocho, a truly native dish with its tropical ingredients, takes the place in the Dominican Republic of the *pucheros* and *cocidos* in cooler Latin-American countries and gives respite from the eternal *Arroz con Frijoles* (see recipes) that's the noontime stand-by throughout the West Indies and Caribbean countries. With it, instead of bread, thin *casabe* (cassava) cakes and yucca meal cakes are eaten in modest homes, with a variety of little rolls, called *panecicos* also made of yucca meal and resembling our corn dodgers.

CUBAN MONDONGO
Tripe

Here is a juicy dish of tripe directly from Spain where it sometimes has other names such as *menudo* in Andalucía and *callos* in Madrid. At home it contains carrots and other Northern vegetables, Spanish sausage and garbanzos, most of which were lost out in the transfer to tropical America, being replaced by indigenous products. It appears as both soup and stew in the Caribbean islands and coastal states, so the following recipe which comes from Cuba serves for Venezuela as well. But Cuba must have the credit, for *mondongo* is so popular there that a special festival called *Veloria de un Mondongo* is held in its honor. Friends gather together during the long hours of the night to sniff the tripe cooking, to sing and dance and keep up the fire.

For ordinary domestic use, however, tripe is sold at Cuban butcher shops already cooked quite tender, just as it is in France and some parts of the United States, thus saving much labor and fuel.

MONDONGO CRIOLLO

After 3–4 pounds of tripe has been cleaned and well washed with hot water scrub with a cut lemon to whiten it. Cut in small pieces. Cover well with cold water. Add 1 calf's foot chopped into several pieces, 2 tablespoons butter, salt, some pieces of green corn, and cook until tender. Then add ¼ pound diced ham, 1 chopped garlic clove with the required number of pieces of cassava, sweet potato and plantain, and for giving it a dark color, add a little *vija* tied up in a little cloth bag. (*Vija*, or *vijao*, are the seeds of a plant whose botanical name is *renealmia exaltata*, containing a sort of black vegetable dye, but a good dash of Kitchen Bouquet will accomplish the same purpose. Of course the bag of *vija* is removed when proper color is obtained.) While vegetables are cooking, grind together 1 teaspoon coriander seeds, 1 teaspoon cumin seeds, a very little saffron, 8–10 blanched almonds, 1 slice moistened bread and a little of the broth from the *mondongo* pot to moisten for easier grinding. Add this ground mixture to the pot with a dozen pitted olives. Let simmer 5 minutes and serve in a hot tureen from which the *mondongo* is dished out into soup plates.

The use of the word *Criollo*, or Creole, in all Latin-American countries is common for any dish adapting native ingredients and technique to Old World recipes, exactly as Creole is a New Orleans cooking term for similar dishes of mixed origin.

LOCROS

ARGENTINE LOCRO

Locro is one of those flexible dishes of everyday country life that can be made with almost any meat or combination of meats, depending on the momentary resources of the kitchen. It resembles Arabian couscous, from which it probably originated, traveling to the Spanish colonies by way of the mother land. Out on the wheat-growing plains of Argentina the main ingredient of *locro* is most often whole grains of wheat, but coarsely milled corn resembling our hominy is equally good. Yellow corn is preferred in many localities because it is supposed to be sweeter, and one asks in the country store for *maiz para locro* (corn for *locro*).

LOCRO DE TRIGO
Locro Made of Wheat

1 pound whole grain wheat	Salt and pepper
2½ quarts cold water	1 pound beef

Cover wheat with water and boil at even temperature until grains are swollen. Season; cut lean, tender beef into finger-sized pieces and add. Boil gently until meat is tender and liquid has become creamy from the breaking up of some of the wheat grains. Serve in a soup tureen and have ready the following sauce:

Sauce for Locro:

3 tablespoons lard	2 tomatoes, peeled and chopped
2 onions, chopped	
2 garlic cloves, minced	1 teaspoon parsley, minced
1 chili pepper, crushed	Salt
(substitute cayenne)	1 teaspoon cumin seeds
Paprika	

Slowly fry onions in lard. Add garlic and continue slow frying. Add chili and tomatoes and continue to cook until thickened. Add parsley, salt, cumin and 1 teaspoon paprika or more. Pour this sauce into center of tureen of *locro* and stir all together.

Instead of beef, this same *locro* may include bits of pork tenderloin, tripe, smoked creole sausages and ½ pound field or black-eye peas, in which case it becomes a company dish, rich enough for any occasion. Also, the dried squash called *chichoca de zapallo* (see recipe) is used for enriching *locro*.

LOCRO DE CHOCLO
Locro Made of Green Corn

6 ears green corn	1 green pepper
½ cup olive oil	Salt and paprika
2 garlic cloves	Cold water
2 tomatoes, peeled and chopped	6 cubes yellow squash
	1 small onion, chopped

Split grains of corn down the rows. Cut off and scrape cream from cobs. Fry garlic cloves in olive oil until brown, then remove garlic. To the garlic-flavored oil add onion and slowly fry until it begins to color. Add tomatoes. Heat pepper under grill until it blisters. Remove skin, seeds and veins. Cut pepper in strips and add. Season. Add corn and sufficient cold water to just cover. Bring to boiling point and add squash. Cook gently 30 minutes. Serve in soup plates.

Whereas wheat *locro* requires many hours of cooking, the green-corn kind is ready in a comparatively short time. There are many individual ways of preparing this hearty *campo* dish, of which the above is typical.

ECUADORIAN LOCRO

Ecuadorian *locro* starts with an onion fried in fat or butter, followed by a large tomato or equivalent in tomato paste. Then a quart of boiling water is added with seasonings and 3–4 cups chopped raw potatoes. When potatoes are soft and all is soupy, milk is added for slightly thinning, and when boiling point is reached 2 slightly beaten eggs are quickly stirred in along with 1–2 tablespoons crumbled white cheese. The soup is removed before it can curdle and is served with fried fish, boiled shrimps or bits of boiled beef.

PARAGUAYAN LOCRO

Everyday *locro*, which Paraguayan rangers boast they can live on without other nourishment beyond steaming gourds full of *yerba maté*, is pretty crude fare consisting of hunks of steer meat fresh from the herd, cooked up with corn and usually served with fried or plain boiled manioc root (cassava) which takes the place of both bread and potatoes. But actually the cattlemen's menu is varied by similar stews with black-eyed peas or Lima beans taking the place of the corn, or included with it, and with sweet potatoes to vary the cooked manioc. Very special *locros* are made for feast days with chicken and pork substituted for beef, and various vegetables added.

MEATS

ARGENTINE FIAMBRES

With meat production for export her greatest industry and boasting the largest refrigerating plant in the world, it is no wonder that Buenos Aires sets the most sophisticated meat table as well. One packing house alone markets over one hundred kinds of preserved, smoked and sausaged beef and pork, including many highly specialized foreign types required by her polyglot population and the European countries with which she trades. With Spanish types of both crude hams and sausages predominating, the list also includes many Italian types of salamis and bolognas, French galantines, Vienna sausages, such German specialties as *blutwurst* and English Oxford sausage.

The average platter of *fiambres* (cold cuts) so characteristic of Buenos Aires eating and usually a feature of the evening meal offers a choice of half a dozen varieties, all equally delicious. They are eaten with bread only—no butter—and the simplest of garnishings—olives, pickles or lettuce leaves.

BIFES

The chief point about *bifes*, *biftec* or *biftek*, however the local spelling runs, is to whale hell out of them with a terrifying weapon that, with all its points and knobs, looks much better suited for a perfect hammer murder than for the preparation of any human food. For beef, from which these little steaks are sliced, is so tough anywhere except in the Argentine and Uruguay that it must almost be pounded to pulp unless it is to be cooked for a long, long time. Since *bifes* appear on nearly every full family menu all Latin America resounds at mealtime with the vicious pounding of these thin little steaks,

as do certain districts in Italy, with the beating of *scaloppini*.
After the *bifes* are fried in fat they are quite toothsome even
though one becomes bored to tears with their monotonous
frequency.

BRAZILIAN CHURRASCO IN BACKWOODS STYLE
Churrasco a Moda de Sertão

Churrasco is perhaps the most popular of Brazilian meats
except the eternal *bifes*. Even when done in a city oven the
flavor is marvelous though the meat itself is a bit tough, both
texture and flavor being partly due to the half-wild cattle
that have been crossed with East Indian zebu strains for many
generations.

The cut used is a big hunk of breast and ribs together, about
6 pounds, and in the country the hide is usually left on. The
meat is well salted with rather coarse salt, then thoroughly
rubbed with much crushed garlic. Preferably it is roasted on
a spit over very hot coals, being turned until brown and crisp
as possible. The fire must be so hot that the inside of the thick
part of the roast remains red in spite of the fact that the outside is so well done.

ARGENTINE ROAST BEEF RIBS
Asado a la Parrilla

This is one of the grand but homely dishes of the Argentine
where even the ribs of beef are especially well furnished with
meat, tender and sweet.

Have about 5–6 pounds of beef ribs cut so there are 3 ribs
to each piece. Season well with salt and pepper and grill over
live coals, turning until outside is crisp and brown. Eat with a
sauce made by frying onion, garlic, chili pepper and tomato
in lard. (See Sauce for *Locro*.) And serve a simple green salad
at the same time.

URUGUAYAN BAKED STEAK
Biftek al Horno

2½ pounds round steak	1 tablespoon salt
2 ounces beef suet	¼ teaspoon cayenne
4 onions	Flour
1 garlic clove	2 tomatoes, sliced
1 teaspoon chili powder	Pepper and salt
1 cup broth	

Fry suet in a pan until no more fat comes out, and remove. Slice 1 onion very thin and fry in the fat. Add minced garlic and chili powder. Take out onion and reserve it for gravy.

Rub salt and cayenne into steak, then dust well with flour. Fry in fat in which onion has been cooked until steak is nicely browned on both sides.

Put steak in a pan which fits it snugly. Slice the other 3 onions and smother steak with slices. Put in oven and bake until it begins to be tender. Then lay sliced tomatoes on top. Season and bake until very tender.

Make gravy with broth, a little flour and the fried onion you have saved. Take up steak. Pour gravy into baking pan. Bring to boiling point and sluice steak with it.

The beef of Uruguay is quite as famous as that of its larger neighbor, Argentina. Wonderful steak dishes like the above are served at the splendid seashore resorts in Montevideo, and beef is shipped from this beautiful port to Spain, Cuba and much of the world besides. Montevideo steaks, indeed, can compete with those of Buenos Aires or Kansas City.

Biftek is both the French and Spanish way of spelling beefsteak, but the Portuguese-speaking Brazilians abbreviate it to *bife*. You will find other spellings on South American menus, however, just as you will find quaint ways of rendering Spanish-dish names on our bills of fare. An excellent example of phonetic spelling is found in a Brazilian approximation of Irish stew—*airixtu* (X is pronounced "sh" in Portuguese).

CHILEAN MALAYA, OR MATAMBRE
Flank Steak, Rolled and Filled

Wash and dry 4–5 pounds thin flank steak (*malaya*). Put in earthenware dish and sprinkle with salt, pepper, thyme, parsley, 1 chopped onion and ¼ cup red wine vinegar. Let marinate 12 hours.

Prepare filling by mixing together 1 cup chopped cooked lettuce or spinach, ½ can green peas, 4–5 carrots. Run through grinder 1½ cups bread soaked in milk, 2 tablespoons grated cheese, 4 hard-cooked eggs, sliced, 4–5 bacon slices. Spread over meat and roll. Sew together and cook 3–4 hours. Drain and cool with weight on top. (From recipes collected by the women's auxiliary to the American Society of Chile.)

Matambre is a familiar dish wherever Spanish is spoken. It means hunger killer, from *matar* (to kill) and *hambre* (hunger). Something like our Southern word "hushpuppy" for corn-meal mixtures that say hush to the little animal howling inside the hungry.

Wine vinegar is specified above because Chile is a wine country *par excellence,* and vintage vinegars as well as vintage clarets are on tap everywhere. There are both red and white wine vinegars, of course, and as with the wines that make them, red vinegar goes best with red or dark meats and white vinegar with white or light-colored meats such as chicken and veal.

Malaya, the alternative name of this dish, is simply Chilean for the flank steak it's made with.

ARGENTINE MEAT ROLL
Arrollado de Matambre

4 whole peppers, crushed	2 pounds round steak
½ teaspoon salt	1 pound veal
2 garlic cloves, mashed	½ pound salt pork
4 tablespoons vinegar	1 onion

Bay leaf

Mix together peppers, salt, garlic and vinegar. Rub this into steak on each side and let lie all night in a cool dry place. Have veal cut in narrow strips and pork cut as for larding. When ready to cook lay steak out on table and arrange on it layers of veal strips, alternating with pork strips. Roll carefully in shape of jelly roll and secure with skewers and string. Barely cover with boiling water. Add onion and bay leaf. Put over low heat and cook covered until meat can be easily pierced with a fork. Take out and put under press to be eaten cold next day. (The broth is saved to add to the next pot of beans.)

ECUADORIAN SAUCED BEEF
Cariucho

Season 2 pounds flank steak. Bake in oven, and when tender put in deep serving dish. Cover with 4 freshly boiled potatoes cut in slices and pour this sauce over:

CARIUCHO SAUCE

Heat 2 tablespoons lard and fry in it 2 minced onions and 1 minced green pepper. When soft add 2 large tomatoes, peeled and sliced, and cook until sauce is smooth and bubbling. Blend in 4 tablespoons peanut butter and slowly add 1 pint scalded milk. Simmer while stirring continuously, and when sauce is thickish serve it, garnished with minced parsley, and 1–2 chopped hard-cooked eggs.

CHILI CON CARNE, I

1 onion, sliced thin	1 pound round steak
2-inch cube beef fat	2 tablespoons flour
2 garlic cloves, sliced	Boiling water
1 tablespoon chili powder	Salt
1 teaspoon marjoram, minced	

Slowly fry onion with sliced beef fat until it begins to color. Add garlic and slowly fry until lightly browned. Remove remains of beef fat and the garlic and add chili powder. Cut steak in very small dice, or chop coarsely. Dredge with flour and add. Fry until meat and onions are browned but not scorched. Cover with boiling water. Season with salt and marjoram and simmer until very tender.

This is the best known of Mexican national dishes, chiefly through its having been adopted by all border and Gulf states of the United States. The manner of its preparation in Mexico varies with the district, the mood of the cook and the means of the household, the basis always being chilies and several other kinds of peppers represented in the chili powder used in this recipe.

It may be eaten with *Sopa de Arroz*, rice cooked according to our recipe for Mexican Rice (see recipe) but left rather moist, which gives it the name *Sopa* or soup. But the most common accompaniment is the same beans that are served with *Chili con Carne* on this side of the Rio Grande, kidney beans, or even white soup beans, cooked separately and added when meat is done. Chili beans for this purpose are put up in Texas (Gebhart brand) and sold not only all over the United States but in Mexico besides.

In using chili powder it is well to remember that to bring out the full flavor it must be allowed to simmer with the other ingredients at least 15 minutes.

Here is a Mex–Tex border recipe for a richer, spicier chili with both Mexican and North American features, since we have adopted this dish for all time.

CHILI CON CARNE, II

1 pound ground beef	½ teaspoon cumin seed
1 large onion	(substitute caraway)
1 garlic clove, minced	1 minced bay leaf
3 tablespoons butter or oil	1 tablespoon chili powder
1 small can tomatoes	⅛ teaspoon basil
1 green pepper, chopped	1½ teaspoons salt
½ teaspoon celery salt	1 pint (or 1 can) cooked
¼ teaspoon red pepper	chili beans

Finely chop onion and garlic and fry for a moment in hot butter or oil. Add beef and fry slowly until brown. The secret of the dish lies in slow frying. Add chopped tomatoes, green pepper and seasonings. Continue simmering over slow fire. Add beans. Cover and let simmer slowly until the juices blend.

TONGUE IN ROMAN STYLE
Lengua a la Romana

Boil 1 medium-sized tongue in about 2 quarts water with 1 bay leaf, 1 sprig marjoram, 4 whole peppers, 1 minced garlic and salt to taste. Cook gently until tender, then take out and remove skin. When cold cut in thin slices. Brown ⅔ cup blanched and shredded almonds in a little butter and mash fine. Stir 2 tablespoons flour in 2 tablespoons butter and gradually add 3 cups strained tongue broth. Simmer 5 minutes and add ground almonds, 2 tablespoons plum marmalade, 1 cup sweet wine, ¾ cup seeded raisins and sliced tongue. Simmer 1 hour over low heat and serve with boiled rice.

Today, when there are more Italians in New York City than in Rome and spaghetti has become an all-American food, we're not surprised to find adopted recipes like the above in such faraway places as Bogota, Colombia, where this hails from.

Plums also suit the Colombian taste and plum marmalade is as necessary here as guava marmalade, or *goiabada*, in neighboring Brazil.

COLOMBIAN TONGUE WITH MUSHROOMS
Lengua con Hongos

1½ pounds beef tongue
1 bay leaf
1 minced garlic clove
1 teaspoon salt
4 whole peppers
1 small onion, minced

2 tablespoons butter
1 tablespoon flour
1 cup tongue broth
1 cup canned mushrooms, chopped
1 cup wine

½ teaspoon parsley

Wash tongue in cold water and let soak 24 hours, changing water 3 or 4 times. Boil in water to cover, about 2 quarts, with bay leaf, garlic, salt and peppers. Cook slowly until tender over slow fire. Remove skin. Slice thin and rearrange on platter in tongue shape. Fry onion in butter until soft. Add flour and cook until lightly browned. Add broth; stir until smooth and add mushrooms, wine and parsley. Let simmer 10 minutes, stirring frequently, and pour over the tongue. Serve with lettuce or watercress salad.

Fresh mushrooms would be better, of course, but they are seldom available in hot countries down around the equator. Both tongue and mushrooms are appreciated delicacies in Colombia, and this dish is made all the richer by cooking it with wine.

ARGENTINE TONGUE IN ALMOND SAUCE
Lengua con Almendras

1 ox tongue, freshly boiled	12 blanched almonds, ground
1 garlic clove, minced	
1 tablespoon olive oil	1 bay leaf, chopped
1 small tomato, chopped	½ teaspoon minced parsley
1½ tablespoons chopped olives	½ cup broth
	Bread crumbs, sifted

Capers

To sauce a freshly cooked ox tongue in expert Argentine style, fry garlic in oil. Add tomato, olives, almonds, bay leaf and parsley. Simmer 10 minutes. Thin with broth in which tongue has cooked and thicken with sifted bread crumbs.

Slice tongue in long thin strips, without spoiling the natural shape of the tongue. Lay it in the sauce to heat and serve on hot platter, surrounded by sauce and garnished with capers.

We have never tasted finer beef than the pampas-grass-fed steers of the Argentine that are bred square and big as piano boxes, to furnish the most cubic meat and cut to the best advantage. Such steers have rich, meaty tongues, fat and juicy, and we shall be happy when Argentine beef and tongues are shipped to this country in quantity.

ROAST SUCKLING PIG
Lechón Asado

Steep a month-old pig in cold water 15 minutes. Then plunge it into boiling water, holding it by the head and shaking until hairs begin to loosen. Remove from water. Rub vigorously with coarse towel until all hairs are off. Cut open. Remove entrails and wash thoroughly in cold water. Dry on a towel and fill with the following forcemeat:

Heart, liver and lights of pig	A few sprigs of parsley
4 cups stale bread	1 teaspoon capers
¼ cup tomato sauce	½ tablespoon salt
¾ cup raisins, soaked in sherry	Red pepper
	Sage
¼ pound chopped roasted almonds	Marjoram
	Salt and pepper
	2 eggs

Cook heart, liver and lights until tender in salted boiling water. Drain and chop fine. Soak bread in water until soft. Squeeze dry in towel and add to meat with remaining ingredients. Mix thoroughly together, seasoning high with red pepper, sage and marjoram. Stuff pig. Sew up and truss to keep legs in place. Brush all over with melted butter. Sprinkle with salt and black pepper and lay pig in a dripping pan just large enough to hold it. Bake 2½–3 hours in moderate oven, 350°. Baste with butter and hot water during first hour, and after that with butter alone. Season with salt and pepper 2 or 3 times during basting. Serve in a nest of lettuce or water cress, with a bright-colored fruit or vegetable in its mouth for decoration.

This is often served with Orange Sauce (see recipe).

In Santo Domingo a hundred years ago Roast Suckling Pig had a place of honor at marriage feasts. The anal ring was cut out carefully and placed on the finger of the most beautiful lady present as a special mark of distinction, similar to the present-day throwing of the bride's bouquet.

MEXICAN PORK CHOPS WITH CHILI
Puerco con Chili

Crush 1 garlic clove. Add to it 1 teaspoon chili powder and work to a paste. Season 4–5 thin pork chops with salt. Rub with garlic-chili mixture. Dredge with flour and fry brown on both sides in fat or butter. Lay in baking dish or casserole, covering each chop with chopped tomatoes that have been seasoned with salt and pepper. Cover closely and simmer or bake 1 hour.

GANSO A LA POBRE
Poor Man's Goose

6 pork chops   A pinch of sage
2 onions, cut fine   Salt and pepper

Lay chops in baking dish. Cover with onions mixed with sage, salt and pepper. Cover with cold water and cook in oven until tender. Thicken gravy with a little flour dissolved in water and cook 5 minutes.

Although this is a Chilean recipe, Poor Man's Goose speaks Esperanto to a world of stomachs.

BLACK LOIN OF PORK
Lomo Negro

Cut 2 pounds loin of pork into thin steaks. Sprinkle with a mixture of lemon juice and water and let lie ½ hour. Put 2 tablespoons fresh lard into frying pan and fry steaks in it to a golden brown on each side. Sprinkle with salt and pepper.

Leave steaks in pan. Add ½ cup vinegar. Cover pan and cook over slow heat until meat is tender and a deep rich brown.

With the French, who call browned butter black, *beurre noir*, the Spaniards call this richly browned pork black, *negro*.

LITTLE LOINS OF PORK (CHILEAN)
Lomitos de Chancho

Cut a loin of pork into steaks and marinate them in a little vinegar with a couple cloves of garlic, a bit of red pepper, a little cumin seed and black pepper. After 1 hour in the pickle remove and let them dry. They can be kept for use in the refrigerator and are usually rubbed over with lard and grilled.

PUERTO RICAN PORK AND POTATO PIE

Boil, mash and season about 5 medium-sized potatoes. Line a piepan with the mashed and seasoned potatoes pressed down like a thick pie crust. (Reserve half the mashed potatoes for the top.)

Make a filling of pieces of pork fried together with sliced onions, sweet red pepper, seasoned with salt and pepper. When the meat is tender add some tomato sauce.

Put the filling in the crust with a layer of mashed potatoes over the top. Brush with evaporated milk and brown in the oven.

WEST INDIAN PIG'S HEAD AND PEAS
New Year's Dish of the West Indies

Have a big pig's head scalded, scraped clean, split in two and the eyes removed. (The brain is saved for some other dish.) Rub pig's head with vinegar and start cooking in cold water with a teaspoon of whole peppers and a tablespoon of salt. Cook very slowly until tender, about 3 hours.

Meanwhile cook ½ pound black-eyed peas in salted water until the water has boiled down and the peas are getting tender. Grate the meat of a fresh coconut. Warm the water or milk taken out of it. Pour it over the grated nut and wring it dry in a strong cloth. Wet the wrung coconut with a little warm water and wring again, until all milk has been extracted. Put ½ to 2 pounds of rice into the cooking black-eyed peas and add the coconut milk. Cook until rice is tender.

Serve on a large platter, the pig's head at one end, the peas and rice at the other. A bowl of pot liquor is placed on the table for those who like to put a spoonful of it over the meat or do a fancy bit of dunking.

POZOLE

A pig's head enters often into Indian ceremonials. In some parts of Mexico a *Kubpal* or *Entrega de Cabeza* (carrying the head) is performed on the third of May, or during the Carnival as ceremoniously as the bringing in of the boar's head in medieval Europe. One of the tribe is elected "Big Brother" to preside at the festival and lead a procession bearing a flower-decked head of pig, preferably a *jabali* or wild pig. (Indian name *covanmetl*.) Behind him an enormous loaf of bread is carried aloft. Then follow other members of the tribe, each leading or carrying a live animal or fowl.

After the parade around the village the revelers return to a leaf-covered bower, where they dance and drink pulque while the animals are killed and cooked. The pig's head occupies the place of honor at the table.

This custom is supposed to have come down from cannibal times, when the Aztec chief carried a human head as is recorded to this day in a Mexican insult: "O que buena cobeza para un pozoli [What a good head for a pozole]." One is reminded of a similar saying from once cannibal Brazil, where it is still a good joke in Bahia to say to a fat man, "E uma boa barriga por uma faca [It's a good paunch for a knife]" from the ancient habit of slitting the enemy's abdomen.

The Zapotecs and Chiapanecs have a special tortilla to serve with pig's head, made of tortilla dough mixed with brown sugar. They bury an olla, or big earthen pot in the ground, fill it with fire, then take the fire out and let the pot cool to the proper temperature. The tortillas are plastered on the inside surface of this primitive oven. They curl up as they bake and come out crisp and tasty.

The pig's head is marinated in vinegar and salt and then stewed with *Molé Poblano*.

CHILI RABBIT, MEXICAN MEZCHILLA STYLE

Joint a plump young rabbit. In a casserole slowly fry until golden 1 large chopped onion in 1 tablespoon olive oil or butter. Add 1 chopped tomato, 1 tablespoon chili powder and continue frying. Dredge rabbit in flour, salt and pepper. Put it in frying mixture. Add 2 cups broth, a little at a time. Keep covered until meat is tender. Garnish with slices of fresh or fried bananas. If fried, cut lengthwise, sprinkle lightly with sugar and fry in butter.

RABBIT, BAHIAN STYLE
Coelho Bahiana

1 young rabbit	Orange peel
1 tablespoon fat	2 green peppers, chopped
Flour	1 tablespoon parsley,
1 cup broth	chopped
¾ cup orange juice	½ cup chopped mushrooms
¼ cup lemon juice	A pinch of ginger

Cut rabbit in joints. Put in a casserole with fat. Sprinkle with a little flour and brown the meat well. Then add broth, orange and lemon juice with a bit of orange peel and all other ingredients. Cover casserole and cook very slowly until tender.

While a good many Anglo-Saxon surnames derive from early trades, such as Smith, Barber, Farmer, etc., in Latin countries quite as many come from animals and birds, and among them Señor Coelho, or Mr Rabbit, is one of the most common in South America.

RABBIT BRAZILIAN, COUNTRY STYLE
Coelho a Moda do Campo

Have rabbit skinned, emptied and cut up. Save blood. Mix with 1–2 tablespoons vinegar and set aside along with rabbit liver to use in the sauce. Pack pieces of rabbit in a bowl that just fits. Pour over them the marinating mixture described below and let stand 24 hours, turning pieces over several times and putting those from the bottom on top to marinate all evenly. Drain rabbit. Dry with a cloth and reserve marinating liquid. Chop 2–3 slices bacon. Start frying in frying pan, and when sufficient hot fat is extracted add floured pieces of rabbit and 10 whole scallions. Fry and turn until nicely browned. Transfer to earthenware casserole or enameled saucepan. Add 3 cups red wine (claret), ½ teaspoon mixed spice (cinnamon, nutmeg, cloves and black pepper in equal proportions), 1 tablespoon sugar and 1 cup of the reserved marinating liquid. Bring rapidly to boiling point. Add salt; cover and simmer over very low heat until rabbit is tender. Mash rabbit liver thoroughly. Mix with reserved blood, ¼ cup pan broth from the rabbit and 2 tablespoon white rum. Add this mixture to pan here and there, shaking pan gently until well combined. Keep below boiling point to prevent gravy from curdling. This gravy should be thick enough, but if it isn't add 1 teaspoon cornstarch blended with 2 tablespoons water. Pile rabbit in hot platter. Pour part of sauce over and serve remaining sauce in a bowl.

To dish up a rabbit in real Brazilian country style pile it on one end of the platter and put a generous heap of *Angu* (see recipe) on the other end to balance.

MARINATING MIXTURE FOR RABBIT AND ALL OTHER MEATS AND GAME
Vinho d' Alho—Wine of Garlic

½ garlic clove, mashed	1 sprig parsley
1 onion, sliced	1 small bay leaf
1 small carrot, chopped	4 whole peppers
1 piece of celery	½ cup vinegar
(or celery leaves)	1½ cup wine

Mix together, using white wine for white meats and red wine for red meats.

BRAZILIAN MEATS

The secret of making Brazilian meat dishes lies largely in the preliminary preparations. Practically all of the recipes begin in the same way whether the meat is to be boiled, pot-roasted, hashed or baked. A tablespoon of butter, fat or oil is heated in a frying pan. Into it is dropped a finely sliced raw onion, which is fried slowly until tender, but not brown. Then a minced clove of garlic is added, and the two are allowed to brown lightly. The garlic is put in after the onions are nearly done because it cooks more quickly. Many recipes call for a chopped tomato at this juncture, which is allowed to cook until the mixture thickens. Then 1–2 cups boiling broth is added or, lacking that, boiling water will do.

A bouquet of herbs follows, consisting of a sprig of parsley, a sprig of celery leaf, a bay leaf, a leaf or two of tarragon, mace, sage or thyme, or all four, depending on the resources of the kitchen. For convenience some cooks tie up the assortment in little bunches, held together with a string, and dry them so they will always be at hand. In North America all these seasonings can be bought in powdered form and a pinch of each put together in a small cloth, tied with a thread, and thrown in to boil with the sauce. One must remember, however, to take it out when the flavor is extracted, or it may be ladled out on a guest's plate and mistaken for a stewed fig.

A wineglass of Madeira or sherry is often added for mutton, duck or kid; a glass of white wine is used for other meats. Portuguese wines, of course, are used in Brazil, differently from the other Latin-American countries which use Spanish, or, in Argentine and Chile, their own native wines.

The resulting wine sauce is used for basting roasts, or is put into the pot in which meat is to be boiled, pot-roasted or sautéed.

It is also used as a gravy to be poured over steaks or chops and is especially delicious when employed in cooking game, as anyone can testify who has eaten the curious wild meats to be found in the Brazilian markets, the *paca* (small wild boar), the *tatú* (armadillo) which tastes like young pig, the *gamba* (a delicate small animal of the opossum family), the *cotia* (a root- and nut-eating creature resembling giant-sized ground squirrels), *macuca* (a big bird something like wild turkey) and various kinds of wild rabbits. (See recipes.)

Many other animals are eaten in the interior of the country where they abound. It is said that the meat of the *anta*, or tapir, is better than pork, and that monkey meat—oh, cannibal thought—is very tasty. But why not? The creatures live on fruits and nuts, and the ordinary varieties have nothing like the intelligence with which they are credited.

Wild parrots are sometimes stewed and dished up in palatable fashion, but as some of them live for fifty years they must be boiled for a long time.

When our ancient pet parrot, *Gordo,* (fat one) was naughty, Alzira, fat and none too young herself, invariably threatened to put him into the pot. And this is always a good joke among South Americans when Polly dirties the week's wash while the cook is talking with the vegetable peddler. Alzira's was only a threat, however, for she was a city woman who wouldn't even touch the haunch of puma meat she once roasted for us. And when the owner of our favorite restaurant sent us a gift of live armadillo for our Christmas dinner, the creature mysteriously disappeared through two feet of solid stone wall and floor, and Alzira went to work for another foreign family who limited their menus to domestic animals.

MEXICAN ROAST KID
Cabrito Asado

1 leg kid, with chops	Salt
4 garlic cloves, shredded	Pepper
Bacon in short barbs	2 tablespoons melted butter
1 onion, minced fine	1 tablespoon seeded raisins
1 bay leaf, minced	½ cup Madeira

Make incisions all over the meat and stuff into each a barb of bacon and a sliver of garlic. Mix salt, pepper, bay leaf and onion and rub over. Mix raisins, butter and Madeira. Place leg in a well-oiled paper bag. Pour in Madeira mixture. Start baking in hot oven, then reduce to moderate heat.

In all Latin countries the meat of the kid is highly prized, right down to the tripe, and once it has been eaten by North Americans it is ever afterward preferred to mutton. Kid is marketed under the fancy trade name of "chevon" in some parts of the United States, and unscrupulous butchers sometimes sell it for mutton to customers who have the absurd Anglo-Saxon prejudice against goat's flesh.

But there is little prejudice against it along our Tex-Mex border where roast-kid sandwiches appear on the very best barbecue stands. (From *The Wine Cookbook*, by the Browns.)

MEAT BALLS, HASHES AND GIBLETS

MEAT BALLS

MEXICAN ALBÓNDIGAS

Every country has its own kind of meat balls, but those of Spain, called *albóndigas* and especially well seasoned and tasty, followed Spanish occupation around the world, in some places to become little sausages, in others changing into meat loaves, always varying to suit local supplies and equipment. In Mexico, where so much Spanish cooking has been altered to include tropical products and Aztec kitchen technique, some of the Spanish *albóndiga* recipes have remained intact to this day. Here is one of them:

MUTTON BALLS, SPANISH STYLE
Albóndigas de Carnero a la Espanola

1 sheep's brain
1 pound leg of pork
¼ pound shelled almonds
1 cup soft bread crumbs
2 eggs, separated
⅛ teaspoon grated nutmeg
1 dash ground cloves
1 dash ground cinnamon
⅛ teaspoon pepper
1 scant teaspoon salt
2–4 tablespoons sherry

2 sprigs parsley
1 sprig yerba buena
   (substitute mint)
1 onion, chopped
2 tablespoons olive oil
4 tomatoes, chopped
1 crushed chili
   (or a good dash cayenne)
1 teaspoon parsley, minced
½ teaspoon yerba buena,
   minced

Juice ½ lemon

Scald brain in boiling water. Remove skin and membranes and chop. Have pork run through meat grinder twice. Blanch almonds. Remove skins and grind, reserving 2 tablespoons ground almonds for sauce. Mix brain, pork, almonds and bread crumbs, and work smooth in wooden bowl with wooden spoon. Add beaten egg yolks, spices and salt, and work together again to a smooth mass. Add slightly beaten egg whites and sherry to moisten. Mix well. Form into balls the size of a walnut and let stand a few minutes for outsides to dry. Drop into boiling water with parsley and yerba buena sprigs and parboil until half done. Meanwhile, fry onion slowly in olive oil until tender but not browned. Add tomatoes and chili, and simmer until thick. (If you do not want a very hot sauce remove chili after 5 minutes.) Press through sieve. Add reserved almonds and sufficient broth from meat balls to make a sauce of proper consistency. Taste and season. Transfer half-cooked meat balls to this sauce and simmer until done, adding minced herbs and lemon juice just before serving.

There are as many recipes for *albóndigas* as there are kinds of meat, for they are constantly on the table and variety is necessary. Especially fine ones are made of chicken and of game, particularly venison. And for fast days there are special codfish balls, made from dried codfish, parboiled, flaked fine, mixed with fried bread, egg yolks and many seasonings including vinegar, made into balls and fried brown in fat.

A Mexican gourmet of the old school looked upon his food with gusto and liked to hear it talked about at the table while it was being consumed. Thoroughly fed up with the refinements of the younger generation and their incessant polite conversation about poetry and the beauties of nature, he burst out at them:

"¡Las flores, esquite! de las frutas, *albóndigas!*" In other words, "You talk about the fruits and flowers! For me, the most exquisite flowers are popcorn, the fruits meat balls."

HAITIAN MEAT BALLS

¾ cup dry bread	1 small hot pepper
¼ cup milk	(optional)
1 pound tender beefsteak	Parsley
2–3 slices bacon	1 teaspoon vinegar
1 garlic clove	Salt and pepper
Thyme	Flour

Soak bread in milk. Let stand awhile. Grind together meat, bacon and spices. Squeeze all milk out of bread. Grind and add to meat. Add vinegar, salt and pepper. Mix very well. Cut this mixture into pieces. Roll each piece in a little flour and with palms form into firm ball. Fry in deep hot oil and drain. Serve hot with the following sauce.

Sauce:

Fry lightly in butter 5 well-cleaned tomatoes and 6 shallots. Add to taste salt and vinegar. Thicken with a pinch of flour. Cook and serve hot on meat balls.

BOLIVIAN EGG MEAT BALLS
Albóndigon de Huevos

1 pound lean beef	1½ teaspoons salt
½ pound lean pork	½ teaspoon pepper
3 eggs, beaten	⅛ teaspoon nutmeg
4 tablespoons dry crumbs	4 hard-cooked eggs
1 cup broth	

Chop beef and pork very fine and mix thoroughly with beaten eggs, crumbs and seasonings. Spread mixture out. Cut in 4 squares. Put 1 hard-cooked egg in center of each and roll meat around. Put in a deep casserole. Add 1 cup seasoned broth. Cover and cook slowly 1 hour.

ARGENTINE MEAT BALLS WITH BROTH
Albóndigas al Caldillo

1 onion, minced	½ pound meat, chopped
2 garlic cloves, minced	2 eggs
1 teaspoon parsley, minced	Salt
1 tomato, chopped	Red pepper
1 tablespoon olive oil	1 slice bread
1 quart meat broth	

Fry onion, garlic, parsley and tomato in olive oil or other fat until smooth and thickened. Stir this into meat. Add eggs, 1 scant teaspoon salt, a little red pepper and bread which has been soaked in water and squeezed dry. Mix all thoroughly and shape into balls, adding toasted crumbs if too moist. Have broth boiling hot in casserole. Arrange balls in it. Cover. Cook 10 minutes and serve.

The word *albóndigas* comes from the Arabian, meaning to swim.

HASHES

PICADILLO

Picadillos cover the whole range of little dishes of finely chopped meats, either cooked or raw, mixed with chopped ham, vegetables, nuts and whatnot, and either served as hashes or used to stuff birds, fish, peppers, chayotes and other vegetables. The combinations are limitless, the following example being typical:

PICADILLO OF PORK WITH SAUSAGE
Picadillo de Carne de Puerco con Chorizo

1 pound lean pork, chopped or ground fine	¼ teaspoon cumin seed, crushed
¼ pound dried smoked sausage	1 tablespoon almonds, chopped, or whole pine nuts
Salt	
1 onion, chopped	½ cup cooked ham, minced
1 tablespoon olive oil	1 chopped hard-cooked egg
1 garlic clove, minced	1 teaspoon parsley, minced
1 tomato, chopped	8–10 olives, pitted
A dash of ground cloves	Pepper, pepper sauce or chili

Vinegar to taste (optional)

Mold uncooked pork into little balls and cook with sausage in salted water. Reserve broth and mash both meats together after removing skin of sausage. Meanwhile slowly fry onion in oil. Add garlic and fry until golden. Add tomato and fry until thick. Add reserved broth, mashed meats, cloves, cumin, almonds and ham, and simmer. If intended for hash, cook until gravy is of a pleasant consistency. If intended for stuffing, cook until nearly dry. Add remaining ingredients.

Meats vary with the locale, veal, lamb, kid, poultry and game all being suitable for a *picadillo*. Seasonings may include chili powder as in Mexico, saffron in true Spanish tradition, paprika, marjoram or any other favored herb. And thickening, if used, may be anything from tortilla dough or cassava meal to mashed bread or wheat flour.

SPANISH ROPA VIEJA
"Old Clothes"

1½ pounds flank steak boiled, cooled and flaked	1 chopped onion
2 tablespoons lard or olive oil	3 green peppers, chopped
	3 large tomatoes, chopped
	Pepper
2 garlic cloves	Canned pimientos

There will be about 3 cups of flaked meat. Heat fat in small deep frying pan. Brown garlic cloves in it and remove them. Add onion and peppers to the garlic-flavored fat and cook gently until soft. Then add chopped tomatoes, stir and simmer, and when sauce is smooth and bubbling add flaked meat, a dash of pepper and salt to taste. Let meat simmer in sauce 10 minutes. A little water may be added, if needed. Serve garnished with slices of canned pimientos.

BRAZILIAN ROUPA VELHA
"Old Clothes"

Heat 2 tablespoons butter in saucepan. Add 2 tablespoons flour. Stir and simmer until nicely browned. Add ½ cup chopped mushrooms, 1 teaspoon minced parsley and ½ garlic clove minced. Simmer together 3–5 minutes, then add 1 cup meat broth and ½ cup white wine, stirring until smooth and thickened. Pull a portion of boiled jerked beef into coarse shreds (like rags, from which the dish takes its name). Add to the sauce and simmer 15 minutes.

Leftover game birds, turkey and chicken are also used for *Roupa Velha*, but most frequently jerked beef that has been cooked in *Feijoada*. It is served with *Tutu* made out of the beans left from *Feijoada*. (See recipes.)

Since this dish with the playful name "old clothes" is popular in both Portugal and Spain, it appears not only in Brazil as *Roupa Velha* but in Spanish-speaking republics as *Ropa Vieja*, and is so well known, in fact, that you'll find it in any Spanish or Portuguese dictionary.

BRAZILIAN PASSOCA

1 pound jerked beef	1 teaspoon parsley, minced
1 tablespoon fat or butter	Pepper
1 onion, chopped	1 cup yellow corn meal
1 garlic clove, minced	Ripe bananas

Soak jerked beef in cold water 24 hours, changing water several times. Drain; cover with fresh cold water. Bring slowly to boiling point and cook until tender. Take out meat and cut fine with a sharp knife. Measure cooking water and add sufficient boiling water to make 1 quart. Meanwhile heat fat, slowly fry onion until it begins to color. Add garlic and continue slow frying until lightly browned. Add to jerked meat broth with parsley and pepper to taste. Bring to rapid boiling point and sift in corn meal, stirring until smooth and thickened. Simmer until very thick. Probably no salt will be needed, but taste and make sure. Add cut-up jerked beef. Pile into a mound on a hot platter. Peel bananas, split in halves lengthwise and lay around edge of platter.

TRINCADILLOS
A Kind of Chilean Croquette

1½ cups cooked meat, chopped
½ cup bread crumbs or boiled rice
2 cups onion, chopped
Salt and pepper
Sage
1 egg, beaten
Water

Mix first 5 ingredients well. Moisten with beaten egg and sufficient water to pat into croquettes. Fry in deep fat.

Picadillo is Spanish for hash, and although the dictionary doesn't give *trincadillos*, probably it means "little chopped things" from the verb *trincár*, to chop.

SPANISH SAUSAGES AND LENTILS

1 pound sausages
1 cup cooked lentils
1 sliced onion
1 minced clove garlic
1 green pepper, skinned and seeded
2 tomatoes, peeled and quartered
Salt and pepper

Fry sausages lightly. Remove and cut in small pieces. Pour off all but about 2 tablespoons of sausage fat and fry lentils, onion, garlic and pepper. Cook slowly, occasionally stirring until all are slightly yellow. Then add tomatoes, salt, pepper and the partly cooked sausages. Cover and simmer until all are tender.

A popular fry wherever Spanish is spoken or eaten.

GIBLETS, ETC.

ITALO–ARGENTINE MIXED FRY
Fritto Misto

Deep fat or oil for frying

Frying Batter

½ cup flour   1 dash cayenne
⅛ teaspoon salt   ⅓ cup milk
                1 egg, beaten

Mix ingredients in order given.

For each person a selection from the following:

¼ slice calf's liver   1 slice yellow cheese
1 slice sweetbread   ¼ slice eggplant, blanched
1 slice calf's brain   1 floweret cooked cauli-
1 slice kid's kidney   flower
    or sheep's kidney   1 slice Italian squash
1 slice lamb's fry   (*zucchini*)
1 cooked artichoke bottom   1 length cooked celery
                Salt and pepper

Soak sweetbread and brain in cold water 1 hour. Blanch, skin and remove large veins. Skin kidney. Season and dip each item separately in batter. Fry in fat. Drain on absorbent paper and serve all together on the same hot platter.

Although such a classically Italian dish as *Fritto Misto* is considered foreign in the outlying provinces of the Argentine, such as Tucuman and San Luis, in Buenos Aires it is quite at home and becomes fully Italo-Argentine by the selection of fine tidbits and giblets from the fat steers and sheep of rich pampas pastures.

And Buenos Aires is not only distinguished for its enthusiastic adoption of such great Italian dishes, but for its per

capita consumption of the choice "innards" of all animals—
prime parts that only Americans and Englishmen are likely to
throw away. At the ancient and honorable La Caracole (The
Snail) on Calle Rivadavia in the capital city, we ate the most
succulent concoctions of every part of almost every beast that
walks, runs, hops or crawls on the ceiling, and came back for
more.

For the salutary fact is that no juicy giblet escapes the
Argentine lover of good eats and lest we, in our Anglo-Saxon
squeamishness, think that marrow, milts, mountain oysters and
tripe of all kinds is hardly ladylike to eat, it is well to remember that these meaty jewels contain the essence of the animal,
and modern doctors say that much of the trouble with our
diet today is that we do not eat the whole of the carcass, that
is, every bit of it, all the way from brains to tail, as our pioneer
fathers did.

We Browns have been lucky in this respect, and just to
prove it, here are some of the good things we enjoyed at the
old Caracole a decade ago, as we jotted them down on the
spot:

> *At the sign of the writhing escargot:*
> *How will you have your pickled tripe?*
> *Will you take frogs' legs still twitching?*
> *We have nice ox innards today,*
> *Or, for forty centavos*
> *You can wrap around thirty-odd feet*
> *of tender young goat's insides—*
> *delicate as new-mown spaghetti.*
> *We heartily recommend the boiled brains*
> *And sweet vine-leaf-fed snails.*
> *Try our pig's liver, cocks' combs,*
> *sounds and tongues, chicken-foot jelly,*
> *lamb's hearts with gizzard gravy.*
> *Sorry, but we're just out of lights,*
> *but the herring milts are exceptionally*
> *soft and slippery this season.*

COLOMBIAN "TOPKNOTS" OF RICE WITH BRAINS
Copetes de Arroz con Sesos

Soak brains 1 hour in cold water and remove membranes. Cook slowly 20–25 minutes in boiling salted water with 1 bay leaf, 1 small minced onion and 1 tablespoon vinegar. Drain and plunge into cold water to firm. Take out. Drain again, and when cold cut in small pieces.

In double boiler cook 1 cup well-washed rice with 1 pint cold water until nearly dry. Then add 1 pint hot milk, salt to taste and let cook dry. Remove from heat. Stir in 2 tablespoons grated cheese, 1 teaspoon butter and ½ teaspoon sugar. With spoon or fingers form small balls of rice with brains in center. Dip in beaten egg. Roll in bread crumbs and fry in deep fat. Serve with tomato sauce.

Copete is Spanish for topknot, curl of hair, toupee or almost anything else that conceals the brains.

COLOMBIAN SOUFFLÉ OF BRAINS
Soufflé de Sesos

2 pairs calf's brains	½ teaspoon paprika
Dry bread	A few gratings of nutmeg
Milk	½ cup cream
½ teaspoon salt	4 egg yolks, beaten light
4 egg whites, beaten stiff	

Wash brains. Remove arteries and membranes and soak 1 hour in cold acidulated water. Cook gently in boiling salted water 20–30 minutes. Thoroughly drain and mash with fork. Soak bread in milk until soft and squeeze dry, enough to make ½ cup. Add to brains with seasonings, cream and beaten egg yolks. Fold in egg whites last. Turn into buttered mold and bake in pan half filled with hot water, about 45 minutes. Serve with white sauce or tomato sauce.

CHILEAN LAMB KIDNEYS
Riñones a la Chilena

6 lamb kidneys	1 small onion, minced
2 cups cooked peas, drained	½ teaspoon parsley, minced
12 small mushrooms, cooked	Salt and pepper
½ cup tomato sauce	4 tablespoons white wine
2 tablespoons butter	1 hard-cooked egg, sliced

Remove fat and skin from kidneys and slice thin. Mix cooked peas with mushrooms and tomato sauce. Keep hot over boiling water until wanted. Heat butter in deep frying pan. Add kidneys with minced onion, parsley, salt and pepper to taste, and wine. Stir and cook 3 minutes over brisk fire, then add hot vegetables and cook a few minutes until kidneys are done. Serve on hot plate surrounded by vegetables and garnished with egg slices. Narrow strips of fried ham are often added.

CHILEAN BROILED BEEF KIDNEY
Guiso de Riñones

Fry coarsely chopped onion a few minutes in olive oil or "color" (lard and Spanish paprika). Cut a beef kidney in small pieces. Add to onion and fry carefully, taking care that it doesn't harden. Sprinkle with bread crumbs and salt. Serve with chopped hard-cooked egg on top.

With plenty of cattle- and kidney-loving Englishmen in Chile such a dish is always in demand, although in the Anglicized port of Valparaiso grilled sheep kidneys would be the thing.

It is interesting to note English cooking influences that have spread out from Chile's chief trading center, called Valpo by resident British (who in the Argentine also abbreviate Buenos Aires to B.A. and pervert the great *Rio de la Plata* to "River Plate"). Such British banalities as Bubble and Squeak (cabbage hash) and English Monkey have been foisted on people who have a much more colorful cuisine of their very own.

MEXICAN TRIPE

Cook 2 pounds tripe with seasonings: 1 bay leaf, 2–3 parsley sprigs, 1 sprig marjoram and 1 sliced onion. When tender make the following sauce:

Slowly fry 1 chopped onion in 2 tablespoons olive oil until it begins to color. Add 1 minced garlic clove and fry until lightly browned. Add 1 tablespoon chili powder and stir well together. Have ready 2 dozen almonds, blanched, peeled and ground fine. Add almonds and stir, then add 2–3 cups broth from tripe. Simmer and stir until well blended. Add well-drained tripe, simmer a few minutes until tripe is flavored with sauce, then serve each portion on a toasted tortilla.

CHILEAN LAMB TRIPE PUDDING
Budín de Guatitas

Tripe from 1 lamb	Milk
4 eggs	Lard
1½ loaves bread	Spanish paprika
	Salt

In this case tripe means the tender young intestines of a lamb. Clean well and boil until done. Then mince fine and mix with eggs, bread soaked in milk, lard, Spanish paprika and salt to taste. Grease pudding mold with lard and paprika. Put tripe mixture in and cook 1 hour in oven.

The tripe of kid is used in the same way and considered a specially fine dish by Italians. Sometimes the intestines are left whole and cooked like spaghetti, which they resemble in appearance though not in taste. Either lamb or kid intestines are excellent food, even more succulent than the more usual beef stomach tripe.

Sheep gambol everywhere among the rich grasses of Southern Chile and the Argentine, where climate combines with lush pasturage to produce the finest of mutton. And every part of the animal is relished, even the blood, which is also cooked by the above recipe, using about 4 cups of blood in place of the lamb tripe and a little more bread to absorb the moisture. Such a scrumptious blood pudding is seldom made in North America, but it's well worth getting acquainted with if you live where fresh sheep blood is on tap.

RAGOUT OF LIVER AND LIGHTS
Chanfaina

This popular Argentine dish is made with the blood and giblets of lamb.

Put 4 tablespoons oil or butter in a casserole over low heat. Add 1 minced onion, 2 sprigs parsley, 2 minced garlic cloves and 1 chopped tomato. Cook slowly until all are soft and well blended, then season with ½ teaspoon marjoram, salt and chili powder to taste. Dice the coagulated blood and add to casserole. Chop the liver and lights and add to casserole with 1 cup broth or water, 2 tablespoons vinegar and 1 tablespoon flour dissolved in a little cold water. Let come slowly to boiling point while continuously stirring. Cover; keep at bubbling point 15 minutes and serve hot.

The red wine of Mendoza is the proper thing to drink with this *Chanfaina*, although some of it is artificially colored with *quebracho* wood extract to make it as ruby red as port; and unfortunately the wines of the Argentine, including the locally popular Criollo (Creole) are not comparable to those of neighboring Chile, just as the wines of Italy, on the whole, cannot compete with those of France.

Argentinians are as fond of hashed lights as are Frenchmen, but unless you've acquired the taste you may mistake them for bits of a chopped rubber bath sponge.

BRAZILIAN MOCOTÓ
Calf's Feet

4 calf's feet	Salt and pepper
1 onion, sliced	¼ cup claret
Herb bouquet (parsley,	1 tablespoon tomato paste
celery leaves, bay leaf)	or ¼ cup cooked
1 tomato, cut up	tomatoes

1 chili pepper without seeds

Have calf's feet prepared by butcher. Cover with cold water, adding onion herbs and tomato, and cook gently until tender, adding salt and pepper during cooking. Take up feet, saving the broth. Remove bones and cut meat into convenient small pieces. Meanwhile boil the broth rapidly until reduced to one half. Add claret, tomato paste and chili pepper, and simmer until well mixed; then strain. Add cut-up calf's feet meat to strained broth and simmer until broth is sufficiently thick to form a sauce. This sauce may be further thickened by stirring in 1–2 beaten egg yolks just after pan is taken from heat. And small pieces of little sour pickles may also be added to sauce at the last moment. Serve in a hot deep dish.

Throughout the United States of Brazil *Mocotó* is easy to make and easy to eat, but here in the United States of America calf's feet are hard to get. In big cities the surest source of supply is a kosher butcher shop, for the Jews, like the Brazilians, know what's good to eat.

Mocotó helped make the fame of the old Villa Barcellos restaurant in Rio de Janeiro which, alas, is no more, although *Mocotó* is carrying on quite handsomely alone.

ITALO–PARAGUAYAN MARROWBONES
Osso Bucco

8 three-inch length mar-   Salt and pepper
  rowbones   1 cup tomato, strained
5 tablespoons butter   1 teaspoon granulated sugar
1 small onion, minced   ½ tablespoon flour
1 small carrot, grated   Rounds of toast
Parsley sprigs

Select bones of young beef, not too thick and heavy. Heat 4 tablespoons butter. Add bones, onion, carrot and seasonings. Cover and slowly fry, basting and turning often. When they begin to color add tomato, sugar and flour mixed with remaining butter. The marrow is cooked as soon as it is heated through. Lay bones in hot dish. Skim fat from sauce and strain over bones. Serve with a plate of hot toast on which the marrow is to be spread. Garnish with parsley.

FOWL

BUENOS AIRES CHICKEN A LA SPIEDO

With chickens grilled on the spit (*a la spiedo*) Argentine barbecue practice has been brought right into the city kitchen. They are always highly seasoned, whether marinated or not, and are a feature of public eating in Buenos Aires where one restaurant, the famous Old Chicken House, has been built up around this dish alone, along with its incidental accompaniments of *taglierini* or other Italian paste, romaine salad, and red Mendoza wine.

Two other very native restaurants in Buenos Aires that tourists do not necessarily discover are La Cabaña, in Calle Entre Rios, which is smart and rather formal, and La Prette, where Argentine gourmets, who love their national cooking and like to get it in real homely fashion, go to eat.

At the old Conte's, turkey was always the specialty, those Argentine turkeys that are forcibly fed until they grow bigger than any we have ever seen elsewhere. Only the *maître d'hôtel* is competent to cut the first slice from a prime roast turkey, and that slice begins logically with the Pope's Nose, carries the two sparkling jewels with it and the long, sizzling, crackling brown turkey back skin with tiny bits of heavenly meat clinging to it. This portion is served to the honored guest by the headwaiter himself while an ordinary waiter carries on, carving the less important breast and drumsticks.

One cannot think of South American turkeys without mentioning an interesting and perhaps useful custom. For home consumption they are invariably bought alive, and while the entire household and a few neighbors gather in the kitchen patio Mr Gobbler is doused with rum or *cachaça* until he struts and gobbles with happiness before falling in a disreputable heap, to remain unconscious during his quick and painless dispatch. His pleasant death by alcohol that pervades his whole system is supposed to account for his especial tenderness when cooked.

ARGENTINE CHICKEN IN GRAPE JUICE
Pollo al Jugo de Uva

Season a jointed tender chicken and fry in 3 tablespoons butter with a little minced parsley until lightly browned on all sides. Meanwhile place 1½–2 pounds juicy white grapes in a bowl and squeeze them with the hands until all juice is released. Then strain in a sieve, pressing out all juice with hands. Transfer chicken to saucepan or earthenware casserole. Cover with grape juice. Bring to boiling point and cook uncovered, for juice to reduce somewhat. Then cover tightly and simmer until chicken is tender. Serve chicken on a platter and the cooking liquid, either thickened or not, in a separate dish.

In Mendoza, where grapes grow gigantic and are better for eating fresh than for making wine, many good Argentine cooks prefer cooking with the freshly squeezed juice instead of wine. It imparts an exquisite flavor to fowl.

ARGENTINE CHICKEN WITH GREEN CORN
Pollo con Choclo

Roast a well-seasoned chicken. When it is beginning to be tender make a sauce as follows: Fry 1 chopped onion slowly in 2 tablespoons olive oil. When it is colored add 2 chopped tomatoes and continue slow frying. Add 1 bay leaf, 1 sprig marjoram (or a little dried marjoram) and 1 cup fresh green corn grated from cob. Thin pan gravy from chicken and add, then add carved chicken. Cover and simmer until all is hot, being careful that entire cooking time after corn goes in does not exceed 10 minutes.

BRAZILIAN CHICKEN IN BROWN SAUCE
Gallinha com Molho Pardo

½ cup vinegar	1 sprig celery leaves
1 roasting chicken, alive	1-2 cups boiling water
3 tablespoons fat or butter	Salt and pepper
1 onion, chopped	1 tablespoon sugar
½ small bay leaf	12 very small onions
2 sprigs parsley	½ tablespoon flour

Pour vinegar into a soup plate. Cut off head of chicken and hang over plate to catch blood. (The vinegar keeps blood from coagulating.) Prepare chicken and joint it. Fry in hot fat until nicely browned. Place pieces in deep saucepan with onion, bay leaf and celery leaves. Add boiling water and simmer. When half done add salt, pepper and sugar, and continue cooking slowly. Add onions ½ hour before chicken is done. When chicken is tender work flour smooth with 2 tablespoons cold water and add, shaking pan to mix well. Simmer 5 minutes. Then stir blood well and add a little at a time, shaking pan to mix. Do not let boil after this or gravy will curdle. Take up at once, and in a separate dish serve rice, either boiled plain or cooked, Spanish style.

Squabs and pigeons are especially delicious prepared in the same manner, squabs being kept whole and pigeons being cut in half before cooking.

BRAZILIAN DISH OF CHICKEN
Manjar de Gallinha

1 hen	2 cups rice flour
1½ quarts milk	Grated rind 1 lime
2 cups sugar	1 teaspoon cinnamon

Cook chicken in casserole with milk and ½ teaspoon salt until tender. Take out. Remove meat from bones and cut into small pieces. Place meat in a mortar and pound to a paste. (Wooden bowl and wooden potato masher will substitute.)

Put paste back into milk; mix well. Add 1¾ cups sugar, rice flour and lime rind. Stir and mix until thoroughly blended, then turn into a buttered pudding dish. Cover with remaining sugar. Sprinkle with cinnamon. Bake in moderate oven and serve hot.

COLOMBIAN CHICKEN IN MUSTARD SAUCE
Pollo en Salsa de Mostaza

Joint chicken. Rub well with salt and pepper. Fry until light brown in butter and put into a casserole with 1 cup water and 1 cup wine. Cover tightly and cook slowly until tender.

Prepare a sauce by beating 2 eggs and mixing with 2 tablespoons vinegar, 1 tablespoon water and 1 teaspoon dry mustard. Cook over boiling water, stirring continuously until smooth and thick. Strain broth from chicken, when done, and stir into egg mixture. Add 1 teaspoon sugar and salt to taste. Return casserole with chicken to slow heat. Spoon sauce over it, and as sauce falls to bottom baste chicken again with it and continue until all the pieces are richly glazed.

CASTILIAN CHICKEN
Gallina a la Castellana

1 chicken	½ tablespoon salt
2 onions, minced	¼ cup seeded raisins
1 green pepper, minced	1 cup rice
1 garlic clove, minced	2 tablespoons butter
1 tablespoon parsley, minced	¼ pound Edam cheese, grated
2 tablespoons butter	
½ cup tomato sauce	4 tablespoons sugar
1 cup wine	3 eggs, beaten

¼ pound roasted almonds

Clean chicken; truss and put in saucepan. Fry onions, pepper, garlic and parsley in butter until soft and smooth. Stir in tomato sauce and wine and salt. Add enough boiling water to half cover chicken and pour it over. Cover pan. Cook slowly until tender, turning occasionally. When chicken is tender remove bones and return meat to sauce in pan. Add raisins and cook slowly 20 minutes. Boil rice in salted boiling water until tender. Drain and add butter, grated cheese, sugar and beaten eggs. Place a buttered mold on baking dish and pack a ring of rice mixture solidly around it. Put in oven to set and brown nicely. Remove mold and spoon chicken and sauce into the rice ring. Sprinkle almonds over and serve piping hot.

This classic Spanish dish from the ancient province of Castile makes a festive dish in Bogotá, Colombia and other proud Latin-American cities. There's a Moorish touch in the liberal use of almonds.

CUBAN CHICKEN MIRAMAR

Cut a chicken into pieces and cook it in butter in the oven in an earthenware casserole. Have some rice cooked in Spanish style, young green peas, pimientos, cooked separately in butter, and mushrooms also separately cooked in butter. Make a good gravy by pouring stock over chicken in the casserole it has been cooked in and slightly thicken with brown roux or espagnole sauce.

Place chicken on serving dish with the rice around it and the peas, pimientos and mushrooms on the rice. Then pour your good gravy over the rice, peas, etc. and serve.

MEXICAN CHICKEN LARDED WITH BACON
Pollo Picado con Tocino

4 slices bacon	⅛ teaspoon ground cloves
2 garlic cloves	1 roasting chicken
1 teaspoon chili powder	Salt and pepper
1 dash cayenne	Minced parsley or marjoram

Have bacon sliced ¼ inch thick. With a wooden spoon crush garlic to paste in a small bowl. Add chili powder, cayenne and cloves. Work smooth and spread over bacon slices.

Cut bacon with scissors into shoestring strips. With larding needle thread bacon strips into chicken. Rub inside of chicken with salt, pepper and minced herbs. Dredge chicken with flour. Lay in pan well greased with bacon fat and sear in hot oven. Then reduce heat and add the following basting sauce as needed for basting:

2 tablespoons melted butter	1 tablespoon almonds, minced
2 cups tomato juice	
1 green pepper, minced	⅛ teaspoon ground cloves
1 small onion, minced	1 teaspoon coriander seeds
1 tablespoon olives, chopped	Salt and pepper

Baste frequently, adding a little boiling water if necessary toward the end. When chicken is tender carve it in the kitchen. Lay pieces on a hot platter and pour pan gravy over.

Mexicans frequently pot-roast this dish after frying the chicken in olive oil or butter, transferring it to an earthenware casserole and pouring basting sauce over. The chicken is turned several times and kept closely covered while slowly steaming. A little white wine is added if the sauce evaporates too rapidly toward the end.

In Guanajuato chicken is prepared in this way without larding. When the dish is ready the bird is covered with grated creamy cheese, put in the oven and left there until the cheese melts.

PARAGUAYAN SOPA
Sopa Paraguaya

This is neither soup nor stew, but a sort of Yorkshire pudding done in Latin-American style.

1 tablespoon fat	2 teaspoons baking powder
1 onion, chopped	1 cup pot cheese
1 tomato, chopped	or ½ cup grated cheese
½ cup boiling water	3 tablespoons shortening, melted
Salt and pepper	
2 cups corn meal	1 cup milk

Heat fat and slowly fry onion until tender and golden. Add tomato and continue frying until tomato is ready to break up. Add boiling water and season. Simmer while mixing remaining ingredients. Mix corn meal, baking powder and ½ teaspoon salt. Stir in cheese, shortening and milk. Add onion-broth mixture and stir smooth. Spread in one end of a dripping pan in which poultry is roasting and bake until nicely browned. Serve like Yorkshire pudding with the meat.

MEXICAN CHICKEN WITH ORANGE JUICE
Pollo con Naranja

1 tender chicken, jointed
Salt and cayenne
3 tablespoons fat or butter
12 almonds
½ cup seeded raisins

1 cup pineapple, chopped
⅛ teaspoon ground cinnamon
⅛ teaspoon ground cloves
2 cups orange juice

1 tablespoon flour

Season chicken and brown pieces on all sides in fat. Blanch almonds. Remove skins; chop and add with raisins, pineapple, spices and orange juice. Cover tightly and simmer until chicken is tender. Work flour smooth with 2 tablespoons cold water and add here and there, shaking pan to mix well. Simmer 5–8 minutes until gravy thickens. Take up chicken on hot platter. Pour some of the gravy over and garnish platter with half-moon slices of avocado and pomegranate pips. Serve remaining gravy in a gravy boat.

MEXICAN CHICKEN WITH FRUITS
Pollo con Frutas

Joint a tender young chicken, such as you would select for Chicken Maryland. Pack the pieces close together in a deep stewpan. Cover with 2 cups water, 2 tablespoons chili powder,

½ teaspoon freshly ground (or pounded) black pepper, ¼ teaspoon powdered cinnamon and 2 tablespoons onion juice. Cook slowly 30 minutes. Add 1 tablespoon salt, and when chicken begins to get tender remove from broth and fry in butter.

To the broth add 1 cup strained tomatoes, or tomato juice, and heat to boiling.

Put fried chicken in a hot, shallow baking dish and pour the broth over. Cover with thin slices of a cored but unpeeled apple, lightly sprinkled with 1 teaspoon sugar, alternating with thin slices of orange. Cook in oven or steamer until apples are tender. Decorate edges of dish with slices of avocado, halved white grapes of the Málaga type and pomegranate pips.

Rice is nice to serve with this for bland contrast. As a matter of fact throughout Latin America when you say chicken you might as well add rice, for chicken and rice is probably the most popular dish all the way from the Rio Grande to Tierra del Fuego.

PUERTO RICAN CHICKEN AND RICE
Arroz con Pollo

Cut a chicken (about 4 pounds) in medium-sized pieces. Rub with salt and pepper. Put about 2 tablespoons of Crisco or lard in a saucepan. Add a dozen olives, 1 tablespoon capers, 1 onion sliced, ½ of a large red sweet pepper cut in pieces, 2 medium-sized tomatoes cut in pieces, salt. Add the pieces of chicken. Cover and cook slowly; stir a few times. Cook until tender. If the chicken is old a little water should be added and the meat steamed to cook it until tender.

Wash 2 cups of rice; put the rice in the saucepan with the prepared chicken. Add about a pint and a half of boiling water. Cover and cook until the rice is done, stirring occasionally.

To serve put the rice on a large platter and around it place the pieces of chicken, over it a can of peas heated with a little butter, and garnish with halves of pimientos.

WEST INDIAN PILAU

3-pound chicken, jointed
3 garlic cloves, minced
2 teaspoons salt
½ teaspoon pepper
½ teaspoon cayenne

3 large onions, sliced
½ pound bacon, coarsely diced
1 large green pepper, sliced
1 tablespoon curry powder

1 pound brown rice

Mix garlic, salt, pepper and cayenne. Rub mixture thoroughly into chicken. Then rub chicken with onion slices. Fry bacon carefully, frying out most of the fat but being very careful that bacon does not scorch. Put bacon and bacon fat in a large kettle. Add chicken with onion slices and seeded green pepper, and stir well until bacon fat has covered chicken. Add curry powder and stir again. Add sufficient boiling water so that water shall stand ½ inch above chicken when all is done. Cover tightly and simmer until chicken is tender but does not fall from the bones. Taste broth and add more salt if necessary. Thoroughly wash rice, drain, and dry in a towel. Increase heat until chicken is boiling rapidly. Add rice, and when it has swollen, reduce heat, cover tightly and simmer 20–30 minutes, letting rice steam until it is dry and grainy, not soupy.

Serve either sweet or sour pickles with this dish.

THE TURKEY
El Guajalote

The turkey has been domesticated in Mexico since pre-Columbian days and *Molé de Guajalote*, or "Turkey in Sauce," is the traditional fine dish of the Aztec Indian.

Many folk tales from prehistoric times have come down to us in which the turkey figures as a sacred bird, and to this day it has kept its ritualistic character in some of the remote districts of Mexico and Peru, which last country gives the turkey its Portuguese name—*peru*. The Spanish call it *pauo* or *pava*, according to sex; Cubans have named it *guanajo* and Mexicans, *guajolote*.

We eat turkey ceremoniously on Thanksgiving, while in Latin America it is the chief food at a number of feasts. In Mexico a fine gobbler decked with wreaths of flowers is often presented by the mother of the bride to the godparents at a wedding, and the importance of a marriage is measured by the number of turkeys killed. Such a feast is called a *Molé*, as is also the celebration of the Saint's Day of a district or city ward.

An American friend tells of going with her engineer husband in the early days to an isolated mining camp in Sonora where they lived comfortably enough in an adobe house furnished by the company. She grew unbearably homesick, and when Christmas came longed for an American celebration with roast turkey, so her husband gave their cook one rifle cartridge and sent him out on the mountain where wild turkeys flocked, explaining that a turkey had become necessary for the happiness of the household. At nightfall the man came back with an enormous bird, standing five feet from the tips of its claws to its bullet-holed head. He was proud of the turkey, but still more proud of his perfect shot.

The next morning the wife was up early to superintend the stuffing and cooking of the fowl. But the cook was earlier still. He had cleaned the turkey, jointed it and had it already stewing in a pot. His mistress was in tears, and the dismayed servant was nearly on his knees in despair over having unwittingly cut it up to prepare it in a style his employers considered most un-American.

It was a sad Christmas morning until the midday meal was served, and the strange dish came on the table. It was the *Molé de Poblano Guajolote*, often simply called *Molé de Guajolote*, which would elevate the cuisine of any country to the Lucullan class. When the family tasted it all their gloom fled, and the cook was the happiest man alive.

Herewith is the recipe, with all 25 ingredients:

TURKEY IN MEXICAN PEOPLES' SAUCE
Molé de Poblano de Guajolote

½ pound pasilla peppers   4-10 chilies
½ pound broad peppers   3 cups olive oil or butter
¼ pound brown peppers   1 large turkey, jointed

Flavorings

1 tablespoon sesame seeds   1 sprig marjoram
½ cup squash seeds   1 sprig thyme
½ cup pumpkin seeds   1 bay leaf
½ cup peanuts   3 cloves
2 tablespoons pine nuts   1 teaspoon cinnamon
1 piece stale tortilla   ½ teaspoon ginger
½ slice white bread   1 tablespoon aniseed
3-6 garlic cloves, minced   ½ cup raisins
3 tomatoes, chopped   Salt
1 ounce chocolate

Remove seeds and veins from peppers and chilies and fry in plenty of oil. If dried peppers are used drop them into hot water to soften and let stand; then drain. Fry turkey in pepper-flavored oil until brown on all sides. Arrange turkey pieces close together, preferably in an earthenware casserole, but a deep saucepan will do. Cover with salted boiling water and cook gently until nearly tender. Toast sesame seeds by shaking over heat in a dry pan. Fry squash and pumpkin seeds but do not brown. Roast peanuts, if not already roasted. Fry tortilla and bread until crisp, then crumble it. Finely grind sesame, squash and pumpkin seeds, pine nuts and bread crumbs. Also grind peppers and chilies together. Slowly fry garlic without browning. Add tomato and fry until tomato thickens. Put all these prepared flavorings together. Mash and work mixture until smooth. Add strained oil from various fryings to herbs, spices and raisins and mix thoroughly, seasoning to taste with salt. Simmer and stir with wooden spoon. Then add turkey and its broth and finish cooking, moving it once in a while with wooden spoon to prevent sticking. Add grated chocolate at last moment and take up when melted and blended.

This long process may be shortened to kitchenette technique by buying a tin of *Molé de Guajolote* at a Spanish store and using it according to directions for the preparation of a small turkey, the vest-pocket kind being bred nowadays to fit the family refrigerator.

And by the way, our Thanksgiving bird is of Mexican origin, domesticated long before white men came to this continent, and not developed from our own wild species.

CHICKEN MOLÉ
Molé de Gallo o de Gallina

This is prepared the same as *Molé de Guajolote*, except that chicken is substituted for turkey.

"*Para molé su gallo viejo*" is an insult hurled at a man whose "fighting cock is too old for battle and fit only for a stew."

PERUVIAN DUCK WITH RICE
Pato con Arroz

Heat ¼ cup fat or butter in frying pan and add jointed duck with 1 minced onion and 1 minced garlic clove. Sprinkle well with pepper and with pounded coriander and cumin seeds. Fry until duck is nicely browned on all sides. Transfer entire contents of frying pan to a deep saucepan. Cover well with boiling water; add salt. Cover pan and cook gently until duck is becoming quite tender. Add ¾ cup well-washed rice. Boil rapidly, uncovered, 5–8 minutes. Then cover very tightly and simmer until rice is tender, about ¾ hour.

This is the dish in Peru that takes the place of the ubiquitous *Pollo con Arroz* (Chicken and Rice) of other Spanish-speaking countries.

BRAZILIAN DUCK WITH OLIVES
Pato com Azeitunhas

1 duck	6–8 whole peppers
2 tablespoons butter	2 cups boiling water
2 slices bacon	1 bay leaf
1 small onion, sliced	2 parsley sprigs
Salt	1 sprig celery leaves

1 cup small green olives

Fry duck in butter with bacon, and as it is growing brown add onion and continue frying and turning until evenly browned all over. Transfer to deep saucepan or casserole. Add salt, whole peppers, boiling water and herbs. Cover tightly and simmer, turning occasionally, until tender. With a sharp knife cut the flesh from each olive in an unbroken spiral. When duck is done take up and keep hot. Strain gravy. Thicken with a little flour worked smooth with 2–3 tablespoons cold water. Scald olive spirals 2 minutes in boiling water and add. Serve gravy separately in a gravy boat.

Brazil uses the small, piquant olives of Portugal in cooking, and we find them tastier than the bigger bland ones of Spain and California.

CHILEAN PARTRIDGES IN PICKLE
Perdices en Escabeche

5 partridges	2 bay leaves
2 whole onions	4 whole peppers, ground
2 carrots	A small pinch marjoram
1 celery stalk	¼ cup vinegar
6 garlic cloves	2 tablespoons olive oil

1 teaspoon salt

Wash, clean and truss partridges. Pour boiling water over and let cool in water. Take from water. Wipe dry and place in a casserole. Add remaining ingredients. Cover with boiling water or broth. Cover casserole and cook until tender, about 40 minutes.

Meats *en escabeche*—pickled or soused—are not so common as fish in the same popular Spanish style. But game birds and venison respond to this somewhat sourish treatment and are leaders on the menus of big Chilean restaurants where game of all sorts is in demand. *Perdices en Escabeche* indeed has been voted the best game dish of the country by many Chilean gourmets.

PARTRIDGE WITH AMERICAN SAUCE
Perdiz con Salsa Americana

1 partridge	2 tablespoons butter
Salt and pepper	½ cup bread crumbs

Joint a plump young partridge. Season with salt and pepper. Brown in a covered pan with butter and bread crumbs and serve with:

SALSA AMERICANA

1 tablespoon butter	1 cup tomato sauce
1 tablespoon flour	½ cup cream

Melt butter, add flour and stir smooth. Add tomato sauce, stir and simmer until thick and smooth. Quickly stir in cream, and serve at once.

With plenty of game and dairy products this rich dish is made to perfection in Chile. The American Sauce was introduced by American ladies in Chile who published their own cookbook in Santiago, from which this recipe is taken.

COLOMBIAN PIGEONS WITH PEAS
Pichones con Petit-Pois

Dress and clean 6 pigeons, leaving them whole. Prepare a marinade with 4 tablespoons olive oil, 2 tablespoons lemon juice, 1 tablespoon orange juice, 1 teaspoon salt and ¼ teaspoon pepper. Rub pigeons well inside and out with marinade and let rest on a platter overnight. Next day heat 1 tablespoon butter in bottom of a deep kettle with tight cover and brown pigeons lightly in it. Add liquid collected in platter, 1 bay leaf, 1 marjoram sprig and 1 cup red or white wine. Put on cover and cook over slow fire until tender. Have ready in hot serving dish 3 cups freshly cooked, drained and seasoned peas. Arrange pigeons on them and strain sauce over.

ARGENTINE OSTRICH
Chaya de Avestruz

The thigh of the small Argentine ostrich, or rhea, is considered the choicest part, and thin steaks are cut from it. These steaks are first washed in salted water and then soaked 1 hour in a marinade made with a little vinegar, mashed garlic, peppers both hot and sweet, chili pepper sauce, marjoram, grated nutmeg, clove and bay leaf, the amount depending on number of steaks. The meat is turned often while marinating.

When ready for cooking put enough olive oil or other fat in the bottom of a deep casserole to just cover it. For 6 steaks, chop up about 3 pints of any desired fresh vegetables with 3 crushed garlic cloves and place in casserole in form of nests. Heat 6 flat round stones very hot. Remove steaks from marinade. Wrap each one around a hot stone and place in center of the vegetable nests. Sprinkle with good olive oil and ground pepper. Cover well with fresh cabbage leaves and press them down. Cover casserole; put over low heat and cook 2 hours. The hot stones help cook the toughish ostrich steaks all the way through and bring out its full savor.

Red or *criollo* wine from the lush province of Mendoza is just the thing to wash down a feast on this common game of the pampas prairies.

And if you must first catch your rhea just borrow one of those braided lariats with lead-filled rawhide balls at the dude

ranch, whirl the three balls around your head at the end of
their short thongs, ride down your prey and let the lasso go
with a yell, aiming to wrap the balls around the bird's long
leaping legs and bring her down for breakfast.

If you find the meat too tough maybe you'd prefer it jerked
in the form of *Charqui*. (See recipe.) And do try a roasted rhea
egg . . . one will be plenty. The eggs of this South American
ostrich are found singly and sometimes a couple of dozen to
a nest. They're considered as great a delicacy in Argentina
and Paraguay as sister ostrich eggs are in Africa. The shells are
thick, hard and ivory colored, strong enough to resist the heat
when put directly on the campfire coals for roasting.

You can also get the makings of an exotic omelet out of one
by piercing the ends and blowing out the raw contents as you
would in fixing a fancy Easter egg. And never throw the shell
away, for it makes a practical and pretty cup by chipping the
top edge away. It holds more than a pint and is greatly fancied
by *maté* drinkers in the interior. The shells are often set in
beautifully wrought silver frames with feet, making attractive
table utensils, and the best of these fetch high prices in Buenos
Aires' antique shops off the Calle Flroida. Every tourist should
bring one back, for it's a choice souvenir of a period of pampas
culture that's now passing, and the rhea may soon be as scarce
as our wild turkeys.

BARBECUES

BARBACOAS

Although our own Southern states throw some pretty swell barbecues and boast many experts at the art most of the traditions are borrowed from the neighbor just south of us, and one must cross the Rio Grande to be in the real home, on this hemisphere, of the most primitive form of meat cookery. And then one can keep going on barbecues alone to the tip end of Patagonia with a continual change of menu from a tiny kid grilled on a spit to a huge ox buried and roasted in the ground.

The very words "kid" and "barbecue" suggest high gastronomic revel, the romance of the Spanish Main, those greedy, colorful buccaneers of old, Captain Kidd and that other pirate, John Silver, who was nicknamed Barbecue by the playful crew. Indeed the mere mention of this most elemental form of feasting has suggested culinary adventure ever since those French corsairs dubbed their favorite catch-as-catch-can cooking style *de barbe à queue*, which translates literally "from beard to tail," referring of course to roasting any animal entire, all the way from its goatee to the final tuft of tail.

And to get into the true swing all you have to do is recall Bo Bo, that great lubberly Chinese boy, the hero of Charles Lamb's "Dissertation on Roast Pig," who burned down his father's hut one day over a "fine litter of nine new farrowed pigs." Thus by accident Bo Bo was first to taste the "crackling" of suckling pig, and after that not only his father's but all the neighbors' huts were burned down accidentally on purpose every time a new batch of pinkies arrived. And Lamb wasn't the only English author interested in this subject, for the poet Pope has one of his characters cry out, "Send me, gods, a whole hog barbecued," while other merry beef eaters of old England record the common custom of roasting oxen in their hairy hides, even sheep in their wool to save the trouble of skinning them.

In our wanderings through Latin-American countries we have tried every kind of barbecued animal at least once, except snake, iguana and alligator, which didn't happen to be on the menu when we chanced in, although these are esteemed delicacies not only in South America but on Florida ranches devoted to raising some of these charming pets. From country to country barbecue styles differed considerably, and we even found some imported from far places, such as the Hottentot way of tendering elephant trunks and feet, which is used all over the Argentine for barbecuing beef. The hide, hair and all is left on in this style and the steer buried whole in a stone-lined pit where it's put to bed at twilight and left to roast all night.

Of the same ilk is the pampas ranger's *carne con cuero* (beef barbecued with its hide on) that Argentine epicures go for, consisting of the tenderest cut of a steer, since he has the whole animal to choose from, buried in a hole in the ground that has been heated and raked clean of ashes and coals. It is eaten very rare, and therein lies the skill, for it takes not only a good cook but the cattleman's instinct to know the exact moment for digging it out.

The same expertness is required of West Indians in preparing their suckling pig in clay. Thickly plastered with his earthy blanket, piggy lies in a bed of hot ashes with a well-regulated fire going over him all day, for he must be well done. When his skin has begun to scorch, as one knows by intuition, the clay covering is cracked off, skin comes with it, and the perfume of sage-seasoned pork is an appetizing start for the barbecue feast.

Another West Indian barbecue trick, shared with Brazil, is to wrap any meat, no matter how tough and forbidding, in papaya leaves and then either bury it in hot ashes or roast it over coals. The papaya leaves contain vegetable pepsin which softens and predigests the meat without affecting its flavor, and it turns out meltingly tender in very short order.

Also, there is the incomparable South Sea Island style, as popular among Chileans as it is with the Tahitians who invented it. In this, appropriate fruits, roots, grains and vegetables, many of them unknown to us, are wrapped separately in big leaves or in *petates*, which are mats woven of fresh palm fronds, and these are laid on top of the meat to steam in its juices. Everything is tamped down with more leaves. Hot stones and coals are heaped on, and finally a close cover of earth. Enough of the essence of the fruits and things seeps down as the savory meat steam wells up, so everything comes out of the hole with a richness of flavor that no other method can equal. It's well worth trying next time you find yourself near a hole in the ground and a well-stocked farm with the farmer away, for almost anybody can make some kind of a *petate* out of plenty of green corn husks.

Among many barbecues we'll always recall that colorful *Asado de Carnero*, sheep spitted in typical Argentine style, with which our small American colony in Buenos Aires celebrated one Washington's Birthday. Many in that party were executives of Armour's, Swift's, Cudahy's and Wilson's, representatives of practically all the big American packing houses which maintain branches down there. They knew their cattle both on the hoof and over the pit fire. There was plenty to choose from—prime pampas-grass-fed steers built as four square as piano cases and marbled through with fat, great waddling sheep with backs as broad and level as pool tables, the kind that wear away blue ribbons from yearly cattle shows in "B. A." And real Gaucho cooks fresh from the pampas, too, where they're weaned on barbecued steaks with the hair on! Deft of hand they were, and unflustered by the clamorings of a thousand ravenous guests.

The sheep were stood upright in circles around a regular Dante's inferno of fires, each carcass speared through from neck to tail by a heavy metal rod sharpened at one end to thrust into the ground over and over again as the animals were turned to the fire to make sure of even roasting. The fore and hind quarters were trussed open by similar rods, giving the effect of being hung on Maltese crosses. Attendant Gauchos told us that these metal spits are such perfect heat conductors that the inside of the meat is cooked as thoroughly as the parts nearer the fire. And this is the great value of all cooking on metal spits, everything's well done all the way through.

Hearty slabs of Spanish white bread, which is much more closely knit than ours and fancily braided as well, served both as sandwich coverings and plates, each portion of meat being garnished with a heaping forkful of coleslaw and sluiced with an *adobo* or sauce that had not only mint, but plenty of pungent capers as well. There was good beer, too, light Quilmes Crystal straight from the keg.

Since ninety-nine per cent of the success of such a picnic can be chalked up to the barbecuers' skill, this one went clear over the top. And by contrast, we remember another that failed in Brazil. Our expatriate colony in Rio de Janeiro, numbering about six hundred, staged a big get-together in the enormous garden of a local brewery, but it was a hollow flop, because the reputed expert cooks turned out to be only novices. The meat was improperly prepared, not sufficiently seasoned and hurriedly roasted. Spits of green wood were used instead of steel, so the meat was raw within as well as burnt and tough outside. And it was hours late besides, while the beer—this time Polonia—flowed and flowed and appetites waxed and waned. The onions which were to have been sliced into an invigorating salad to top the meat never even got peeled and finally were handed out whole. Soon even the dignified fathers of our far-from-home community, lacking anything better to do, began heaving those Brazilian apples at each other, and then the barbarous chefs, catching stray ones on the conk, took this as their cue to seek safe hiding places, while most of us left in disgust and went to restaurants to get a square meal.

MEXICAN BARBECUE SAUCE

½ cup olive oil	½ tablespoon salt
1 onion, chopped	2 large tomatoes, cut up
1 garlic clove	2 tablespoons chili powder
1 chili pepper, minced or cayenne	¼ cup vinegar
	¼ cup water

Heat 1 tablespoon olive oil. Add onion and slowly fry until lightly browned. Add garlic, chili, salt and tomato and simmer until thickened. Add remaining ingredients and cook 5–8 minutes, stirring constantly. Use as a basting sauce while grilling or roasting meats.

Heat 1 tablespoon olive oil. Add onion and cook over medium heat. Add garlic, chili, salt and tomato and simmer until thickened. Add remaining ingredients and cook 25 minutes, stirring occasionally.

SAUCES

MEXICAN SAUCES

Even when made by the humblest Indian woman over her outdoor fire, Mexican sauces are very sophisticated, technique and seasonings going back to days of Aztec culture before Spanish occupation, and so closely resembling East Indian curry making that ethnologists may find in this cooking art good proof of racial relationships. Unlike the mild and simple sauces of Spain, a Mexican sauce, or *molé* is stinging hot with chilies and contains an astonishing variety of well-balanced flavorings. Recipes are highly individual, each cook and household varying proportions to suit personal taste and the dish to be dressed.

The Aztec word *molé* (also used with varied spelling and pronunciation in India, Portugal and sometimes in Spain) is applied as well to a dish accompanied with a sauce. *Molé de gallina,* or "chicken molé" as it is called in the hybrid language of foreigners in Mexico, is chicken in sauce; *molé de guajolote* is turkey in sauce, etc. This same word appears in combination to denominate many native dishes characterized by their sauces. *Chimolé* (Aztec *chil-molé*) is a sauce with chili, still known as *chil-molé* in some districts; *guacamolé*, avocado with sauce (*ahuacatl* in the Aztec language, corrupted to *aguacate*, being the word for avocado), is made of avocados mixed with ripe tomatoes, onions and mashed green chilies, seasoned, combined with olive oil and vinegar, and served either as a salad or a sauce. *Clemolé*, eaten several times a week by those who can afford it, is a meat and vegetable stew with its own tasty sauce spiced with chili.

It is always wise to taste Mexican sauces while making them and adjust the quantity of chilies and pepper accordingly or they may turn out too hot for the unaccustomed palate. A number of the best are now put up in tins and can be purchased at Spanish stores. The grocer, or grocer's wife, will explain how to use them in case any assistance is needed beyond the instructions on the labels. A tiny can of *Molé de Guajolote* will prove a prized adjunct in any kitchen, for a little added to meat sauces and gravies imparts a mysterious and delightful aroma.

ORDINARY MEXICAN COOKING SAUCE

1 onion, chopped	1 teaspoon chili powder
1 tablespoon olive oil	1 large tomato, chopped
1 garlic clove, minced	1 cup meat broth

Salt and pepper

Slowly fry onion in oil until it begins to color. Add garlic and continue very slow frying until golden. Add chili powder and stir well together. Add tomato and continue to slowly fry and stir until tomato thickens. Add broth; bring to boiling point and simmer 10 minutes, stirring often enough to blend well. Thicken, or not, with a little tortilla dough or flour.

Since this sauce is good with all meats and nearly all vegetables it is the stand-by of the Mexican cook, who always seems to have it simmering before every meal. In place of the chili powder, however, fresh pepper paste made of several kinds of peppers and chilies is often used. Meat served with this sauce is called *entomatado*, or "dressed with tomatoes."

SIMPLE MOLÉ POBLANO

½ pound broad peppers	2 tablespoons sesame seeds
¼ pound pasilla peppers	1 cup cooked tomatoes
4 tablespoons olive oil	Salt
2–4 garlic cloves	Tabasco
2 tablespoons coriander seeds	1 dash ground cloves

Fry peppers in oil until browned but not scorched. Peel and remove seeds and veins. Lightly brown garlic in same oil and remove. Fry coriander seeds in same oil a moment and remove. Toast sesame seeds in dry pan, being careful not to scorch. Finely grind peppers, garlic and seeds together. Mash tomatoes and then mash together with ground mixture. Add salt, Tabasco and cloves and simmer a few minutes to blend well.

MEXICAN RED SAUCE
Molé Colorado

1 onion, chopped	1 tablespoon ground almonds
3 tablespoons olive oil	2 tablespoons sesame seeds
2 garlic cloves, minced	1 tablespoon ground peanuts
4 tomatoes, chopped	1 clove
4 red sweet peppers, emptied and chopped	⅛ teaspoon ground cinnamon
¼ pound ground ham	⅛ teaspoon ground ginger
2–4 red chilies, crushed	⅛ teaspoon ground mace
	1 tablespoon sugar

½ teaspoon salt

Fry onion very slowly in olive oil without browning. Add garlic and continue slow frying but do not brown. Add tomatoes, sweet red peppers (substitute canned pimientos), ham and chilies (substitute Tabasco or cayenne) and simmer until thick. Blanch almonds; remove skins. Toast sesame seeds in dry frying pan. Run almonds, sesame seeds and peanuts all together through grinder twice, using finest blade, and add with remaining ingredients. Simmer a few minutes, stirring to blend well.

This peppery sauce is thick enough to be called a spread, and it is used as such to make *enchiladas* and a score of other Mexican dishes. Or it is thinned somewhat with a little hot broth or water and used as a regular sauce for meats and vegetables. It keeps well when stored in the refrigerator.

MEXICAN GREEN SAUCE
Molé Verde

This sauce must retain its green color when finished, so care is needed not to brown or overcook any of the ingredients, and thus spoil the fresh appearance.

Begin by frying 1 cup squash seeds in 2 tablespoons olive oil without letting them brown. Squash seeds can be bought already toasted at corner stands in cities, or they may be retrieved from any well-developed squash opened in the kitchen. After frying, run them through the grinder, using finest blade. Take seeds and veins from 6 green chilies (purchased from any foreign greengrocer or pushcart market). Also remove seeds and veins from 6 green peppers. Discard the tough bitter tips from 3 spring onions or an equal bulk of chives. Finely grind chilies, green peppers, onions (using both green and white parts) and 2–3 parsley sprigs. (Coriander sprigs are more Mexican if you have an herb garden.) Chop a very small green tomato and fry in 1 tablespoon olive oil without browning. (If tomato is beginning to get red use only part of it or you will spoil the color.) Chop spinach very fine, enough to fill 1 tablespoon. Place all these prepared ingredients in an enameled saucepan with 1 clove, 1 cup chicken or veal broth, salt to taste, and simmer and stir until nicely blended but still bright green.

MEXICAN SAUCE FOR MEATS OR VEGETABLES

2 tablespoons olive oil	½ cup ground almonds
1 onion, chopped	4 tomatoes, chopped
1 teaspoon chili powder	1 bay leaf
2 stalks celery, chopped	1 pint broth
¼ teaspoon cayenne	1 sprig parsley
or a seeded chili pepper	Salt

Heat olive oil. Add onion and fry very slowly without browning. When onion begins to color stir in chili powder.

Then add celery, almonds, cayenne (This quantity will make it very hot.), tomatoes and bay leaf. Simmer until well blended and thickened. Add broth from either meat or vegetables, and parsley. Season with salt to taste and simmer and stir until well blended. Then strain and reheat. This sauce requires patience to bring it to the right consistency, for it has no thickening except almonds and tomatoes, but the result is worth the trouble.

MEXICAN SAUCE FOR FISH

2 tablespoons olive oil
1 onion, chopped
1 garlic clove, minced
2 tablespoons ground cooked pork or uncooked sausage meat
4 tomatoes, chopped
6 olives, chopped
⅛ teaspoon ground cinnamon
⅛ teaspoon ground cloves
½ teaspoon minced parsley or marjoram
Salt and pepper
Pan liquor from fish
Juice ½ lemon

Slowly fry onion in olive oil. Add garlic and continue slow frying until they begin to color. Then add meat, tomatoes, olives and spices. Simmer until blended and thickened. Strain, pressing soft ingredients through sieve. Add a very little fish pan liquor until of proper consistency and reheat. Season; add parsley and lemon juice.

MEXICAN BARBECUE SAUCE

See under Barbecues.

COLOMBIAN YELLOW SAUCE (FOR FISH)
Salsa Amarillo

Heat 1 cup milk or broth with 1 tablespoon butter, 1 teaspoon salt, 1 teaspoon sugar, 1 dash of pepper and ½ teaspoon minced parsley. When boiling, stir in 1 teaspoon cornstarch, dissolved in a little water. Stir and simmer 3 minutes. Add 2 beaten egg yolks. Stir until smooth. Then remove from heat; add 1 tablespoon vinegar, and it's *pronto!*

BRAZILIAN FISH SAUCE
Molho do Peixe

Rapidly boil the liquid in which any fish has been cooked, and to make it rich and tasty, add bits of shredded leftover fish. (It is presumed that your fish broth is already seasoned with salt, pepper, dried celery sprigs, fresh parsley sprigs and 1–2 onion slices, and that the fish head was cooked with the fish in order to give proper gelatinous consistency.) Thicken broth with butter kneaded with flour, allowing 1 tablespoon butter and 1 tablespoon flour to each cup of broth, and stirring bits of mixture in until all is incorporated and sauce thickens. Or thicken to desired consistency with toasted *farinha de mandioca* (cassava meal). Serve with eggs, fish or sea food.

PUERTO RICAN FISH SAUCE

See under Baked Tuna.

COLOMBIAN SEASONING SAUCE
Salsa de Aliños

Chop fine and grind together 2 parts tomato and 1 part onion. Fry slowly in a little butter with lemon juice, salt and pepper. Stir to keep from sticking and cook until you have a soft, thickish sauce.

This simple Colombian seasoning sauce is used as we use catsup in cooking. Usually it is made in sizable quantity and kept on hand for countless seasoning purposes. (See Colombian Lentil Soup.)

CUBAN SAUCE FOR MEATS
Salsa Cubana

1 green plantain or	1 teaspoon capers, drained
2 large bananas	1 teaspoon parsley, minced
Lemon juice	Yerba buena or mint
1 cup stock	1 tablespoon lard
2 garlic cloves	2 tomatoes
1 sweet green pepper	Salt and pepper
1 minced onion	1 egg, beaten

Peel plantain or bananas. Sprinkle with lemon juice. Mash to smooth pulp. Add stock and stir until creamy. Chop together as fine as possible garlic, pepper, onion, capers and herbs. Put lard into a hot saucepan and fry seasonings until lightly browned, then add tomatoes, peeled and chopped, and simmer until smooth and thickened. Add plantain pulp. Stir until well blended. Season to taste and continue simmering until sauce is of proper consistency. Stir in beaten egg just before taking from heat.

ECUADORIAN PEANUT SAUCE FOR MEATS

See *Cariucho* Sauce under Ecuadorian Sauced Beef.

BRAZILIAN SAUCE FOR ALL MEATS

1 onion, chopped	1 garlic clove, minced
2 tablespoons olive oil	Herb bouquet
	Meat gravy or white wine

Slowly fry onion in olive oil. When it begins to color add garlic and continue slow frying. At this point a chopped tomato may be added. Add herb bouquet, consisting of 2 parsley sprigs, 1 sprig celery leaves and a bit of either thyme, marjoram or tarragon. Add meat gravy or white wine and simmer. Strain and add 1 tablespoon Madeira if you wish.

The above mixture is the secret of the excellent meat preparation of all Brazilian cooks. Little steaks and cutlets are fried along with the onion and garlic and finished by simmering with the herbs and gravy or white wine. All pot roasts—beef, chicken, duck, kid, even pork—are first browned in olive oil with onion and garlic and then slowly simmered in remaining ingredients; and this same mixture goes into practically every roasting pan, with onion perhaps sliced instead of chopped, and garlic left whole, both to be removed or strained out of pan liquor before gravy is thinned with wine and thickened with flour or cassava meal. This technique originally came from Portugal, and is similar to the general cooking sauce of Spanish origin that is used in nearly all of Latin America.

Brazilian cooks know how to make the famous French sauces, Maître d'Hôtel, Bechamel, Robert, Bernaise, etc., and occasionally employ them, but they prefer cooking their meats in the sauce described above, which is really a gravy, and placing on the table for good measure an additional appetizing little sauce, such as these three:

PORTUGUESE SAUCE
Molho Portuguese

Slice 1 onion and 1 green pepper in thin rings. Fry together very slowly in a little olive oil or butter. When tender but not browned add 1 unpeeled tomato, sliced thin, salt, pepper and 1 teaspoon minced parsley. Cook very gently 10 minutes, keeping tomato slices whole. Add a little hot water or meat broth and a dash of vinegar. Slide out of pan into hot gravy boat without breaking onion rings and eat with fried or reheated meats.

The same sauce, uncooked, is eaten with cold meats, and made thus:

Place thin onion rings, green pepper rings and slices of tomato in a shallow dish. Sprinkle with salt, freshly ground pepper and minced parsley, and pour over ¼ cup vinegar thinned with ¼ cup water. Let stand 1 hour before serving.

BRAZILIAN PEPPER SAUCE
Molho de Pimenta

Crush a dozen hot green chilies in the juice of 1 lime and add a bit of salt if desired. Or mix some red chilies with the green for a more colorful effect.

This is a very hot sauce that appears in a small dish at all Brazilian meals, and the little dish in which it is served is provided with a wooden mustard spoon with which the smallest quantity is sprinkled over meats or *feijoada* (black bean stew). It is considered good only when freshly made, often at the table.

ORANGE SAUCE
Molho do Laranja

Simmer 1 hot green chili in 1–2 tablespoons wine or cider vinegar until flavor is extracted but chili is only half cooked. Stir 1 tablespoon cornstarch into strained juice of 1 orange and add. Bring slowly to boiling point, stirring constantly. Add boiling water to thin somewhat. Stir in 1 tablespoon butter and add salt to taste. Serve hot with meats.

CHILEAN ORANGE SAUCE FOR ROAST DUCK
Salsa de Naranja para Pato Asado

2 teaspoons bacon, finely chopped	Salt and pepper
	Juice of 1 orange
2 teaspoons onion, finely chopped	½ cup port wine
	Duck gravy

Fry bacon and onion together 5 minutes. Season; add orange juice, wine and gravy from roast duck. Heat and serve piping with duck.

A heavy sweet red wine would be used instead of port in Chile, because importing any kind of wine to Chile would be bringing coals to Newcastle. Like California, at the other end of the Pacific coast, Chile runs with wine of all types and is, in fact, the producer of the very best wines in all the Americas, and a great deal of it is used in such sauces as the above.

ORANGE SAUCE FOR ROAST PIG
Salsa de Naranja para Lechón

Heat in a saucepan 1 cup water with 1 tablespoon sugar, juice of 2 oranges and 1 lemon, 1 tablespoon butter, 1 teaspoon salt and a little white pepper. When hot stir in 1 teaspoon corn-starch which has been mixed with a little water and 1 beaten egg yolk. Stir and cook gently until sauce thickens.

In Latin America the sour orange (*naranja agria*) is commonly used in place of lemons, which are not as common as they are in this country. The Brazilian lemon is round and green and milder in flavor than ours.

RICE AND BEANS

(Or, more accurately, Beans and Rice, for there are always beans though rice may be scarce.)

RICE AND BEANS
Arroz con Frijoles

Throughout Mexico, Central America, the West Indies and most of South America rice and beans are the mainstay of the people. Beans are almost invariably of the kidney variety, ranging in color from white through tans and browns to chocolate and black, depending on local crops and taste, with a majority vote for the darker ones. They are seldom cooked with meat, but boiled plain until soft and soupier than our Boston Baked. And being boiled with nothing but salt, pepper and perhaps a few herbs, they would be rather tasteless if it weren't for the fact that usually they're finished off with a little sauce made as follows:

SEASONING FOR PLAIN-BOILED FRIJOLES

Heat 2 tablespoons fat. Add 1 chopped onion and slowly fry until golden. Add 1 minced garlic clove and slowly fry until lightly browned. Add 1 large chopped tomato, seasonings and minced herbs—always including a little wild marjoram. Fry until tomato thickens. Add a few cooked beans and a little bean liquid to this mixture. Stir and mash together and throw all into the bean pot to simmer until well mixed.

Rice appears on the table in a separate dish but is always put on the plates to be mixed with beans at will. It is seldom just plain boiled, but is cooked in gay Mexican or Spanish fashions (See recipes.), made pink with tomatoes and paprika, or yellow with saffron.

The ubiquitous beans and rice of Latin America are alike in being served either quite plain or pretty rich.

To be at their best beans should not be soaked, as is too

often done, for this robs them of flavor and color. To be sure it takes longer to cook unsoaked beans, but the result is well worth the time.

Leftover beans are never thrown away, but made into:

RE-FRIED BEANS
Frijoles Refritos

Mash beans a little in a skillet with plenty of dripping and some browned flour. Add a little water if too dry. Serve with or without rice and garnish with green onions and radishes.

HAITIAN RICE AND BEANS
Pois et Ris

1 pound red kidney beans	Garlic, minced
Lard	Thyme
Salt pork, or ham or little peppery sausages	Salt and pepper
	Butter
1 pound rice, well washed	

Boil kidney beans until soft to pressure of fingers. Drain off water and save. Heat lard in frying pan. Add beans and cut up meat or sausages and fry until slightly browned. Add bean water, and if insufficient, add a little boiling water. Add garlic, thyme and seasonings. Heat to rapid boiling point and add rice with butter to taste. Boil rapidly at first until rice is swollen and mixture is becoming dry. Then reduce heat; cover and simmer over very low heat until thoroughly done.

Rice and Beans can be considered the national dish of Haiti. No one has definite measurements for the ingredients, but the result always tastes good when an Haitian woman makes it. It is served with meat sauce or alone.

In the French words of Haiti the dish is *Pois et Riz*, which leads to the mistaken idea that it's made with peas instead of beans.

RICE AND BEANS
The Daily Food of Most Puerto Ricans

Boil 1 cup of kidney beans until tender. In another saucepan put some lard in which achiote seeds have been heated (Do not add the seeds.), 1 medium-sized onion, sliced, part of a pimiento, some small pieces of cured ham or a little *salchichón* (smoked sausages), 1 or 2 tomatoes. Cook all these ingredients together to form a sauce and add to the beans.

Wash 2 cups of rice. Put with the prepared beans. Add about 3 cups water. Stir often and cook until the rice is done.

GANDULES
Pigeon Peas, Much Used in Puerto Rico

Prepare in the same way as the above recipe for rice and beans. The *gandules* are often served as a vegetable without the rice.

JAMAICA COAT OF ARMS

Little red beans are soaked overnight for this dish and cooked with salt pork and a good piece of beef. The beef is taken out and served separately with an onion and tomato sauce. Grate a fresh coconut. Squeeze out the juice and add it to the beans for the accompanying dish.

This is a Sunday special and must be eaten the day it is made or the coconut will become rancid.

COLOMBIAN BLACK BEANS

Select plump black beans. Wash well and soak overnight in cold water. Drain in morning. Cover again with cold water. Bring slowly to boiling point. Add salt to taste and let simmer until tender. There should be little liquid left. Drain this from beans.

Heat lard in a frying pan. Fry a minced onion in it. Add

drained beans and a sprinkling of black pepper. Turn beans in seasoned fat until coated. Add just enough milk to cover. Bring slowly to boiling point and serve.

TEZCUCANA "FAT BEANS" WITH PEPPERS
Frijoles Gordos con Chili a la Tezcucana

Parboil 1 quart large soup beans with ½ teaspoon soda until skins slip. Drain and wash beans with hot water. Cover with salted boiling water and start cooking gently. Cut fat from 1 pound fresh pork shoulder. Dice it and fry it until crisp; remove from frying pan and add to beans along with lean pork. Fry 1 whole pepper in pork fat until skin blisters. Remove skin, seeds and veins. Chop pepper and return to frying pan with 1 minced onion and 1 minced garlic clove. Fry until everything is lightly browned and then turn entire contents of frying pan into beans. Add salt and 1 or 2 chilies (or cayenne). Cook until beans are tender and fairly dry. Take up in a hot deep platter, placing pork in center, and sprinkling beans with grated cheese. Garnish edges of platter with small lettuce leaves, slices of avocado, little mounds of chopped radishes and mounds of chopped green peppers, all interspersed with olives.

No country is more bean conscious than Mexico, and each variety has its own name, in this case *Frijoles Gordos,* which translates "fat beans" or "suet beans." So Tezcucans literally live on the fat of the land.

MEXICAN FRIED BEANS
Frijoles Fritos

4 pork sausages	Mexican Red Sauce
2 tablespoons olive oil	Green peppers, or tinned
1 garlic clove, minced	pimientos
1 tin Mexican beans	

Remove skins and fry sausage in 1 tablespoon olive oil. Separately fry minced garlic in other tablespoon olive oil. When brown add sausages and their gravy. Turn beans into mixture and mash and fry them, turning frequently. Make a loaf of the mashed fried mixture. Let bottom brown a bit, pushing and lifting continually with cake turner so it keeps together and doesn't stick. Slide this bean and sausage loaf out on a hot platter and pour hot Mexican Red Sauce over. (See recipe.) Garnish with slivers of green peppers, bits of tinned pimientos, or serve with Mexican Stuffed Peppers.

A little incident well illustrates Mexican respect for the national beans: A *hacendado* (landed proprietor) was acting as host for a large dinner party when he noticed that his young and beautiful daughter ate almost nothing and even turned down the familiar bean dishes with disdain, denying her usual healthy appetite in order to appear a delicate lady before company. He watched her refuse one fine dish after another and then burst out: "Come frijol', Margarita, come frijol'"— "Anyway eat some beans, Margarita," motioning to a servant to pass the beans again. Whereupon Margarita served herself with a dainty spoonful, ate them, and her father beamed satisfaction. Being a patriotic Mexican he believed everyone should eat beans if they ate nothing else, even at a banquet. And it is said by calumniators of our neighbor's cuisine that some Mexican banquets consist of nine or ten courses—all of them beans.

Yet, on the other hand, Cortes wrote that the Emperor Montezuma served 300 different dishes at a banquet—and all of them meat!

BEANS YUCATAN STYLE
Frijoles a la Yucateca

3 cups black beans	½ teaspoon fine salt
1 tablespoon kitchen salt	2 cups pork broth
½ cup olive oil or fat	A few slices boiled pork
1 onion, chopped	2 onions, sliced thin
1 garlic clove, minced	1 small chili, crushed

Grated cheese

Soak beans several hours; drain. Cover well with cold water. Add kitchen salt and boil gently until beans begin to be tender. Drain and wash beans with hot water. Heat oil in a casserole. Add chopped onion and slowly fry until it begins to color. Add garlic and fry a few minutes but do not brown. Add fine salt, pork broth, pork, 1 sliced onion and chili (or cayenne to taste). Simmer until beans are ready to break up. Sprinkle with grated cheese and garnish with rings of remaining onion.

This dish is always served with a bottle of olive oil beside it to enrich it further if desired.

TUTU

This is a dish made of leftover Brazilian *Feijoada* (see recipe), consisting chiefly of black beans and their soupy gravy. Fry ½ cup diced bacon crisp in frying pan. Pour off most of fat and take up bacon. In fat left in pan fry 2 table-spoons minced onion and 1 small minced garlic clove. Mash 2–3 cups of the leftover black beans and add with the crisp bacon and 1 teaspoon minced parsley. Stir in at once toasted cassava meal and continue to stir and simmer until the soupy beans and cassava meal form a purée thick as mashed potatoes. It is eaten plain or with meat, and often served in the center of a hot platter garnished with sections of boiled cabbage to make a fine dish with reheated jerked beef, pork roast or boiled tongue.

CHILEAN LENTILS
Lentejas

Grind 2 cups cooked lentils with 1½ cups bread soaked in water, 2 red pimientos, 2 egg yolks, parsley and a little onion fried in "color" (lard "colored" with Spanish paprika). Moisten with a little wine vinegar. Heat and serve with grated cheese scattered over.

While most Chilean cooking "color" is made of lard well mixed with *aji,* ground dwarf red peppers, hotter peppers are often used, and as noted before, Spanish paprika is about the best substitute we have at hand to mix with lard for the indispensable "color."

Because every kind of legume, from Chile beans to chickpeas, has its enthusiastic following in Latin America, the lentils which we so often overlook come into their own in Chilean and neighboring cuisines all the way down to Mexico.

LENTIL SALAD
Ensalada de Lentejas

Soak 1 cup lentils several hours in cold water and drain. Cover with fresh water and let cook just below boiling point, adding 1 teaspoon salt. When tender, drain. Add a French dressing, seasoned well with pepper, and let stand an hour to absorb dressing before serving.

MEXICAN RICE

1 cup rice	1 green chili, minced
3 tablespoons olive oil	1 teaspoon parsley, minced
1 onion, chopped	or marjoram
1 garlic clove, minced	1 teaspoon chili powder
1 tomato, chopped	1 teaspoon salt
1 green pepper, chopped	Olives

Wash rice through many waters and dry in a towel. Heat olive oil. Add rice and fry until golden. Add onion and garlic. Stir and fry until all begins to brown. Add tomato, green pepper and seasonings, and pour over just enough boiling water so rice will be dry when done, about 1 quart, quantity depending on how long rice has been stored. Boil rapidly until rice is becoming tender, then reduce heat and cook slowly until tender and sufficiently dry. Pile into a wide shallow dish, and garnish with olives.

This is the classic rice dish from Spain that appears with only slight modifications all over Latin America. It may have a bit of ham in it, or a light yellowing with saffron, but the basic principle is always the same. Rice is grown widely in Latin America today, so in many places it is almost as cheap as native corn with which it competes as a food of the people. In the days when it was an imported luxury it was consumed mostly in middle class and rich families.

BRAZILIAN RICE

2 tablespoons olive oil
1 onion, sliced thin
1 garlic clove, minced
1 tomato, chopped

1 teaspoon parsley, minced
3 cups boiling water
1 cup well-washed rice
2 teaspoons salt

A dash of cayenne pepper

Heat oil in metal pan until it smokes. Cool for a moment. Add onion and fry slowly until onion colors. Add garlic and continue slow frying until onion is tender but not browned. Add tomato and continue slow frying until mixture thickens. Add parsley, boiling water and seasonings. Bring to rapid boiling point and gradually add rice that has been washed through many waters. Cover and boil rapidly until rice is swollen, then place over asbestos ring and cook slowly until rice is tender. Remove pan cover and let rice become dry and fluffy.

RICE WITH PALM HEART
Arroz com Palmito

1 tablespoon olive oil
1 medium onion, chopped
1 tomato, peeled and
    chopped
1 herb bouquet
    (bay leaf, parsley, celery)

½ pound smoked sausage
3 slices salt pork, cut thin
1 cup boiling water
½ cup rice, well washed
3 cups palmetto, sliced
    thick

Heat oil. Add onion and slowly fry until lightly browned and tender. Add tomato, herbs, sausage and pork. Cover and let simmer, stirring occasionally. Add water and rice. Cover and continue slow simmering. When rice is swollen add more boiling water and increase heat. Boil rapidly until rice is tender and fairly dry, frequently shaking pan to make sure it does not scorch.

Meanwhile cook palmetto in salted boiling water, or if canned palmetto is used heat it in its own liquor.

Arrange rice on hot platter, using cut-up sausage and pork as a garnish, and heap drained palmetto in center.

Palmettos and hearts of palm are the creamy inside meat of young palm shoots and the buds of cabbage palm and other palms, including the royal. During ten years in Brazil we ate different kinds of palmettos every day in every way, and they always made a hit with guests from home. Frederick Stief, author of *Eat, Drink and Be Merry in Maryland* met his first palmettos there and liked them so well he used to cable us several times a year to ship him a few tins with which to thrill Baltimore guests. But domestic palm hearts can be had in plenty from Florida today, where they're looked upon as almost as necessary a vegetable as potatoes.

John Crashley, an Englishman who ran the only Anglo-Saxon bookshop in Rio de Janeiro used to tell us of his first encounter with palmettos when he was a youngster fresh from London. Employed on a Brazilian farm in Nicteroy, just across Rio's beautiful bay, it was his job to row the farmer's green stuff across to the city market every morning. There he saw for the first time piles of palm shoots selling at very good prices and recalled that he'd seen similar sprouts on an apparently abandoned island en route.

So one morning he cut down a boatload of them and took them to market on his own, expecting to earn a month's wages in one day. But the marketmen laughed at his ignorance—for he'd cut down a farmer's whole field of newly planted banana palms, which are inedible.

BRAZILIAN RICE WITH PALM HEART
Arroz com Palmito

Fry a chopped onion brown and tender in 1 tablespoon olive oil or cooking fat. Add a chopped tomato, a bay leaf, a sprig of parsley, a celery leaf, salt and a piece of smoked sausage large enough to serve a small portion to each person. Add 3 thin slices of salt pork. Cover and cook slowly. When well heated add 1½ cups boiling water, 2 cups sliced palmetto (fresh or canned) and ½ cup well-washed rice. Mix well. Cover tightly and simmer until rice is fluffed and tender.

BRAZILIAN RICE WITH CLAMS
Arroz com Mariscos

Place a bouquet of herbs in 1 cup cold water and bring water to boiling point. Bouquet should consist of 1 sprig parsley, 1 sprig celery leaf, 1 bay leaf, ½ dozen chives or 1 scallion and 1 sprig marjoram if you have it. Let cook 5 minutes to extract flavor, then remove herbs.

Have ready 2 dozen clams which have been well scrubbed and allowed to stand in water for 1 hour or more to precipitate sand. Add them to herb-flavored water and cover tightly. Let steam 10 minutes or until shells have opened. Take clams out on plate. Be sure there is no sand in bottom of liquid. Put into it 1 cup rice which has been washed through many waters. Probably no salt will be needed, but taste and make sure.

If there seems to be too little liquid, that is, if clams are not sufficiently juicy, add a little boiling water. The rice must have absorbed all water when it is done. Add 1 peeled and chopped tomato. Keep rice boiling rapidly, and while it is cooking remove meats from clam shells and drop them into rice when nearly done.

Reduce heat and let cook until rice is tender. If not yet dry enough place, uncovered, over asbestos ring.

Have ready balls of butter, ½ teaspoon butter to each ball.

Work finely chopped parsley into some of them and paprika into others. Turn rice out onto hot platter and dot top with butterballs.

Some Brazilian *mariscos* are as small as your little fingernail and it takes about an hour to pick the meats out of a quart, but they're sweet, nutty and well worth the trouble.

TAMALES, HUMITAS, HALLACAS, ETC.

CORN AS PREPARED AND EATEN BY THE MEXICAN PEOPLE

No secrets are hidden by the Mexican cook from the public eye. The traveler sees every process going on in the open air. All that is necessary to set up a cookshop or to establish a complete family life is a frying griddle (any chance sheet of iron will serve), a globular earthen fireproof olla, a cooking pot with a smallish opening, a water jar, a fireproof bowl, a mixing bowl, a bowl of wood hard enough for crushing spices with a wooden pestle, a few stones on which to set them over and around a fire of sticks or charcoal, some gourds for food containers, a wooden spoon or two and of course the eternal stone *metate*, slanting like a washboard, on which the cook works the corn dough up and down with another stone, shaped something like a rolling pin and called a *metlatpilli*. Hours and hours every day are spent over the *metate*, scrubbing tortilla dough up and down, a labor every bit as hard as the dreariest washing of the dirtiest clothes.

But the brown-skinned cooks of Mexico do this self-ordained task smilingly, chattering all the while, working in the good will without which no cooking in the world is worth the salt that's put into it. Four hours a day is the least amount of devotion to this kneading and grinding operation which the mother of an ordinary family should give. And the more the better. If there is a festival pending, or someone is going on a journey, she will stay up all night in order to make a more delectable dish, or prepare a quantity to last for several days. And if she dares to shirk a dread disease is supposed to attack her knees, called "laziness of the knee joints," and then everyone will know what a careless housekeeper she is.

As far as the general populace is concerned, the basis of Mexican cooking is the tortilla dough made in this arduous way from corn boiled in lye, like our old-fashioned lye hominy, washed well or boiled again in fresh water to take out surplus lye. The corn is first mashed to a pulp with a little salt, then worked and worked until a fineness of texture is obtained which is satisfaction enough for the back-breaking work. And since most *metates* are made of volcanic rock a good deal of grit comes off in the dough, and the constant eating of stone-ground tortillas wears the teeth down to the gums.

Corn furnishes the necessities of life to the Mexican Indian. Out of the stacks he builds his fragile shelter. He uses the husks to wrap his tamales, but still more important, it supplies the basis of his diet, his drink and food. According to the views of our most modern ethnologists who trace the character of a race to its grain supply, this native maize has given the Mexican Indian his very nature.

Spanish explorers found the Indians handling their native corn in the same manner five hundred years ago, and wrote home about it. There is no change to this day. The expensive electric tortilla mixing machines in the homes of the well to do stand idle in favor of the proper dough bought from a neighbor who makes it by hand. And the product turned out by shops which deal in such things is bought only by the indolent or those hard pressed for time.

Cooking varies in the different states. One would not expect the rich Eastern coast to be like the high plain of Mexico City, eight thousand feet above. Nor the heated tropical Isthmus of Tehuantepec, where foodstuffs grow without planting and even fence posts send out sprouts, to be like the Northern desert where little but cactus can be wrested from the soil. People even distrust the cooking of a district just a few miles away, and when going on a visit will take enough of their own trusted food with them to last until their return, with no intended insult to their host. But the tortilla grinding goes on everywhere the same.

So far as we were concerned, after traveling the full length of the country, crossing the continent twice at different latitudes, and visiting nearly every state during three sojourns, there was no detectable difference between the machine and the handmade tortilla dough. In fact some of the most delicious dishes we ate were concocted in the houses of our foreign friends from the despised corn meal, a statement which will make a true Mexican weep for our lack of taste.

A tourist, buying out of the windows of trains or stopping in chance inns, where he must eat what is carelessly at hand or go hungry, complains bitterly of what is perhaps the worst eating in the world. But if he happens to be entertained in a Mexican family, whether rich or poor, or if he stays with American residents who have learned the true Mexican cuisine, he is likely to develop a sudden taste for the peppery hot succulence of the dishes which will haunt him for many a day.

The spices and peppers are peculiarly Mexican and Spanish-colonial, and do not occur in the mother country where the food is mild and cool. Only in India and the countries under the influence of East Indian culture does one find the counterpart of the Mexican chili in the many varieties of curry, where a similar climate and soil, and perhaps race, have evolved a similar taste and materials. These hot seasonings serve to disinfect foods where they are none too well handled and there is an absence of refrigeration. The capsicum contained in the chilies is said to stimulate the digestive organs and aid digestion, and so it is even sprinkled on oranges, for much the same reason that our fathers peppered their ice cream. Certainly there is a minimum of digestive ills among the Mexicans.

A volume could be written about Mexican peppers alone. There are the small red-hot chilies and the small green or unripe hot ones. There are broad red peppers and long dark peppers, peppers nearly black, half-hot peppers and sweet pimientas, just as many varieties of peppers as there are of maize, and nearly as many as there are of beans with which they are invariably cooked. More than the Spaniards' three: pimiento hot, pimienta sweet and pimenton for ground black pepper.

You will not want to learn to cook iguanas or their eggs, or *iguaracu* (alligators) or the green worms of maguey (*gusanos de maguey*), those grassy-tasting parasites living in the century plant, nor to make cactus sandwiches, and perhaps you would never care for sour oranges cut in half and eaten with salt and a thick smear of biting pepper. These peculiarly Mexican specialties are not liked by foreigners even when they have lived in the country for years.

But there are many dishes from the Mexican kitchen which are so delectable that they have spread across our border and become incorporated in our menus in the Southwest and in California—dishes reflecting the culture of old Spain modified by Aztec customs, which demand little skill in preparation and are relished by everyone. And there is something festive about them, an air of guitar playing and holiday making which makes them adapted to party giving.

Many of the recipes look long and complicated. But a second glance shows most of the ingredients to be seasonings, and the hastiest perusal proves them to be no more complicated than our own.

From the tortilla dough half a dozen entirely different kinds of food are made: first, tortillas themselves, which not only take the place of leavened bread but serve as fork, spoon and plate in the poorer families where the household boasts only a knife and the wooden spoons used for cooking. They are stuffed or rolled around, or covered with a hundred different mixtures of meat or vegetables to make *enchiladas, tacus* and *chalupas*.

Then there are tamales, sweet or hot, made of tortilla dough dressed up in corn husks or plain.

And the *clacoyos*, meat or dessert cakes in various versions made from the dough modified with shortening.

Also *atoles*, or cereal drinks, flavored with anything from onions to chocolate.

Besides there are the *molés*, sauces in which meat is cooked or served, which are usually thickened with tortilla dough as we thicken gravies with flour.

TORTILLAS

In nearly all of our large cities there is a Mexican colony, recruited partly from families who have lost everything but their lives in one revolution or another, and whatever they do without they must have their tortillas, which an expert tortilla maker cooks and markets, all ready for toasting and filling. Sometimes they can be bought from Spanish grocers, who in any case will be able to furnish the address where tortillas are made to order.

Our advice to the hostess about to go Mexican is to buy them ready made if possible; but here are suitable recipes in case she prefers to make them herself—without the *metate* and grinding labor of course.

MASA I
Dough for Tortillas

3 cups whole white corn	½ cup lard
1½ cups wood ashes or	½ yeast cake
½ cup quicklime	Salt

Pepper

Boil corn with wood ashes until tender, then wash through 4 waters. Rub off hulls and mash. Add lard, yeast cake, dissolved in a little warm water, and seasonings. Beat and knead, then let stand in a warm place 2 hours. Knead and beat again, working in 1 tablespoon more lard. Pat out the thinnest possible cakes and fry in dry pan.

MASA II

Boil 3 cups prepared hominy until tender. Drain, saving some of the water, and mash to a dough. Beat and work 15 minutes. If necessary add a little bit of the water in which hominy was cooked. Dissolve 1 yeast cake in a little warm water. Mix in with the dough, then mix in ½ cup lard. Beat and knead thoroughly. Let rise 2 hours, then knead and beat again. Pat out tortillas as thin as possible between the hands and bake on a hot dry griddle.

MASA III

Boiling water	1 yeast cake
3 cups corn meal	½ cup lukewarm water
1 teaspoon salt	2 eggs

½ cup lard or butter

Add boiling water to corn meal and salt to form a soft dough. Stir well and cool. Dissolve yeast cake in warm water. Beat eggs; mix the dissolved yeast and eggs into dough, then mix in lard. Let stand 2 hours. Work again and pat out the tortillas.

If you should happen to feel very primitive the first recipe can be tried. It most nearly approximates the real article, and with the help of the yeast it will not be necessary to scrub the dough in a *metate* for 4 hours, in true Mexican style. Simple but generous kneading will be enough.

The second recipe saves the trouble of boiling the corn with lye, since the softening process has already been done by the cereal company that put up the hominy.

The third recipe presents no more difficulty than any bread biscuit made with yeast, and the resultant tortillas are wonderfully good—only do not by any chance serve them to a Mexican guest who fondly hopes he is going to a real native treat. He will be able to tell the difference at the touch of the tongue, even if your other friends cannot.

MASA OUT OF A CAN

Drain 1 can cooked hominy, letting it stand in colander or sieve until liquid has dripped out. Add salt to taste. Mash thoroughly in wooden bowl with wooden spoon, adding 1–2 tablespoons fine corn meal and cold water a few drops at a time until a stiff dough is formed. Knead with hands to even consistency.

After the dough is prepared by one or another of these methods a few minutes practice will teach the secret of *echando tortillas* (throwing tortillas). Take a ball of dough the size of a small hen's egg. Flatten it out between the hands, then play patty-cake with it, first with one hand on top then the other, patting, patting, until it is of a fine thinness. The hands must be occasionally moistened with cold water.

Bake like pancakes on a dry griddle and stack them in the same way on top of each other as they are done. North Americans and many other foreigners like best tortillas that have been toasted a second time and are served hot.

But probably you will want to make them into *enchiladas,* since keeping the table supplied with hot tortillas, either made in the kitchen or over an electric toaster on the table is a task, and accounts for the fact that Mexican men and their women seldom eat together.

PLAIN ENCHILADAS

Prepare Ordinary Mexican Cooking Sauce (see recipe) and have it piping hot. Dip 12 tortillas, one at a time, into hot deep fat, taking them out at once with a perforated skimmer to let them drain, and then dropping them into the hot sauce. When well covered and soaked with sauce transfer to a hot platter. Have ready a well-salted mixture of finely minced onions and grated cheese in equal parts. Lay across each tortilla 1–2 tablespoons of this mixture. Roll tortillas and pile up rolls, like little logs, parallel to each other. Pour remaining sauce over, reheat in oven, sprinkle with remaining onion-cheese mixture and serve.

ENCHILADAS WITH MOLÉ POBLANO

Make like Plain Enchiladas, substituting *Molé Poblano* (see recipe) for Ordinary Mexican Cooking Sauce.

ENCHILADAS COLORADAS

Make like Plain Enchiladas, substituting Mexican Red Sauce for Ordinary Mexican Cooking Sauce. In place of chopped onion and cheese, the stuffing may be minced cooked meat, chopped hard-cooked egg and chopped avocado in equal proportion.

ENCHILADAS STUFFED WITH LETTUCE

Purchase at a Spanish store 1 ounce tomato paste, 1 small tin powdered *molé* (put up for use with turkey, chicken or pork) and 1 small tin of liquid *molé de guajolote*. Then prepare or purchase 1 dozen tortillas.

Add 1 cup hot meat broth to tomato paste and stir smooth. Stir in 1 teaspoon powdered *molé* and 3–4 tablespoons liquid *molé*. Mix well and taste. If not hot enough add a minced chili or a few drops of Tabasco. Add 1 tablespoon olive oil or butter. Heat to boiling point and simmer 10 minutes. Shred 1 dozen tender green lettuce leaves. Finely chop 1 large onion. Chop 1 dozen large olives. Drop each tortilla separately into hot fat or butter. Drain and put at once into sauce. When well soaked transfer to hot platter. Lay a portion of lettuce across each tortilla. Sprinkle with chopped onion and chopped olives, then with a few drops of the sauce. Roll and stack. Pour remaining sauce over them. Set in oven for a few minutes to heat. Sprinkle with remaining chopped onion and chopped olives and serve.

AMERICAN BORDER ENCHILADAS

Fry tortillas in butter. Dip in hot tomato sauce seasoned with chili powder and Tabasco. Spread with minced chicken heated with a little of the same tomato sauce. In a buttered baking dish stack one tortilla on top of another like pancakes. Heat in oven and garnish with onion rings, shredded lettuce and whole olives.

ENCHILADAS STUFFED WITH SAUSAGES
Enchiladas con Chorizo

Make Ordinary Mexican Cooking Sauce (see recipe) and have it hot. Fry 1 dozen smoked pork sausages until nice and brown. Fry 1 dozen tortillas a moment in deep hot lard or butter. Drain and soak in the sauce. In each tortilla place 1 fried sausage. Sprinkle with minced chopped peppers, a bit of minced chili or a drop of Tabasco and 1 teaspoon minced onion. Roll; place in buttered dish. Reheat; pour remaining sauce over and serve.

CHILI RABBIT ENCHILADAS

Prepare a rabbit by cooking according to recipe for Chili Rabbit, adding 1 minced garlic clove with the frying onion. When rabbit is cooked tender remove bones and dice meat. Add 1 slice ground fried bread and a little chopped sauce to pan gravy. Put meat back in gravy. Heat and roll into toasted tortillas. Pour gravy over and serve.

TACOS

Technically, *enchiladas* are tortillas filled with a simple chili mixture, as the name indicates. A number of the preceding more complicated recipes for *enchiladas* are really *tacos*, a word taken from the cotton used in ramming old-fashioned firearms. It means anything stuffed daintily. But foreigners are so accustomed to including all filled tortillas under the designation of *enchiladas* that the recipes would not easily be recognized under their more correct designation.

TACOS DE TINGA POBLANO

Heat finely hashed chicken in *Molé Poblano*. (See recipe.) Fry some tortillas well. Dip tortillas in the sauce to soften. Fill with the chicken hash. Roll and serve.

This dish is very popular in Mexico City, where the *Tinga Poblano*, or chicken hash in *Molé Poblano*, is often served alone without the accompanying tortilla.

BARBECUE TACOS
Tacos de Barbacoa

Pat out small raw tortillas and fill with chopped barbecued meat in Green Sauce. (See recipe.) Then fold and stick edges together with egg to make little turnovers. Fry in deep fat. Cover with mashed avocado pear and grated cheese, and they're ready for munching.

QUESADILLAS

Make as for *Tacos de Barbacoa*, but in place of the meat mixture, fill with grated cheese mixed with any chopped left-over vegetables and meat.

EGG TACOS
Tacos de Huevos

Heat 1 cup ground cold meat in 1 cup Red Sauce. (See recipe.) Scramble half the number of eggs that you have of tortillas, putting into the eggs as they cook 1 tablespoon of Red Sauce to each egg. Fry tortillas. Dip in the sauce until softened. Take out; spread scrambled egg on each and lay 1 heaping tablespoon of meat mixture on top. Roll and serve hot.

LITTLE TACOS
Taquitos

Mix together 1 small chopped onion, ½ avocado pear, diced, ½ cup mashed Mexican beans and moisten all with Red Sauce. Roll in small buttered hot tortillas, and heat in the oven or serve cold.

CHALUPAS

The only difference between *enchiladas* and *chalupas* is that the former are rolled around the sauce and stuffing, and the latter are left open without having been dipped in sauce. The name comes from the way a tortilla crisps up around the edges when fried in hot fat, making a little *chalupa* (boat) which is a perfect small container for any food. A favored mixture to put into it is mashed leftover beans, shredded lettuce and grated cheese, well drenched with any of the Mexican sauces.

MEMELITOS

Pat out tortillas ¾ inch thick. Cook slowly on a griddle until done through. Then with a thin-edged spoon filled with butter make cuts in tops of the hot crusts, and slip in bits of the butter. Prepared in this way, the tortillas will be extra good even when cold. They somewhat resemble our hoecake.

Sometimes they are slit open and stuffed with chili and green peppers ground fine, mixed with plenty of chopped onion and grated cheese, the mixture made into a paste and all worked into the slit *memelitos* with a spoon.

ATACATES

Work 1 tablespoon butter into 2 cups tortilla dough. Knead thoroughly. Then pat out and bake.

The word *atacate* (Aztec *itactl*) means "store of food." They are peddled by Indian women on the trains, for they keep moist as unshortened tortillas do not, and are supposed to be practical for travelers. *Atacates* are made in great quantities for the Week of All Saints, cut out in the shapes of stars, dogs, pigs, birds, etc. They are offered to the dead as well as the living on All Soul's Day.

CLASCOLES

Clascoles are sweet *atacates* made for the Week of All Saints. They are also cut in fancy shapes.

Mix 2 cups tortilla dough, 1 cup sugar, 1 beaten egg, 2 table-spoons cream cheese worked to the consistency of butter, 1 teaspoon bicarbonate of soda, 1 teaspoon cinnamon. Roll thin; cut and bake on the griddle and shape as your fantasy directs.

MICAJES

2 cups tortilla dough   1 cup meat paste
A few drops Tabasco

Knead together. Season; pat thin and bake on the griddle.

CLACLOZO

2 cups tortilla dough   2 tablespoons butter

Work together. Cook tortillas. Mash Mexican beans. Wet with a little sauce. Place some of the beans in each tortilla; double over and bake on the griddle.

DESSERT TORTILLAS

DAINTY LITTLE TORTILLAS
Tortillitas de Regalo

1½ cups fine corn meal   3 hard-cooked egg yolks,
½ cup sugar   sieved
½ teaspoon salt   1 teaspoon orange flower
½ cup butter   water
1 raw egg, well beaten

Sift dry ingredients together. Cut in butter as for pastry. Add egg yolks, whole egg and orange flower water. Knead well. Separate balls of the dough. Pat out into thin cakes and leave until next day. Put all dough together again and knead and beat until smooth. Pat out thin cakes again and bake in slow oven, taking care they bake evenly without burning. Dip in syrup. Lay drained and chopped fruit preserves in center of each, or fill with mixture of chopped candied fruits and chopped nuts, and roll.

Tortillitas is the diminutive, affectionate form of tortillas and anyone can become quite fond of these dainty little fellows. The word, besides meaning dainty, denotes pleasure and is also the name for a present, so the whole matter radiates that happiness which good digestion waits upon.

TORTILLAS MADE OF WHEAT FLOUR
Tortillas de Harina de Trigo

3 tablespoons sugar	2 egg yolks, beaten light
1½ cups flour	1 egg white, beaten stiff
½ teaspoon salt	2 tablespoons melted butter

Dissolve sugar in ½ cup lukewarm water. Mix flour and salt. Then mix all ingredients together to make a stiff dough, adding a little more tepid water if necessary. Pat out tortillas and bake on dry griddle.

These, like *Tortillitas de Regalo,* can be filled with preserved or candied fruit, or they may be eaten like pancakes, with honey, or syrup. But, being made with sugar and white flour, they are considered dessert tortillas even when eaten plain, in the same way that the black-bean eating Brazilians call our Boston baked beans "dessert beans," because of the molasses.

GORDITAS
Little Fat Ones

Make tortillas ½ inch thick. Cook slowly on a dry griddle, turning frequently so that they will not burn. (These are twice the thickness of ordinary tortillas and will take much longer to cook.) Have ready a sauce made as follows:

8 tablespoons Green Chili Sauce (see recipe) and 1 teaspoon chili powder cooked together. When cool add the mashed pulp of an avocado pear.

When *gorditas* are done split them open. Lay in a slice of

cheese and smear generously with the avocado mixture. Put the 2 halves together, making a sandwich.

Pulque is usually drunk with this snack which is a great favorite at fairs and festivals.

GORDITAS DE ANIS
Aniseed "Little Fat Ones"

1 pound flour	⅓ cup butter
1 egg	¼ teaspoon salt
⅓ cup sugar	½ teaspoon anise flavoring

Mix ingredients in order given. Work dough smooth. Roll out on a floured board until ¼ inch thick, then cut with a cookie cutter the diameter of a drinking glass. Cook on an oiled griddle, turning several times to keep from burning and to make sure they are cooked through. Eat at once.

Gorditas can be made ready in the kitchen and cooked at the table on an electric hot plate after a Mexican dinner, to serve for dessert.

GORDITAS DE VIRGEN
The Virgin's "Little Fat Ones"

Make dough with 1 pound corn flour (*tamelina*), 3 tablespoons brown sugar (the darkest kind), ½ coffee spoon powdered cinnamon, 3–4 egg yolks, a tiny pinch of salt and butter. Pat out into thin cakes. Fry in a pan with just enough butter to keep them from sticking. Move them about while frying, and serve piping hot.

TAMALES

Tamales have been the fiesta dish of the Mexican Indian since pre-Columbian days, when Aztec priests molded tamales with their own hands as offerings to the gods, much as Tibetan monks model butter for their butter festival.

When the Spaniards arrived in Mexico the use of tamales as a sacred food was transferred to the Christian festivals of Easter

and Christmas, and a variety is still made called *Tamales de
Muerto* (for the dead) which perpetuates the pagan custom of
offering food to the departed, corresponding to the shrine gifts
of rice and *saki* with which the Japanese sustain the spirits of
their ancestors. Some tribes, the Otomies in the Mexican state
of Querétaro, for example, actually place tamales filled with
cheese in the coffin at a funeral, and make a rite of setting out
this food beside the graves in the cemetery on Halloween.

Tamales, like the curries of India, differ in different parts of
Mexico, those of Oaxaca being among the most celebrated. The
best are made from the dough of blue Mexican corn softened
and shortened with lard, spread thin over a board and used to
envelop a tender piece of chicken or meat well moistened with
Green or Red Chili Sauce. This stuffed roll of dough is then
wrapped in cornhusks and steamed for hours. Ordinary tamales
are made of tortilla dough beaten in one of the round low clay
bowls (*pozele*) used by us for decoration, and wrapped around
(1) beans (2) meat (3) squash (4) small fish or (5) mushrooms.

Sweet tamales are flavored with brown sugar or honey and
cinnamon. Sometimes tamales are even made plain, flavored
only with salt; but the favorite tamale of the Aztecs was one
filled with cherries, with which they drank *tepoche* or *pulque*
mixed with honey.

Most of the recipes that follow have been adapted to American use in kitchens where it is difficult to secure real tortilla
dough. And since it takes considerable practice to roll up
tamales in cornhusks and turn in the ends so a tight little packet
is formed in true Mexican style, directions are given to tie the
ends tight in order to keep contents safe during cooking—a
sacrilege for which we ask dispensation.

TAMALE DOUGH, OR MUSH

The heavy dough, which is the chief ingredient of all
tamales, is plain corn-meal mush made by scalding corn meal
with boiling salted water and cooked until very thick.

TAMALE HUSKS

Fresh cornhusks make the best cases for tamales because they are more pliable than dried ones. But since only dried husks are available in winter they are softened in warm water before using. Dried husks are stocked in Spanish stores.

BEAN TAMALES
Tamales de Frijoles

Make tamale dough as above, using 2 cups corn meal. Mash 1 small tin Mexican beans with 1 chopped tomato, 1 chopped onion and 1 minced chili. Spread tamale dough quickly on flattened cornhusks. Put bean mixture in center and roll. Tie ends of husks tight so nothing will spill out, and steam 1½ hours.

MEAT TAMALES
Tamales de Carne

1 hot pepper	1 medium tomato
1 sweet pepper	½ pound lean pork
1 tablespoon cumin seed	1 tablespoon oil or butter
1 garlic clove	Salt

Tamale dough

Finely grind peppers, cumin seed, garlic and tomato together, running them through grinder several times until well blended and mushy. Dice pork and fry brown in butter. Mix with ground mixture. Season with salt and simmer 5 minutes. Spread tamale dough on flattened cornhusks. Put in each tamale 1 heaping teaspoon pork with some of its sauce. Roll and tie securely. Steam at least 2 hours.

TAMALES DE POLLO
Chicken Tamales

Use 2 cups cold tamale dough mixed thoroughly with ½ yeast cake dissolved in a little tepid water. Set to rise 2 hours in a warm place. Add 4 tablespoons olive oil to raise dough and knead it in well.

Make 1 cup ordinary Mexican Cooking Sauce. (See recipe.) Add to it 1 chopped bay leaf, 3 chopped chilies and 1 teaspoon any chopped herb—parsley, coriander or marjoram preferred— and strain the sauce.

Cut 1 cooked chicken breast into 6 long strips. Lay in strained sauce and heat thoroughly until flavors penetrate.

Flatten out cornhusks and spread thickly with tamale dough. Place 1 strip chicken and a little sauce in each one, with the 2 halves of seeded olive. Roll; tie ends with twine and trim them. Make sure tamales are well rolled and tied so contents will not escape. It may be necessary to use 2 shucks for each tamale. Steam 2 hours.

This makes 6 tamales, which would serve about 3 New Yorkers, 2 Mexicans or 1 Texan.

HOT TAMALES

Here is a delicious American version to serve 15 to 20 people at a hot-tamale party.

The meat ingredients are a 5-pound hen, boiled with 2 onions and seasonings to make a rich broth, and 1½ pounds chuck steak, boiled tender with salt, pepper and 2 garlic cloves.

Shred white meat of chicken. Grind rest of chicken meat with the cooked beef and add 1 large bottle tomato catsup, cayenne pepper, *polvo para molé*,* with salt and black pepper to taste.

Strain both broths together. Bring to boiling point and stir in yellow corn meal until you have made a very thick mush. Cook 20 minutes. Have ready husks of green corn. If it is winter and you have neglected to dry some during the summer, they can be bought at Spanish stores and soaked in water until soft.

Flatten out a cornhusk. Spread thick with corn meal. Lay a

Polvo para molé can be bought at Spanish stores, or chili powder can be used as a substitute.

thick line of the ground meat and some shredded chicken down the middle and put a stuffed olive in the center. Roll and tie up tight at both ends. They should be about 1½ inches thick. If cornhusks are small you may have to use 2. With scissors cut off superfluous cornhusk at ends. Place in a steamer. Steam 1 hour and serve very hot. Cut strings before serving.

Tamales can be prepared in the afternoon and be set to steam after the guests arrive.

SQUASH TAMALES
Tamales de Calabaza

Cut into finger sizes ½ pound yellow squash or pumpkin and boil in salted water until just tender; drain well. Add ¼ cup honey and ⅛ teaspoon cinnamon. Make corn-meal dough. Powder 2 macaroons and work into it. Place in each tamale 1 piece squash and drizzle a little honey on.

FISH TAMALES
Tamales de Pescado

Make tamale dough. Mash together ½ green chili and 1 tiny sprig marjoram for each tamale. Make rolls of dough 1-inch thick and of suitable length to receive a small fish. Flatten out rolls. Lay on each 1 small fresh fish, or a bit of fillet from a large fish. Season with salt and a daub of the chili-marjoram mixture. Fold dough around fish and fry slowly in butter until the tamale is brown, or wrap in cornhusks and steam until fish is done.

MUSHROOM TAMALES

Grind 2 green peppers. Cook ½ pound mushrooms in butter in an earthenware casserole. When done chop them and add 1 green chili ground with 1½ tablespoons coriander seed. Add ground peppers with ½ cup boiling water and cook about 20 minutes.

Have ready squash seeds cooked 15 minutes in weak lye

water and then well washed. Add seeds to mushroom mixture. Simmer until thick and use for tamale filling.

SWEET TAMALES
Tamales Dulces

To 3 cups tortilla dough (see recipe) add 1 cup sugar and ¼ teaspoon cinnamon and work well together. Fill tamales made from this dough with spoonfuls of chopped candied fruits.

The dried cornhusks in which sweet tamales are wrapped are often colored pink with the harmless cochineal dye native to Mexico. This adds gaiety to fiestas where drinks likewise are colored with pomegranate juice to a hue which puts our pink lemonade in the shade.

GREEN CORN TAMALES

1 small chicken	2 teaspoons chili powder
18 ears green corn	½ cup minced ripe olives
½ cup oil or melted butter	½ teaspoon dried marjoram
¼ cup minced onion	½ cup seeded raisins

Salt and pepper

Steam chicken until tender. Then cut the meat in 2-inch lengths. Shave off corn kernels and scrape the creamy pulp from the cobs. Slowly fry onion in oil until it begins to color. Add corn kernels and cream and fry 5 minutes. Mix all ingredients together and divide into 12 equal portions. Roll in cornhusks. Tie securely and steam 20 minutes.

PORK TAMALES IN CABBAGE LEAVES
Tamales de Puerco en Hojas de Col

Grind very fine 1 pound lean cooked pork, preferably loin or fresh ham. Fry in 3 tablespoons olive oil with 1 chopped onion and 1 minced garlic clove, stirring constantly. Add 1 cup strong beef, 1 tablespoon chili powder, 1 teaspoon salt and a dash of Tabasco. Cook down until very thick.

To make tamale dough scald 2 cups corn meal with salted water in which has been dissolved 1 teaspoon chili powder. Spread on large cabbage leaves and fill with the meat mixture. Roll leaves, doubling in ends like a paper parcel. Tie securely with string and steam 1½ hours.

If the center veins of the leaves are thick it may be necessary to shave veins thin so ends can be folded.

These are related to the *dolmas* of the Near East and to similar stuffings in grapevine leaves.

In the lowlands of Mexico tamales are sometimes wrapped in banana or plantain leaves, just as *hallacas* are in the Caribbean countries. And sometimes they are not wrapped at all, especially along the Tex–Mex border where American influence is strong. There they're merely molded in long rolls and fried or set in the oven to bake.

Most of the above recipes can be turned into tamale pies, which seem to be a gringo invention.

NICARAGUAN NACTAMALES

2 pounds white corn	¼ pound bacon
1¼ pounds potatoes	12 olives
2 cups shortening	Chick-peas or garbanzos
3 pounds boned chicken or	1 teaspoon salt
2½ pounds fresh pork	Pepper

Boil corn until soft and hulls begin to come off. Drain; put through fine grinder and then through flour sieve. Boil potatoes. Grind when cold and mix with sieved corn. Work shortening into this to form a dough. Cut meat into inch squares. Dice bacon; stone olives and have garbanzos previously soaked. Divide dough into 6 portions. Roll out and fill each with remaining ingredients, portioning them equally. Wrap filled dough in Patapar or waxed paper. (Nicaraguans use banana leaf.) Secure well and cook 1½ hours in boiling water.

HUMITAS AND HALLACAS

CHILEAN HUMITAS

18 ears green corn	3 tablespoons fat or butter
Cornhusks	1 teaspoon salt
1 onion, chopped	1 tablespoon sugar

Grate corn from cobs and save cobs. Also save the freshest and largest cornhusks and cover with boiling water to soften. Fry onion in fat very slowly until tender and nicely browned. Add corn and remaining ingredients and cool. Spread cornhusks on table and lay 2–3 tablespoons corn mixture in center of each. (If husks are small you may need to use two husks for each *humita*.) Roll; tie securely with strips of cornhusk and trim ends. Lay cobs in bottom of wide deep saucepan. Add boiling water to barely cover. Lay *humitas* on top of cobs. Cover pan tightly so no steam escapes and cook 30 minutes. Remove from heat for a few moments, then take up, untie and stack on a hot platter without opening husks. Sprinkle with sugar or not before eating.

Obviously the *humitas* of South America are sisters under their cornhusks to the tamales of Mexico. Compare this recipe with Tamales of Green Corn, with its characteristic Mexican seasonings.

EQUADORIAN HUMITAS

2 cups corn meal	2 tablespoons melted butter
1 teaspoon sugar	2 eggs, separated
½ teaspoon salt	2 tablespoons cottage cheese
	Cornhusks

Mix meal, sugar and salt. Work in butter and then add cheese. Add well-beaten egg yolks and stiffly beaten whites. Pour boiling water over cornhusks to soften, then drain and wipe dry. Lay out on table and place 2–3 tablespoons mixture in each husk, using 2 husks if necessary. Roll loosely to allow for swelling. Tie securely and trim ends. Steam 1 hour and serve very hot in the husks.

Of course this also is a tamale, so the question of which came first, the *humita* or the tamale, becomes a chicken-or-egg conundrum.

Argentine and Uruguay have their *humitas* also, but they have done considerable tinkering with the aboriginal recipes, much as has been done with the Mexican tamale when it is turned into a tamale pie for which recipes are common in Yankee cookbooks and newspaper columns. The true *humita* rolled in cornhusks is still on the River Plate menu, but the following recipe is the more common huskless variation:

ARGENTINE HUMITAS EN CHALA

Select 1 dozen ears fresh green corn. Remove husks and reserve the best and most tender ones to wrap corn paste in. Scrape corn from cob and season to taste with salt and sugar. Fry ½ minced onion in 4 tablespoons oil or butter. Add 1 chopped, skinned and seeded tomato. When smooth add scraped corn and 3–4 leaves of sweet basil, minced. Allow 2 husks, one overlapping the other, to each *humita*. On these place 2 or 3 tablespoons of corn paste and 1 thin slice of good cheese. Fold leaves to make oblong package and secure with a strip of cornhusk. Put a thick layer of the scraped corncobs in a deep casserole. Nearly cover with salted boiling water. Arrange *humitas* on cobs and cover with thick layer of husks. Cover casserole and steam 20 minutes over a quick fire.

These are served and eaten like their tamale cousins.

ARGENTINE HUMITAS WITH MILK
Humitas con Leche

12–15 ears green corn
3 tablespoons lard
1 onion, chopped
2 tomatoes, chopped
2 green peppers, chopped

Salt and pepper
1 teaspoon parsley, minced
2 tablespoons sugar
Plenty of paprika
½ teaspoon cinnamon

Milk

Grate corn from cobs. Heat lard and very slowly fry onion until tender and golden. Add tomatoes and peppers and continue slow frying until tomatoes thicken. Add grated corn, seasonings, parsley, sugar, cinnamon and sufficient paprika to color everything pink. Continue slow frying until all is bubbling, being careful not to overcook. Thin by adding milk a little at a time until about 1 cup is used, amount depending on maturity of corn. The finished dish should be thick enough to eat with a fork. It makes a good vegetable course or may be served with meat.

In both Argentina and Uruguay this recipe is frequently carried a little farther by covering the mixture with grated bread crumbs, dotting with butter and browning in the oven.

VENEZUELAN HALLACAS

1½ pounds dried corn
1 pound beef, diced
1 pound lean pork, diced
2 onions, chopped
1 garlic clove, minced
Lard
2 large tomatoes, chopped
1 green pepper, chopped
1 tablespoon sugar
Salt and pepper

½ cup wine
2 tablespoons wine vinegar
Paprika
Banana leaves or paper
¼ pound salt pork
     cut in strips
Capers
Raisins
Pimiento
Almonds, blanched

Olives, pitted

Cover dried corn kernels with plenty of cold water. Slowly bring to boiling point, then remove from heat. Add cold water to reduce temperature and let stand until following day. Drain; rinse several times with cold water and grind over and over again until reduced to a paste, or if you have a mortar pound the corn in that, in true Venezuelan fashion. Meanwhile slowly fry beef, pork, onions and garlic in 4 tablespoons lard until very lightly browned. Add tomatoes and green pepper and slowly fry 5–10 minutes. Add sugar, salt and pepper, wine and wine vinegar. Cover tightly and simmer until tender. Spread banana leaves on table. Salt the ground corn and make it pink with paprika, then mix with sufficient lard to spread easily. Spread corn mixture on banana leaves ¼ inch thick, using a broad knife. On ½ of the corn-covered banana leaves place 2–3 tablespoons of the meat mixture. Garnish each with a salt pork strip, a few capers, raisins and pimiento strips and put 1 almond and 1 olive in each. Lay a corn-covered banana leaf over each meat-filled one, with corn side down. Tuck in all edges to make a flat, square package about 1 inch thick. Cover with another wrapping of banana leaves and tie with several strands of heavy thread running around in both directions, so no water can seep in. (Packages should be about 1 inch thick and 6–8 inches square.) Steam or boil 2 hours.

Yellow corn is preferred, but American big hominy that comes in a package will do, and even corn meal serves for the dough when scalded with boiling salted water to form a thick mush. In Venezuela, as in Mexico, this corn dough, or *masa*, patiently ground to a fine consistency, can be purchased ready made in the markets, rolled into small balls for convenience in handling. If you have no banana leaves handy Patapar, or well-oiled heavy paper, can be used instead, but the fresh leafy flavor will be missing, of course.

Wine vinegar is used because there are no apples in South America for making cider vinegar.

Hallacas, like the rich tamales of Mexico, are a holiday dish that appeals especially at Christmas time when they're made

with a filling of chicken instead of beef and pork. Such festive
hallacas made a big hit in the Venezuelan pavilion at the New
York World's Fair.

Colombia also has *hallacas*, usually made of white corn, at
least in the Magdalena River districts, where sometimes a
broad-leafed plant growing along streams and known as *biao*
furnishes the wrapping. The procedure is the same as above
except for the filling and here is the recipe:

COLOMBIAN HALLACAS

Dough of white corn
½ pound cooked pork loin
¼ pound salt pork
1 cooked potato, chopped
   fine
1 cup cooked chick-peas
   (garbanzos)

2 small onions, chopped
1 garlic clove, minced
2 tablespoons lard
1 tablespoon paprika
2 hard-cooked eggs,
   chopped
Olives, pitted

Salt and pepper

Use white corn and prepare dough according to recipe for
Venezuelan Hallacas. Chop pork and salt pork. Mix with
potato, chick-peas, onions and garlic. Heat lard. Add paprika
and stir until well mixed, then add meat mixture. Season and
heat together. If too dry add 2–3 tablespoons meat broth. Then
add chopped eggs. Spread out in banana leaves and place in
refrigerator to season until next day. When you make your
hallacas according to the Venezuelan recipe above, put 1 pitted
olive in each *hallaca*. Season with salt and pepper. Tie the packages tight and steam or boil 2 hours.

HAITIAN HALLACAS

Mush:
  1 cup corn meal
  4 cups boiling water
  1 teaspoon salt

Meat Mixture:
   1 pound beef
   ½ pound pork
   1–2 hard-cooked eggs
   Salt and pepper
   Olives, raisins, almonds, capers

Make corn-meal mush and cook until thick. Dice meats. Chop eggs and mix, seasoning with salt and pepper. Spread mush on banana leaves, then spread meat mixture on top. Arrange stoned olives, seeded raisins, blanched and peeled almonds and capers on top. Roll; tie securely. Drop into boiling water and cook about 2 hours.

This is a rich sort of tamale. Because of appetizing tidbits in the way of olives, raisins, almonds, capers, eggs and meats, the opening and dissection of a well-made Haitian Hallaca is like a study in biology.

JAMAICAN STAMP–AND–GO

Stamp-and-Go are really small mush cakes without filling, made of thick corn-meal mush with a little flour to hold it together and a little lard to shorten it. When the mush is cold it is molded out in convenient cakes and is used as a hunger stayer, like the old American "journey cakes" or johnnycake, when undertaking a journey. The name is a nautical order meaning "heave up the anchor and get under way."

MEXICAN POLENTA

3 pints boiling water	1 tablespoon butter
Salt	1 pound ground round steak
1½ cups yellow corn meal	2 teaspoons chili powder
1 onion, chopped	2 cups canned tomatoes
Pepper	

Add 1½ teaspoons salt to rapidly boiling water and slowly sift in corn meal. Stir until thickened. Reduce heat and continue cooking ½ hour or longer until quite thick. Meanwhile slowly fry onion in butter. Add ground steak and fry rapidly, stirring constantly until nicely browned and adding chili powder and salt when half done. Cover and keep hot. Pour half the mush into a buttered baking dish. Spread meat over mush. Drain tomatoes. Cut up and arrange over meat. Season with salt and pepper. Pour remaining mush on top and bake 30–40 minutes until nicely browned.

This substantial one-dish meal, although of Italian origin and enthusiastically adopted in such Italian-influenced republics as the Argentine, becomes authentically Mexican the instant that chili powder goes into it.

PARAGUAYAN CHIPÁ

3 cups cassava meal or fine corn meal	2 whole eggs
½ teaspoon salt	1 egg yolk
1 scant cup lard	⅓ cup milk
	½ pound cheese, grated

Mix meal and salt. Beat eggs and egg yolk, 1 at a time, into slightly softened lard. Then add milk, cheese and salted meal. Knead until well mixed. Separate into small portions. Knead again and pat into thinnish cakes. Place on banana or other pleasantly flavored leaves and bake.

This is the simple or everyday *chipá*. A Paraguayan specialty for fiestas is *chipá-guazu*, in the Guarani language "a large cake," but literally a pudding made of corn, lard, onions and chopped meat.

ARGENTINE MAZAMORRA

1 quart boiling water	2 teaspoons salt
1 pound coarsely milled corn (hominy grits)	

Sprinkle corn into rapidly boiling salted water. Cook until thickened. Reduce heat and simmer until done—about 1 hour.

When made according to Argentine country tradition, this cereal dish is stirred with a fig-wood paddle, to keep it from burning and give it proper flavor. Pour into a mold. Let it get cold. Eat with milk and sugar while munching dried figs, or eat curdy white cheese as an accompaniment.

Fruit syrups instead of milk and sugar are often served with cold cereals and simple puddings, syrups made of pure fruit juices cooked with sugar until slightly thick. There are so many South American fruits that there is always a great variety, but cherry syrup and plum syrup are favorites. These same syrups simply thinned with water, and iced or not, make the most refreshing of summer drinks, called *refrescos*.

Mazamorra is not only popular as a *campo* supper dish in the Argentine, but its consumption is so universal in Peru that Spaniards call it Peruvian Pap.

TUCUMÁN MOTÉ

Cover 2 cups big hominy with plenty of cold unsalted water and cook 1 hour. Add salt, short lengths smoked sausage, ¼ pound bacon, 1 small portion smoked tongue and ¼ pound raw ham cut in finger sizes. Season, and 30 minutes before meats and hominy are done add 1 very small cabbage, coarsely chopped, and required number of whole small white potatoes. Serve in a big platter with baked potatoes laid around the edge.

In the Argentine province of Tucumán, from which this dish comes, whole corn is used in place of prepared hominy. It is boiled with wood ashes until hulls are loose, then washed and rubbed through several baths of hot water until all hulls are removed and the taste of ashes gone—a process reminiscent of hominy making in the early days of New England and our Midwest.

ARGENTINE API
Hominy

Wash corn. Cover with cold water and let soak overnight. In morning put over heat in same water. Cook and stir continuously with a wooden spoon, preferably one made of fig wood, until corn is tender. Let stand to ripen. Serve cold or warm with milk and sugar, honey or fruit syrup.

About the only difference between this Argentine hominy and our own is that it should be stirred with a fig-wood stick.

VEGETABLES

MEXICAN GREEN BEANS
Ejotes

Drop 1 pound string beans into salted boiling water and cook until tender. Drain and add 1 tablespoon butter, ⅛ teaspoon mixed ground cinnamon and cloves, 1 tablespoon toasted and pounded cumin seeds and cayenne pepper to taste. Shake pan until butter melts and seasonings are well blended.

Although *frijoles* are beans in Mexico and *verdi* means green, it would never do to ask for *frijoles verdes* when you want *ejotes*. As a matter of fact beans go by half a dozen pet names, differing in almost every South American country, so the traveling marketer must learn a new word for them often. One of the most amusing is *habitualas*, meaning "the usual" or "the same old thing."

STRING BEANS WITH CHILI
Ejotes con Chili

1 pound string beans	⅛ teaspoon ground cinnamon
2 tomatoes	
1 green chili	1 cup boiling water
1 teaspoon salt	1 teaspoon flour

Cut beans in short pieces. Peel and chop tomatoes. Take out seeds and mince chili. Heat tomatoes, chili, cinnamon and salt together until tomatoes break up. Add boiling water; stir and cook together 5 minutes. Work flour smooth with 1 tablespoon cold water and add. Stir and cook until slightly thickened. Add beans. Cover tightly and cook gently, about 30 minutes, until beans are tender, lifting beans from bottom of saucepan to top once or twice so that all will be equally flavored with the sauce.

MEXICAN LIMA BEAN CAKES
Tortas de Habas

Shake 1 cup cooked Lima beans in moderately hot dry frying pan until skins can be easily removed. Remove skins and grind or mash beans to powder. Add 1 tablespoon grated cheese (or Mexican cheese curd, if obtainable), 1 well-beaten egg, salt and cayenne. Mold into little cakes between the hands and fry in fat or butter. 1 tablespoon cooked tomato, 1 tablespoon minced onion, a tiny bit of crushed garlic and a few cumin seeds toasted in a dry frying pan may be added to these *tortas* to improve their flavor.

Such little vegetable cakes take care of many leftovers in the Mexican kitchen—carrots, cauliflower, rice, squash, chick-peas, whatever is at hand, either alone or all mixed together. If mixtures are too wet the addition of a few dry crumbs solves the problem and makes them possible to mold. These tasty hot cakes are often served with sauces highly seasoned with onion and chili powder.

CAULIFLOWER, ITALIAN STYLE
Coliflor a la Italiana

Separate a head of cauliflower into its flowerlets. Cook in milk and water. Drain and marinate in olive oil, salt and pepper. Dip in batter. Fry in deep fat. Serve hot.

Batter:

1 cup flour	2 egg yolks, beaten
⅔ cup milk	1 tablespoon olive oil
	1 egg white, beaten stiff

This Italian specialty has been adopted in both Chile and the Argentine.

BRAZILIAN XU–XU (CHAYOTE)
Pronounced shoo-shoo

Xu-xu is a pale green single-seeded squashlike vegetable that grows on a vine. It's the size and shape of a large pear and is covered with soft, flexible prickers. In Spanish-speaking countries it is known as chayote and under this name it has been naturalized in Florida as a commercial crop. It is prepared like squash, as follows:

Pare off prickly skin. Remove seed and cut in 2-inch cubes. Cook in salted boiling water until tender. Drain. Sprinkle with freshly ground pepper and pour melted butter over, or lay cooked pieces in buttered baking dish. Cover with white sauce. Sprinkle well with grated Parmesan and brown in hot oven.

The Brazilian cook grinds or pounds whole peppers daily in order to have fresh seasoning, either using a tiny pepper mill, or twisting the whole peppercorns in a bit of cloth and pounding them until coarsely powdered.

MEXICAN STUFFED CHAYOTES
Chayotes Enchaladas

Peel chayotes; split lengthwise and remove seeds. Drop into salted boiling water and cook until they begin to be tender. Drain. Make a stuffing with equal quantities of finely chopped nuts, candied fruits and raisins. Hollow out chayote halves. Mash the chayote thus removed and add to stuffing. Stuff halves. Sprinkle with crumbs. Dot with butter and set in buttered baking dish, adding ¼ cup water to dish. Bake until chayotes are tender and lightly browned.

STUFFED CHAYOTES, PUERTO RICAN STYLE

Cut ripe chayotes (as many as desired) in half lengthwise and boil until tender. Remove flesh from skins. Take out seeds.

Mash; season with salt and pepper. Add grated cheese and a little milk. Put the filling back in the shells (skins). Cover with grated cheese and bake light brown.

Minced meat and tomato sauce may be added to the mashed chayotes and baked in the chayote shells or in a casserole.

CHAYOTES WITH CHEESE SAUCE

Cut chayotes in half lengthwise and boil until tender. Remove skins and dice the flesh. Over the diced chayotes put a layer of medium-thick cream sauce in which American cheese has been grated and melted. Cover all with finely ground dry bread crumbs and bits of butter. Place in a medium oven until the crumbs are golden brown.

MENDOZA CORN PUDDING
Pastel de Choclo

Put ½ cup lard in casserole and fry in it 4 thinly sliced white onions, 1 seeded red pepper, salt, a little marjoram and a few ground cumin seeds. When onions are soft add ⅔ pound ground veal. Stir and cook until meat is slightly browned and remove from heat. Scrape corn carefully from 8 fresh green ears. Place in another casserole over slow fire. Stir until heated through. Add 1 cup hot milk. Stir and cook 5 minutes and let cool.

At this point the Argentine cook makes a stiff hot water dough, kneads it smooth and beats it with an iron pestle until it blisters. But any plain meat pie dough will answer. Roll out thin and line a greased pudding dish with it. Spread meat mixture on the bottom. Put a layer of pitted olives and slices of hard-cooked eggs over meat. Beat 3 eggs, whites and yolks separately and then together, and fold into the cooled corn. Spread this over olives and sliced eggs. Sprinkle with sugar and cinnamon and bake 30 minutes in hot oven.

This generous Argentine dish is enough for 8 servings and may easily be halved.

COLOMBIAN CORN PUDDING

6 ears green corn	¾ cup milk
1 teaspoon salt	¼ cup butter, melted
1 teaspoon paprika	3 eggs, slightly beaten
⅛ teaspoon black pepper	Cheese

Cut and scrape kernels from cobs into a bowl. Add rest of ingredients except cheese and mix well. Pour ½ of mixture into buttered baking tin. Place over it thin slices of cheese and cover with remaining half. Bake in slow oven, 325°, until firm.

CHILEAN GREEN CORN PIE
Pastel de Maíz

12 ears green corn	1 onion, minced
4 tablespoons fat	¼ cup meat broth
4 tablespoons sugar	¼ cup seeded raisins
Salt and pepper	10 olives, stoned
1 cup chopped cooked meat	2 hard-cooked eggs, sliced

Grate corn and fry 5 minutes in fat. Add 3 tablespoons sugar and seasonings. Mix meat, onion, broth, raisins and olives and arrange in buttered baking dish with seasoned egg slices. Spread corn over top. Sprinkle with remaining sugar and brown in oven.

CHILEAN GREEN CORN MEAT PIE
Pastel de Choclo

Heat ¼ cup lard or dripping in frying pan. Fry a red pepper in it and remove. Fry 1 large thinly sliced onion in seasoned fat, and when soft add ½ pound finely chopped beef or fresh pork. Fry and stir meat until done. Add 1 teaspoon salt, ¼ teaspoon red pepper and 1 tablespoon flour mixed with a little cold water. Cook and stir 10 minutes, and just before taking from heat add a few stuffed or whole olives, ground cumin seed and ½ cup raisins, previously soaked in water.

Set aside, and when cool fill a deep buttered pie dish half full with mixture.

In separate pan heat 2 tablespoons lard or dripping. Fry soft 1 minced onion in it. Add 2 cups grated fresh corn, 1 crushed bay leaf and salt to taste. Turn corn in fat. Fry lightly and spread over meat. Put in hot oven to brown, 10–15 minutes.

VENEZUELAN GREEN CORN CAKE
Torta de Jojotos

12 ears corn	½ cup grated cheese
3 eggs	2 cups milk
4 tablespoons butter	Sugar
	Salt

Grate kernels from cobs and put through colander. Mix with all other ingredients, using sugar and salt to taste. Put in well-buttered baking dish and bake until golden brown.

CHILEAN CUCUMBERS AU GRATIN
Pepinos au Gratin

Pare desired number of fresh cucumbers. Boil in salted water until tender, then cut in dice. Arrange in buttered ramekins, alternating layers of cucumbers and grated cheese. Moisten with cream. Cover with buttered crumbs and bake until brown.

Chile does itself well with both cucumbers and tasty cheeses, so a dish of *Pepinos au Gratin* as served in Valparaiso or Santiago de Chile is something to remember.

CHILEAN STUFFED EGGPLANTS
Berenjenas Rellenas

2 small eggplants	2 tablespoons butter
Boiling water	1 cup dry bread crumbs
1 green pepper, chopped	1½ teaspoon salt
1 onion, chopped	Pepper

Scoop pulp from eggplants weighing about 1 pound each, leaving shell ½-inch thick. Cook shell in salted water 5 minutes. Chop eggplant pulp. Mix with chopped green pepper and onion and fry in butter 10 minutes. Then add ¾ cup bread crumbs, 1½ cups boiling water, salt and pepper. Fill eggplant shells with this mixture and sprinkle remainder of bread crumbs over top. Put in pan with a little water and bake 30 minutes.

We don't know why, but eggplant seems to be the most popular vegetable in widely separated parts of South America, such as Chile and Colombia, and it appears on the table in dozens of attractive ways we seldom see at home.

BRAZILIAN EGGPLANT WITH TOMATOES
Bringella com Tomates

1 medium eggplant	4–5 small tomatoes
Salt and pepper	½ teaspoon sugar
3 tablespoons bread crumbs	1 tablespoon melted butter
1 tablespoon grated Parmesan	

Peel eggplant and cut in ½-inch slices. Drop into boiling water with 1 tablespoon salt. Parboil 10 minutes and drain well. Arrange in buttered baking dish. Sprinkle with 2 tablespoons bread crumbs. Peel tomatoes, or use drained tomatoes out of a can and lay on top. Sprinkle with salt, pepper and remaining ingredients, and bake uncovered in medium oven 20 minutes. If there is too much liquid from tomatoes continue baking 5–10 minutes longer to dry out.

EGGPLANT, PUERTO RICAN STYLE

Wash, slice and fry eggplant until slightly brown. Place a layer of fried eggplant in a casserole, then a layer of corn, another of tomatoes and a sprinkling of cheese. Repeat the process and top everything with a little tomato sauce and grated cheese. Bake in oven until slightly brown.

OKRA WITH TOMATOES
Quiabos com Tomates

4 large ripe tomatoes	⅓ cup fine bread crumbs
2 cups sliced okra	Salt and freshly ground
1 medium onion, sliced thin	pepper
2 tablespoons butter	

Peel tomatoes and cut in thin slices. Wash okra free of any sand and cut in ¼-inch slices. Place a layer of tomato slices in bottom of buttered baking dish, then a layer of okra, a few onion rings, a sprinkling of crumbs and seasonings. Repeat until all are used, finishing with a layer of tomatoes topped with crumbs and dots of butter. Bake 1 hour or a little longer, uncovering at end of baking time to let brown. Canned tomatoes, drained and cut up, may be substituted for fresh.

Okra must always be young, tender and freshly picked.

PALM HEARTS

See Rice with Palm Hearts and Brazilian Rice with Palm Hearts, under Rice and Beans.

PEAS, CUBAN STYLE
Chicharos a la Cubana

1 quart green peas	2 green peppers, skinned
1 teaspoon salt	and seeded
1 tablespoon oil or butter	1 bay leaf, minced
2 onions, minced	A few raspings nutmeg
1 teaspoon parsley, minced	1 teaspoon vinegar

Cook peas tender in as little water as necessary, with salt. Heat oil in a frying pan. Start frying onions in it. Add parsley. Chop peppers and add with bay leaf. Cook slowly until everything is soft and lightly browned, then add nutmeg dissolved in the vinegar. Carefully stir these fried seasonings into the cooked peas until they are well coated and serve hot.

BRAZILIAN INDEPENDENCE DAY PEPPERS
Pimentoes Sete de Setembro

3 medium carrots, diced
½ cup cooked tomato
2 medium onions, sliced thin
Salt
1 tablespoon butter

1 garlic clove, minced
3 large green peppers
6 tablespoons cooked peas
2 hard-cooked egg yolks
White pepper

Cook carrots with tomato and 1 onion as lightly as possible in salted boiling water, keeping saucepan covered until carrots are done and then uncovering to let cooking water evaporate.

Meanwhile start preparing a sauce by heating butter in frying pan and slowly frying remaining onion until it begins to color, adding garlic, and continuing slow frying until lightly browned. Split peppers, leaving a bit of stem on each half. Remove seeds and veins. Cook peppers in a separate saucepan of rapidly boiling salted water 10 minutes, then take up and drain.

To fried onion and garlic add ½ cup cooking water from peppers, and simmer. Pile carrots in pepper-shell halves. Place 1 tablespoon hot green peas in center of each pile of carrots. Strain over each 1 tablespoon of liquid from onion mixture and top peas with a tiny cone of sieved egg yolks.

The resulting dish is bright yellow and green, the Brazilian national colors. It was invented and named to celebrate Brazil's Independence Day which falls on *Sete de Setembro* (the seventh of September).

The following menu also carries out this holiday's color scheme, each dish being either yellow or green:

Vatapá, Bahia Style
Tempura Shrimps
Independence Day Peppers
Lettuce Salad with Mayonnaise
Avocado Ice Cream
Yellow Cheese
(Coffee)

MEXICAN STUFFED PEPPERS
Chiles Rellenos

3 green peppers
6 sardines
1 small tomato
1 small onion, minced
1 tablespoon fat
1 small garlic clove, minced

1 tablespoon olives, minced
3 tablespoons grated cheese
½ teaspoon salt
1 dash cayenne
¼ teaspoon chili powder
½ cup Red Sauce

Roast peppers under grill until they blister. Pull off skin. Split lengthwise; remove seeds and veins. Skin; bone and shred sardines. Peel tomato. Cut crosswise. Remove seeds and chop. Slowly fry onion in fat without browning. Add garlic and slowly fry until tender. Mix sardines, tomato, onion and garlic with olives, 1 tablespoon cheese and seasonings, and stuff peppers with mixture. Sprinkle remaining cheese on top. Set in baking dish. Surround with Red Sauce (see recipe) or with well-seasoned tomato juice, and bake about 30 minutes or until peppers are tender.

These are fine with Mexican beans.

CUBAN FRIED PLANTAINS

Cut green plantains in very thin slices. Drop into hot deep fat and fry like potato chips. Drain on paper and sprinkle at once with salt. They should be crisp even when cold.

Plantains often appear in city markets in the United States. They look like elongated green bananas. In Latin America, especially in the West Indies, they're an indispensable vegetable.

PERUVIAN POTATOES WITH TOMATOES
Papas con Tomates

Peel potatoes. Cook with a small piece of pumpkin and drain well. Separately fry onion in lard and red pepper. Add to-

matoes and green corn as desired. When done pour tomato
mixture over potatoes in a tureen. Add a little hot milk and
water. Mix well, mashing half of the potatoes and leaving the
others whole.

Whether you say "tomayto" or I say "tomatto," neither of us
is pronouncing it exactly like the Aztec original—*tomatl*, or
the Spanish derivative, *tomate*.

This dish dates back thousands of years, for Peru is the
first home of both potatoes and tomatoes, from whence they
spread to all other American countries. Peruvian Potatoes and
Tomatoes is therefore as natural a combination as Chilean
Squash with Corn or our own succotash, which we learned
to make from the Indians.

All along the West coast of South America epicures esteem
the flavorsome yellow-meated potato of Peru. There are, indeed, enough spuds of other flesh and skin colors, including
purple, to complete a rainbow, but the one with yellow flesh
is best.

In the high Andes frozen potatoes are relished and *chuno*,
the national dish of Bolivia, is started by dancing on frozen
potatoes to tender them.

• CHILEAN POTATOES WITH RICE
Papas con Arroz

Cook 5 peeled medium-sized potatoes with 1 piece pumpkin
(4 inches square) in salted boiling water to cover. Wash ½
cup rice through many waters and dry in a towel. Heat 2
tablespoons cooking fat with 2 teaspoons Spanish paprika. Stir
until bubbling hot. Add rice, 1 small minced onion and 1
parsley sprig. Then slowly fry until rice has lightly browned
under its paprika coating. When potatoes are done take out
1 only. Mash it fine with the pumpkin and put it back with
the 4 whole potatoes, which have boiled nearly dry. Add
fried rice, 6 whole black peppers, a little salt and sufficient
boiling water mixed with milk to cover. Cover pan and sim-

mer until rice is tender. Serve with a generous sprinkling of grated cheese.

MEXICAN POTATOES DRESSED WITH OLIVE OIL
Papas Guisadas con Aceite

1 large onion, sliced thin	3 potatoes, sliced thin
3 tablespoons fat	1½ teaspoons salt
1–3 green chilies (optional)	Tabasco
1 large firm tomato	2 tablespoons olive oil
1–2 teaspoons vinegar	

Fry onion very slowly in fat without browning. Remove seeds from chilies. Mince fine and add. Peel tomato; coarsely chop and add. Do not stir after adding tomato, for pieces must remain unbroken if possible, but shake pan gently to prevent scorching. After frying a few minutes add thinly sliced potatoes—there should be about 3 cups. Add salt and Tabasco to taste. Cover closely, and when potatoes are hot sprinkle olive oil over them. Keep uncovered until potatoes begin to fry. Sprinkle on vinegar, a few drops at a time. Slide entire contents of frying pan into baking dish. Cover and finish cooking over steam or in oven until potatoes are tender.

ECUADORIAN LLAPINGACHOS

4 cups mashed potatoes	Fat for frying
1 tablespoon butter	1 onion, chopped
Salt and pepper	1 cup cooked tomatoes
2 tablespoons cream cheese	Fried eggs

Have potatoes freshly boiled and mashed. Add butter, seasonings and cheese. Beat and form into potato cakes. Fry brown on both sides. Meanwhile slowly fry onion in 1 tablespoon fat until tender and lightly browned. Add tomatoes. Season and stir until bubbling and thickened. Place some of the tomato mixture on each potato cake and set a poached egg on top.

SWEET POTATO DISHES

See under Desserts.

MEXICAN BAKED SPINACH
Espinaca al Horno

½ pound spinach
2 green peppers, chopped
2 cups cooked celery, chopped
2 cooked onions, chopped
2 tablespoons raisins, chopped
2 teaspoons salt
⅛ teaspoon cinnamon
1 teaspoon sugar
1 chili, minced or 3 dashes cayenne
1 teaspoon chili powder
2–4 tablespoons tomato juice
Grated cheese
Butter

Have spinach well washed and stems removed. Cook slowly with peppers in covered saucepan, using no other water but that which clings to leaves. Drain and chop fine. Mix with other vegetables, raisins and seasonings, adding tomato juice to moisten. Place in buttered baking dish. Cover with grated cheese. Dot with butter and bake in hot oven 10–15 minutes.

CHILEAN SQUASH WITH CORN
Calabaza con Maíz

Peel and remove seeds from a crookneck or other summer squash. Add a chunk of pumpkin. Put in saucepan; cover and cook. Fry a little onion and some fresh green corn in "color" (lard "colored" with paprika). Add to squash and simmer until tender. When ready to serve stir in lightly beaten eggs and grated cheese.

Almost any squash or pumpkin is called *calabaza* in Spanish, and Chile and Peru have endless varieties of both, since they originated in these parts. Summer squashes are sold whole as in North America, but pumpkins usually are marketed by the piece and used in small chunks to add their flavor to soups and dishes made with less tasty sister squashes. An average piece of seasoning pumpkin weighs about ½ pound.

"Color" is the same word in both Spanish and English, but Chileans use it aptly as the name of lard rendered with red pepper until it is highly "colored" and seasoned through. You can buy either white lard or red lard ("color") in many South American countries, and the best substitute for it here is to use plenty of Spanish paprika with the lard in cooking. Spanish paprika is better than Hungarian for this purpose because it is sharper.

The combination of squash with corn is as indigenous as Lima beans and corn in succotash, for both the beans named after Peru's capital and the original Indian maize got their start on the West coast of South America, not a stone's throw from Chile.

COUNTRY BAKED SQUASH
Aboboreira no Forno

Cut out a 5-inch circle from the top of a yellow winter squash that's not too big, slanting the knife toward the center of the circle in such a way that the top piece will afterward fit like a cover. Remove seeds and fibers. Rub salt and pepper lightly over the entire inner surface. Pour in a cup of sugar and turn the squash until as much of the sugar adheres to the sides as will. Dash a generous pinch of cinnamon over this. Replace cover and pin it down with 2 or 3 small skewers; or lacking these, wire nails will do. You may have to use a hammer anyway, if the rind of the squash is hard. Set in a slow oven and bake until tender. Serve whole, digging out the interior with a spoon. To be eaten with butter, like baked potato.

This is a sort of self-contained squash or pumpkin pie, and is best when the squash is picked field fresh and popped right into an outdoor clay *forno*, although any kind of an oven will do. This was the favorite method of our old Brazilian cook, Eva, who when asked what should be bought at the market would always begin thoughtfully with "abob-era," then string along a few other needs and brightly inject "and abob-era" three or four times during the daily ordering, just to make sure she'd get her pet squash.

COLOMBIAN SQUASH SOUFFLÉ
Souflé de Calabaza

1 pound summer squash	½ pound shrimps,
1 tablespoon butter, melted	boiled and peeled
½ cup thick white sauce	4 egg yolks, beaten thick
Salt, pepper and nutmeg	4 egg whites, beaten stiff

Peel firm summer squash. Cut in quarters. Cook tender in salted boiling water. Drain; dry and mash. Add butter and white sauce. Season to taste with salt, pepper and a little nutmeg. Stir in shrimps with a little of their own liquor and beaten egg yolks. Fold in beaten egg whites. Turn into buttered baking dish and bake 25 minutes in moderately slow oven, 325°. Serve with tomato sauce.

CHILEAN STUFFED SQUASH
Zapallitos Rellenos

6 small squashes	Grated cheese
Bread crumbs	Milk
1 egg	Butter

Take 6 small squashes. Split in half and cook in boiling water for about 15 minutes. Then carefully scoop out the pulp and mix with equal amount of bread crumbs, 1 egg and a small quantity of grated cheese. Moisten to a very soft consistency with milk. Brush squash shells with butter before filling with mixture. Dot with butter and put in oven until browned.

MEXICAN SQUASH CAPIROTADA
Capirotada de Calabacitas

3 young yellow squash
1 tablespoon butter
2 onions, sliced thin
2 cups milk
½ teaspoon salt

⅛ teaspoon cinnamon
⅛ teaspoon ground cloves
Toast fingers
½ cup grated cheese
2 tablespoons sifted crumbs

Slice squashes and cook barely tender in salted boiling water. Drain and lay on linen towel to dry. Heat butter and slowly fry onions until they color. Add 1 cup of milk, salt and spices. Cover bottom of a buttered baking dish with toast fingers. Place a layer of squash on top. Scatter a few onion slices over and wet thoroughly with milk. Then another layer of squash and more onions, repeating until all are used. Add remaining milk. Cover with grated cheese. Sprinkle with crumbs and bake in oven until nicely browned. Sometimes sugar takes the place of cheese on top of this dish, and dots of butter top the sugar.

Capirotadas are little fast day dishes made of vegetables without meat, and recipes vary greatly to give variety during Lent. Potato *Capirotada*, for instance, is made as above, substituting potatoes for squashes and well-seasoned tomato juice for milk.

TURNIP CAPIROTADA
Capirotada de Nabos

3 white turnips, sliced
2 garlic cloves, minced
3 tablespoons butter
2 cups meat broth

Salt
1½ cups cooked chick-peas
    (garbanzos)
Sifted crumbs

Toast fingers

Cook turnips in salted boiling water until just tender. Drain and dry on a towel. Fry garlic slowly in 1 tablespoon butter until lightly browned; add broth. Cover bottom of a buttered baking dish with toast fingers. Place a layer of turnips on top, then a layer of chick-peas (from a tin), seasoning lightly with salt. Wet well with broth. Then another layer of turnips and another of chick-peas, repeating until all are used. Add remaining broth and cover with crumbs. Brown remaining butter in frying pan and sprinkle over. Bake until nicely browned.

SQUASH SANDWICHES
Calabaza Frito con Queso—Squash Fried with Cheese

Cook unpeeled young yellow squashes in salted boiling water until just tender. Drain; cut into slices ¾ inch thick and about 3 inches long and dry in a towel. Make sandwiches by putting 1 thin slice of cheese between 2 slices of squash, using white Mexican cheese if obtainable, otherwise yellow store cheese. Beat 1 egg white and 1 egg yolk separately. Mix together, adding 1 tablespoon water, a dash of salt and cayenne and thicken slightly with flour. Dip squash sandwiches in mixture and fry in deep fat, or fry in butter in a frying pan until brown on both sides. Serve with Red Sauce (See recipe.) or with highly seasoned tomato juice.

Eggplant Fried with Cheese (*Berenjena Frito con Queso*) and Sweet Potatoes Fried with Cheese (*Camotes Frito con Queso*) are made the same way, both eggplant and sweets being previously cooked and peeled.

ARGENTINE CHICHOCA DE ZAPALLO
Dried Squash

Cut Hubbard or any tasty winter squashes in two. Remove seeds and membranes and stand in the sun. When halves have dried a little so they can be cut more easily cut around and around in narrow strips of regular size, about ¼ inch thick. These endless spirals are called *chichocas*. Sprinkle well with salt. Put in sun to dry, but bring them into the kitchen at night. When dry pack in boxes and cover well with paper to protect them from moths.

This dried squash is much esteemed in winter when there is a scarcity of fresh vegetables in Southern Argentina, whose winter is, of course, the reverse of ours. It is put into meat stews, *locros* and *carbonadas*. It needs to be steeped only a few minutes in hot water before using.

STUFFED TURNIPS
Nabos Recheados

Peel required number of young turnips. Hollow out centers and cook in salted boiling water until tender. Drain and save cooking water. Meanwhile wash enough shrimps to fill turnips. Drop shrimps into salted boiling water with 1 chopped garlic clove, 1 chopped small onion and a bouquet of herbs (parsley, celery leaves and 1 bay leaf) and cook 10–15 minutes. Drain and save cooking water. Cut up shrimps. Fill turnip cups with them and arrange in buttered baking dish. Combine 1 cup turnip water with 1 cup shrimp water. Bring to boiling point and pour over 2 beaten egg yolks. Add 1 teaspoon minced parsley and pour all over the stuffed turnips, letting surplus, if any, flow into dish. Sprinkle with crumbs. Dot with butter and brown in hot oven.

Celeriac and small green squashes may be cooked and stuffed in the same manner.

MEXICAN VEGETABLE CAKES
Frito de Legumbres

Chop together equal quantities of cooked carrots, cabbage, cauliflower and onions. Add a few leftover green peas and part of 1 beaten egg. Season with salt, pepper and a pinch of chili powder and mold into flat cakes. Dip in remaining egg beaten with 1 tablespoon water. Then dip into sifted crumbs and fry in fat or butter. Or dip in egg batter until well covered and fry in deep fat. Serve with any Mexican sauce.

GAZPACHO

The usual *gazpacho* that turns up in various Latin-American republics is made as follows, with variations to suit local taste:

Chop 1 onion, 1 large tomato, 1 green chili (A pickled chili from a pepper sauce bottle will serve.) and ½ cucumber. Crumble 1 slice bread without crust and lay it in bottom of a garlic-rubbed bowl. Season chopped vegetables and add with sufficient water to cover and let stand 15 minutes. Then add ½ cup or more French dressing, well seasoned with paprika. Chill; stir and serve in soup plates. It should be quite soupy, and may be used as either a first course or a salad. (For a similar dish see Mexican Gazpadeo.)

ARGENTINE GAZPACHO

Lay 2 pilot crackers in a dish. Cover well with warm water and let stand until soft. Drain and break into pieces. Place a layer of soaked crackers in a dish. Cover with well-chopped tomatoes, minced onion and chopped green pepper. Lay on top a thin layer of boned and shredded sardines. Then another layer of pilot crackers, etc., repeating as often as you wish. Make sufficient French dressing to wet all ingredients, seasoning dressing with plenty of paprika and a little minced parsley. Pour over contents of dish and garnish with olives and hard-cooked egg slices. Serve as either a first course or a salad.

CUBAN HOT GAZPACHO

Remove skins from 1 cup cooked Lima beans. Blanch and peel ½ cup almonds. Grind beans and almonds with 1 garlic

clove and stir in 2–3 tablespoons olive oil. Add 1 quart cold
water, salt, pepper, paprika and 1 slice stale bread cut in 1½-
inch squares. Bring to boiling point. Cover and cook gently
until well blended.

This is a typically Andalusian dish transplanted to the New
World. It is served as a soup, or course, differing from other
gazpachos in that it is eaten hot.

A BRAZILIAN TYPE OF GAZPACHO

Dice ½ loaf white bread and simmer golden in 4 ounces
butter. Add 4 peeled tomatoes and 1 can Lima beans, drained.
Season. Add ½ cup chicken broth or stock and simmer 20
minutes.

Although Brazil's language, Portuguese, has no equivalent
for the Spanish *gazpacho*, the borrowed dish is frequently
served in Rio de Janeiro.

MEXICAN GAZPADEO

3 slices bread   1 garlic clove, minced
⅓ cup olive oil   2 tablespoons vinegar
1 small onion, chopped   2 tablespoons water
              1 green pepper, chopped

Lightly toast bread and cut in finger sizes. Heat olive oil.
Add onion and fry slowly until it begins to brown. Add garlic
and green pepper. Continue frying until all are brown. Then
push vegetables to one side of pan. Quickly dip toast fingers
in vinegar thinned with water, being careful they do not become too wet. Drop them without delay into the hot oil and
fry brown on both sides. Take up. Drain on paper and sprinkle

minced browned vegetables over. Serve as a garnish for meats or as a separate course in place of a salad.

Gazpadeo differs from the more common Spanish *gazpacho* in being a knife-and-fork dish, rather than a thick bread soup that calls for a bowl and spoon.

MEXICAN CHILI SPAGHETTI

2 tablespoons fat or oil
1 small onion, chopped
¼ pound spaghetti
1 cup cooked tomatoes

½ teaspoon salt
1 chili pepper or
   several dashes cayenne
1½ cups boiling water

Heat fat in a casserole. Add onion and spaghetti broken into 2-inch lengths. Fry slowly until lightly browned. Add tomatoes and seasonings and continue slow frying, stirring until tomatoes break up. Then add boiling water and simmer until water is absorbed and spaghetti is tender.

This meeting of Italy and Mexico is celebrated all along our own Tex–Mex border where chili-flavored spaghetti is always in demand.

AVOCADO COCKTAIL
Cocktail de Aguacate

2 or 3 ripe avocados
½ cup tomato sauce
½ cup cream
1 teaspoon celery, minced

1 teaspoon Worcestershire
   Sauce
1 tablespoon vinegar
1 teaspoon salt

Dash of pepper

Dice avocados and fill small glasses. Blend remaining ingredients. Pour over diced fruit and chill before serving.

Aguacate is only another Spanish name for avocado, which last, curiously enough is also the word for lawyer. The

Portuguese-speaking Brazilians call it *abacate*. In any case the original word was Aztec, *ahuacatl*, testicle, which the fruit resembles in appearance, and from this name it got the reputation of being an aphrodisiac.

STUFFED AVOCADOS
Aguacates Rellenos de Picadillo

For each avocado:

2 tablespoons ground cooked pork
1 small tomato, chopped
3 capers
Salt and pepper

¼ teaspoon minced marjoram or parsley
½ egg, beaten
Bread crumbs
Butter

Tomato sauce

Peel avocados, which should not be too large. Cut lengthwise and remove seeds. Mix pork, tomato, capers and marjoram. Season and stuff avocado halves. Cover with beaten egg, then with crumbs, and fry in butter until browned all over. Lay in baking dish. Cover with tomato sauce and finish cooking in oven. Serve as a vegetable.

NICARAGUAN AVOCADOS STUFFED WITH CHEESE
Aguacates Rellenos de Queso

Peel and cut avocados as above. Stuff with cheese—any fresh cream cheese will do. Nicaraguans use their own special curd cheese. Dip in beaten egg, then in crumbs. Fry brown in butter or fat. Cover with tomato sauce and finish cooking in oven. Serve as a vegetable.

CENTRAL AMERICAN SANDWICH

Mash ripe avocados. Season with salt, black pepper, Worcestershire, onion juice and French dressing. Spread generously between bread slices and toast the sandwiches. (From *The Vegetable Cookbook*, by the Browns.)

BRAZILIAN AVOCADO SANDWICHES

Whip pulp with sugar and lime juice, as above, and mix with ½ cup cashew nuts, crisped in oven and put through grinder. Spread on thinnest slices of unbuttered bread and scatter a few crumbs of chopped nuts on top.

Cashew nuts, by the way, are not nuts at all, but a tropical fruit that's inedible until roasted to get rid of its cardol content, cardol being a fierce caustic oil from which indelible ink is made.

The many ways of using avocados in Latin America would fill another book. They're good dressed up as appetizer, salads, desserts or just plain, since the avocado is a natural vegetable butter. Bread is often spread with them, and they're commonly called "Midshipman's Butter" or "Sailor's Butter" in the tropics.

Until California's recent concern with these "alligator pears" we North Americans have been inclined to eat them too green and only cut them up in salads, or use pieces to garnish soup. But to get their full flavor they must be dead ripe, and that's not determined by pinching them, which bruises and discolors the flesh beneath the hard skin, but by shaking them to make sure the big seed rattles inside, proving that they're ready to eat.

MEXICAN GUACAMOLE

2 avocados, chopped very fine
1 tomato, chopped
1 chili pepper, minced
1 small onion, minced
French dressing
Tortillas

Mix vegetables together adding French dressing made with lemon or lime juice and plenty of salt. Eat with tortillas.

There are almost as many recipes for *Guacamole* as there are cooks in Mexico. Incidentally the original spelling, often still encountered, was *Aguacamole*, from *aguacate*, Spanish for avocado.

CHILEAN RAW ARTICHOKE SALAD
Ensalada de Pencas

Use the heart of small, tender young artichokes, cutting away the tough parts of leaves and the choke. Cut into small pieces and drop into cold water with lemon juice to keep them from turning black. Quarter these pieces and put the fine bits back into water. When ready to serve drain and wring them dry in a napkin. Serve with plenty of olive oil, lemon juice and bits of garlic.

A taste for raw artichokes in this manner doesn't have to be acquired, yet California is the only other place besides Chile where this salad is commonly relished.

BRAZILIAN SALADS

Brazilians serve the usual green salads, lettuce, romaine, chicory, cress, etc. and tomatoes, with French dressing generously seasoned with onion juice or crushed garlic. And lime juice is sometimes used in place of red vinegar. So if you are giving a Brazilian dinner any of our simple salads will be in tune.

A pleasant variation of salads to be served with fish is made by mixing threads of anchovy into the dressing, a touch which is especially good with potato salad. Shrimps, crab meat or cold fish are served in mayonnaise usually as an hors d'oeuvre, accompanied by a salad of a cooked green vegetable, or a mixture of several, with French dressing. Olives, sliced green peppers and parsley sprigs are used for garnishing.

AVOCADO SALAD
Salada de Abacate

Split avocado lengthwise. Take out seed. Place in each half 2 tablespoons French dressing made with lemon or lime juice instead of vinegar. Serve one half to each person. Eat like a cantaloupe by digging out with a teaspoon. The fruit should be ripe, the consistency of hard butter.

SHRIMP SALAD
Salada de Camarões

Combine 2 cups chopped cooked shrimps, ½ cup chopped olives and 1 cooked and chopped green pepper. Mix with mayonnaise. Pile on lettuce leaves. Sprinkle with chopped hard-cooked egg and garnish each pile with a dab of mayonnaise.

COOKIES, CAKES AND SWEETS

CHILEAN MOLASSES COOKIES
Masitas de Chancaca

¾ cup sugar	2½ cups flour
½ cup lard	½ teaspoon soda
2 eggs, well beaten	½ teaspoon salt
½ cup *chancaca* molasses	½ tablespoon ground ginger
	½ cup boiling water

Cream sugar and lard together. Add eggs and molasses and beat well. Sift dry ingredients together and add. Gradually stir in boiling water and beat thoroughly. Drop by spoonfuls on greased baking sheet and bake 12–15 minutes in hot oven.

Chancaca is crude native molasses for which Puerto Rican molasses may be substituted.

TACUBAYAN RUM ROLLS (MEXICAN)
Panecitos de Tacubaya

Work ¼ pound of almond paste with 4 tablespoons rum until it forms a smooth wet paste. Add ⅛ teaspoon powdered cloves, then work in confectioners' sugar until paste is thick enough to mold. Roll into tiny tidbits and eat as is.

Literally *panecitos* are little rolls of bread, in this case playfully applied to little rolls of almond paste.

MEXICAN MOUTH–SLAPPERS
Tapabocas

2 cups flour	4 tablespoons lard
4 tablespoons sugar	1 ounce grated fresh cheese
4 tablespoons butter	1 egg
	1 wineglass sherry

239

Sift flour and sugar together. Work in butter, lard and cheese, and then the egg and sherry. Work to a smooth mass and put into a pastry tube. Squeeze out in small spirals and bake in moderately hot oven.

Tapaboca is Spanish for "a slap on the mouth," and it would be hard to imagine a pleasanter one.

ALMOND TWISTS
Roscas Almendra

2 cups ground almonds	3 tablespoons grated lemon
3 tablespoons granulated	rind
sugar	3 egg whites

Mix together lightly almonds, sugar, lemon rind and egg whites, beaten until stiff but not dry. Put in pastry bag and squeeze out in little twists on greased baking sheet. Bake a rich brown in moderate oven, 350°.

BRAZILIAN ALMOND TOOTHPICKS
Palitos de Amendôas

2 eggs	1 teaspoon aniseeds
1 cup sugar	2 cups flour (about)
1 tablespoon butter	¼ cup chopped almonds

Stir eggs and sugar and butter together, stirring in one direction only until light and creamy, then stir in aniseeds. Sift flour and add gradually to mixture while continuously stirring until dough is stiff. Roll out thin on floured board. Cut in short narrow strips and let dry 24 hours at room temperature. Sprinkle with chopped almonds and bake in moderately slow oven, 325°, on buttered tins.

This recipe resembles one used by Germans for their gay little square cakes that have designs embossed upon them with a springerle board, except that almonds are added.

MEXICAN SOLETAS
Stocking Soles

3 egg whites   7 egg yolks
½ cup sugar   1 cup cornstarch
                ¼ teaspoon salt

Beat egg whites until stiff but moist. Add sugar gradually and continue beating. Add egg yolks, beaten until thick and lemon colored. Fold in cornstarch mixed and sifted with salt. With teaspoon put batter in globs on buttered baking sheet. Sprinkle sugar thickly on top of each and tap pan sharply on bottom to make sugar settle. Bake in moderate oven, 350°, about 12 minutes. Remove and stick together in pairs while hot.

These flat white cakes that come in pairs are amusingly called *soletas* because of their resemblance to linen stocking soles.

LOVE IN PIECES (BRAZILIAN)
Amor en Pedaços

½ cup sugar   8 tablespoons rice flour
¼ cup butter   2 egg whites
5 eggs   2 tablespoons sugar
                ½ cup chopped almonds

Cream sugar and butter. Beat in 1 egg and 2 tablespoons rice flour. Beat in another egg and 2 tablespoons flour. Repeat twice more, until all rice flour has been used, then add last egg and beat thoroughly. Bake in greased shallow pan. When done cover with a meringue made with egg whites and sugar. Sprinkle with almonds and bake a delicate brown. Cut into squares or break into small pieces.

Playful names, such as "Love in Pieces" and "Little Mother-in-Law Kisses" Brazilians bestow on their many light sweets, and thus increase their appeal to both imagination and appetite. Most of them are of Portuguese origin.

SIGHS
Suspiros

2 cups granulated sugar
¾ cup water
4 egg whites
1 pound almonds, blanched
Grated rind ½ lemon

Boil sugar and water until it forms a soft ball in cold water. Beat egg whites until stiff but not dry, and beat syrup slowly into them. Fold in blanched almonds, cut lengthwise into fine strips. Mix in grated lemon rind. Drop by teaspoonful, not too closely together, on a baking sheet covered with oiled paper. Bake in a moderate oven, 350°, until delicately browned.

GYPSY'S EMBRACE
Brazo de Gitano

3 eggs
½ cup granulated sugar
Grated rind 1 lemon
½ cup flour
Cinnamon
Powdered sugar

Beat egg yolks until thick and lemon colored. Gradually beat in sifted sugar and grated rind. Beat egg whites until stiff but not dry. Fold ½ of them into mixture, then ½ of the sifted flour. Continue alternating until both are used. Pour into a greased shallow pan and bake in a moderately hot oven, 375°, about 25 minutes. Sprinkle with cinnamon when done. Cool; spread with Spanish Cream Filling and roll as for jelly roll. Dust with powdered sugar.

SPANISH CREAM FILLING
Crema Española

1 cup milk
1-inch stick cinnamon, crushed
1 teaspoon lemon rind, grated
¾ cup granulated sugar
⅛ teaspoon salt
¼ cup flour
2 tablespoons butter
4 egg yolks

Bring milk with cinnamon and lemon rind slowly to boiling point and strain. Mix sugar with salt and flour and add strained milk gradually. Cook 15 minutes in double boiler, stirring constantly while mixture thickens, then occasionally. Add butter and egg yolks, well beaten, and cook 2 or 3 minutes longer. Cool and use.

SPANISH CREAM PUFFS
Hinchares

1 cup water	4 tablespoons granulated
¼ cup butter	sugar
1¼ cups flour	3 eggs, unbeaten
Cooking fat	

Put water into saucepan with butter and sugar. Bring to boiling point and stir flour briskly until you make a smooth paste. Remove from fire and stir a few seconds longer until dough forms a ball and does not stick to pan. Let it stand 2 or 3 minutes, then stir in, with a wooden spoon, one egg at a time, until all are used. Have ready a kettle of hot oil or lard. When it is almost smoking hot drop the mixture in by the spoonful, but only a few at a time to allow for swelling. Fry, not too quickly, until they are brown all over and twice their original size. Take out with skimmer. Drain on brown paper. Open at one side and fill with sweetened whipped cream or any preferred filling. Sprinkle liberally with icing sugar.

To bake: Let dough stand ½ hour. Stir a little and drop by tablespoons on buttered pans, about 2 inches apart each way. Bake 15–20 minutes in a moderately hot oven, 375°, being careful that they do not burn.

SWEETS OF PARADISE
Dulce del Paraiso

½ cup almonds and filbert nuts	4 eggs, well beaten
1 cup granulated sugar	12 ladyfingers
2 tablespoons cornstarch	Flower or fruit syrup
1 quart milk	Powdered sugar
	Cinnamon

Grind almonds and filberts to a fine meal. Mix with sugar and cornstarch and stir in the milk and eggs thoroughly. Cook over boiling water, stirring mixture continually, until a bubble forms on top. Have the ladyfingers, previously soaked in a fruit or flower syrup, arranged in a serving dish. Pour cooked mixture over them. Powder with sugar and cinnamon on top and decorate with the fresh fruit or flowers the syrup is flavored with.

ALMOND STRAWS
Pallitos de Almendras

3 cups flour	2 tablespoons butter
½ teaspoon salt	2 cups blanched almonds
1 teaspoon baking powder	6 eggs
1¼ cups sugar	1 tablespoon anis liqueur

Sift flour, salt and baking powder together. Add sugar, butter and eggs. Flavor and work to a smooth dough. Roll out and cut in long, thin, strawlike shapes. Brush with egg yolk saved out for that purpose, and sprinkle with chopped almonds. Bake in moderate oven, 350°.

CHRISTMAS TARTS
Tortas Finas de Navidad

1 cup olive oil	Cake flour
½ cup brandy	Sifted powdered sugar

Combine oil and brandy in a mixing bowl and add enough flour to make a firm dough. Roll out ¼ inch thick and put in small forms lined with oiled paper. Bake in moderately hot oven, 375°. Powder thickly with sugar when done. Grated sweet chocolate or finely powdered hard candies may be used in place of sugar. (From the Spanish section of *The European Cookbook* by the Browns.)

TARTS IN NESTS
Tortas de Camadas

2 cups butter
2 cups granulated sugar
2 egg yolks, beaten until thick

1 teaspoon vanilla
1 cup almond meal
½ cup brandy
3 cups sifted flour

2 egg whites, beaten to a stiff froth

Cream butter and sugar. Add beaten egg yolks, vanilla, almond meal and brandy. Stir in flour and beat thoroughly. Fold in beaten whites last. Put in small buttered, narrow forms and bake in moderate oven, 350°. Brush over tarts with Syrup of Granada. Pile in layers of 3, with marmalade or chopped almonds, filberts or pine nuts mixed with icing between.

SYRUP OF GRANADA
Almibar de Granada

Remove skin from half a dozen blushing pomegranates. Break sections apart and extract the ruby juice without crushing the seeds, which would embitter everything. The best way is to bruise the pips lightly. Cover with water and heat until juice runs out. Then strain through cheesecloth, and to each cup of juice add 2 cups of sugar. Cook to a rather thick syrup, but remove before it reaches the soft-ball stage, and skim it religiously.

Serve with puddings, or pour over small cakes like Tarts in Nests.

GUATEMALAN CHEESECAKES
Quesadillas de Guatemala

½ pound rice flour
1 cup sugar
1 cup butter

1 whole egg
7 egg whites
9 egg yolks

Sift together rice flour and sugar. Work in butter and whole egg, then beat until bubbles form. Beat egg whites until stiff but not firm. Beat egg yolks until thick. Mix together and cut into the dough, mixing as lightly as possible. Place in little paper forms or in lined gem pans and bake in a moderate oven.

CHILEAN CREAM TURNOVERS
Empanaditas de Crema

Mix 1 beaten egg yolk, 1 cup warmed milk, 2 tablespoons melted fat and ¼ teaspoon salt with enough flour to make a stiff dough. Knead until smooth. Roll out very thin and cut in rounds, 3 inches in diameter.

Make filling as follows: Add 3 tablespoons sugar to ½ cup scalded milk. Pour over 3 slightly beaten egg yolks. Add ½ teaspoon vanilla and cook in double boiler until thickened, but not long enough for eggs to curdle. Lay a portion of filling in each round of dough. Fold; pinch edges securely together. Fry in deep fat. Drain on paper and sprinkle with sugar.

It is interesting to note the resemblance between these turnovers and the classic North American chess pies which are also of Spanish origin.

ECUADORIAN LEMON PANCAKES

1 cup flour	Salt
2 eggs	Browned butter
1 teaspoon sugar	Lemons, in quarters

Add water to flour, eggs, sugar and salt to make thin batter. Butter a large frying pan and cover bottom with batter to make a wide, thin pancake which is served covered with browned butter and quarters of lemon for flavoring to taste, with or without sugar.

COSTA RICAN BAPTISMAL CAKES
Manon del Bautismo

½ pound cornstarch	¼ teaspoon cinnamon
¾ cup sugar	6 egg yolks
	6 egg whites

Sift together cornstarch, sugar and cinnamon. Beat egg yolks until thick and egg whites until stiff and mix together. Add dry ingredients to egg mixture a little at a time. Place in small buttered tins and bake 30 minutes in moderate oven.

These cakes are eaten with hot chocolate at baptismal functions in Costa Rica and other Central American republics, as well as in Mexico. The name *Manon* suggests that they are considered celestial manna.

BUÑUELOS AND FRITTERS

Buñuelos

The *buñuelo* has such a wide range of interpretations in Spanish-speaking countries that the foreign traveler shopping in bakeries and ordering from menus is completely confused after a time, for enough *buñuelo* recipes could be assembled between the Rio Grande and Tierra del Fuego to fill a small cookbook, especially if one includes the *bolinhas* of Brazil which are sisters under their crusts, but with Portuguese names. Mexico alone has over forty varieties, many of them without duplicates in the other republic. A number come directly from Spain, especially the round unsweetened "puffs of wind" called *Buñuelos de Viento* made of cream-puff dough (See recipe.), and also several kinds of doughnuts—nuts of dough, to use the old English phrase—always associated with fiestas in Spain when these *buñuelos* are both fried and sold in the streets.

Mexico has a similar holiday custom, but the bits of *buñuelo* dough that hop into the hot deep fat are often as thin as paper, and the resulting cakes that look something like cookies are so crisp they melt on the tongue, leaving mostly the taste of the sugar and cinnamon with which they were sprinkled after they were done. Most of the Latin republics have *buñuelos de arroz, buñuelos de papas* and *buñuelos de pan* which are, respectively, our familiar rice cakes, mashed potato cakes and a similar cake made of bread crumbs massed together with beaten egg.

BUÑUELOS DE VIENTO

2 cups flour
Cold water
½ teaspoon salt
½ cup olive oil or fat

2 egg yolks, well beaten
1 whole egg, well beaten
1 tablespoon orange flower
    water

Deep fat

Mix flour with salt and enough cold water to make a stiff dough. Knead; place in a bowl. Cover with a napkin and let stand at least ½ hour. Warm oil over low heat. Add dough and mix quickly and thoroughly, beating vigorously and being careful not to scorch. When cool work in egg yolks and whole egg, 1 at a time, along with the orange flower water. Knead dough, which should be very stiff, until it is smooth and satiny. Mold into small balls and fry in deep fat. Drain on paper.

These *buñuelos* may be simply sprinkled thickly with powdered sugar, but the favored way is to roll them in thick sugar syrup flavored with wine or with orange flower water, and then sprinkle them with powdered sugar mixed with finely chopped almonds.

MEXICAN BUÑUELOS

The following recipe is for a popular kind sold in the streets in Mexico during the Week of All Saints:

Sift 3 cups flour with 3 tablespoons sugar and ½ teaspoon salt. Beat whites and yolks of 4 eggs separately until very light. Then mix them together and add the dry ingredients, sprinkling in 3 tablespoons of finely chopped pecan meats. Roll out by hand in finger sizes. Fry in deep fat.

TRANSPARENT BUÑUELOS
Buñuelos Transparentes

5 egg yolks	Melted butter
1 egg white	⅙ pound grated cheese
⅓ pound flour	1 cordial glass anis
1 teaspoon baking powder	(Spanish aniseed liqueur)
¼ teaspoon salt	Butter for frying

Beat yolks and white of egg separately, then put them together. Mix in dry ingredients and enough melted butter so the mixture can be beaten. Beat thoroughly. Don't shirk. Add cheese and anis. Drop batter from a spoon in hot butter and fry golden. Drain on paper and let cool.

Make a sugar syrup deep enough to receive several *buñuelos* at a time. Boil until it threads. Flavor with a pinch of cloves or cinnamon. Drop *buñuelos* in and boil until they look clear. Lay in a dish and pour remaining syrup over them.

SWEET POTATO BUÑUELOS
Buñuelos de Comote

Peel and mash 3 boiled sweet potatoes, removing any fibers. Measure and mix with ½ the quantity of flour and ½ teaspoon of salt. Add well-beaten yolks of 3 eggs. Knead well until the dough clings together and is spongy. Form into balls the size of an egg. Flatten out to the thickness of ¾ of an inch. Fry slowly in butter on both sides and serve with syrup or honey.

LIME BUÑUELOS
Buñuelos de Lima

Mix ½ pound flour with 4 beaten eggs, ⅛ pound butter and the juice of 1 lime. Dissolve a pinch of soda in a tablespoonful of tepid water. Work well into dough. Work and beat dough thoroughly, then cut out small spoonfuls. Place in hot butter in a frying pan, flattening them out a bit with a spoon. Fry on both sides slowly until brown.

YAUTIA FRITTERS

Grate 1 pound of raw yautia. Add 1 unbeaten egg, salt, ½ of a grated lime peel, about 2 ounces of cream cheese and 1 tablespoon sugar. Mix well. Drop by spoonfuls into hot deep fat and fry until light brown.

Serve hot as a garnish around a meat course.

COLOMBIAN BUÑUELOS

1 cup corn meal	4 eggs, well beaten
2 cups thick sour milk	½ teaspoon crushed aniseed
½ teaspoon salt	2 tablespoons fat

Fat for frying

Mix corn meal with sourmilk and salt and beat. Add eggs, aniseed and fat and beat thoroughly. Drop heaping teaspoonfuls into hot lard and fry. Serve with sugar syrup poured over and dropped apple or other fruit sprinkled on top.

Other types of *buñuelos* are made exactly like our fritters. In Cuba, for instance, such fritters are sometimes made of apples imported from the States, but the batter in which the pieces of apple are enclosed is well seasoned with Cuban rum. Santo Domingo has a similar *buñuelo* made with our familiar fritter batter concealing pieces of *mamey*, that big orange-fleshed fruit with a rusty leathery rind that's now shipped to New York markets from the West Indies. Another West Indian specialty in the same form is cheese *buñuelos*.

Then there are all sorts of fancy *buñuelos* that pop up everywhere on special occasions, containing raisins, chopped nuts, etc., etc.

CRILLON SQUASH FRITTERS IN SYRUP
Picarones Pasados en Chancaca

1 pound squash	1 pound flour
1 teaspoon salt	1 tablespoon baking powder

Brown sugar syrup, flavored with cinnamon

Cut squash or sweet pumpkin into thick slices. Cook soft in small amount of boiling salted water and press into a bowl through purée sieve. Add baking powder to flour and sift into squash purée (about 1½ cups), stirring with wooden spoon until dough no longer clings to sides of bowl. Let stand in warm place 2 or 3 hours. When ready to fry pull off small pieces. Roll into strips. Twist them or pinch points into a hoop and fry in deep fat. Drain and dip while hot into syrup.

This is a chef's choice from the many fine native dishes served at the Hotel Crillon in Santiago de Chile. It's as distinctive a sweet as our pumpkin pie and quite as luscious.

ARGENTINE FRITTERS
Soparpillas

3 tablespoons fat
¼ teaspoon salt
Boiling water

1 egg, well beaten
3 cups flour
2 teaspoons baking powder

Put fat and salt into a cup and fill to top with boiling water. Sift flour and baking powder together twice. When first mixture is lukewarm stir in beaten egg and work in flour mixture, kneading to a smooth elastic dough. Roll out thin. Cut in any shape desired and fry in deep hot fat. Drain and powder with sugar.

COLOMBIAN ORANGE PUFFS
Hojuelas de Naranja

½ pound flour
2 tablespoons butter
½ teaspoon salt

2 tablespoons sugar
Juice of 2 oranges
Cold water, if needed

Mix ingredients to a smooth dough. Roll out thin as possible. Cut in any desired shape. Fry in deep fat. Drain and powder with sugar.

SWEET BREADS

PETROPOLIS BREAD
Pão de Petropolis

Mix to a dough 1 small yeast cake, dissolved in a little warm water, with 1 pound flour, 3 tablespoons sugar, 1 teaspoon salt and 1 pint milk. Leave the dough well covered and in a warm place, but not hot, until next day. Then add 1 tablespoon each of butter, lard, sugar and 6 eggs. Knead in sufficient flour to make firm loaves. Let stand in warm place to rise 4–5 hours. Bake in hot oven.

Petropolis is the summer capital of Brazil, named after Peter, the first emperor. It lies in the cool mountains above Rio de Janeiro and was originally the home of many Germans who introduced this delicate sweet bread which is also much esteemed in Rio de Janeiro.

BRAZILIAN BREAD OF THE NORTH
Pão do Norte

1 pound flour	1 tablespoon butter
6 egg yolks, beaten	½ cup lard
6 egg whites, beaten	½ yeast cake
4 tablespoons sugar	1 cup milk

Mix ingredients and knead until dough separates from the mixing bowl. Put into greased bread pan, and when it has risen bake in hot oven, 400°.

Although there are several such fine sweetish breads in different localities, Brazilians regard them more as cakes. Relatively little loaf bread, as we know it, is eaten in Brazil. Either rolls or long, crusty French "flutes" are provided for breakfast coffee and sandwiches, but manioc meal is commonly sprinkled on the national dish of beans and rice, and that supplies almost enough starch.

(For Sweet Tortillas see Dessert Tortillas.)

WEST INDIAN CASSAVA CAKES

2 cups cassava meal	1 tablespoon butter
½ teaspoon salt	1 tablespoon sugar
¾–1 cup milk	2 eggs, well beaten

Mix meal with salt and then with milk and let stand until softened. Cream butter with sugar. Add eggs and mix with beater. Spread in buttered baking sheet and bake in moderate oven.

Leftover cassava cakes are made into bread pudding by pouring custard over them, topping with a blanket of freshly grated coconut and baking until custard sets. A meringue may be added or not after pudding is done.

GILDED SLICES
Fatias Douradas

Remove crust from bread 2 days old. Dip slices quickly into wine. Drain and dip into egg yolk beaten with a little cold water. Drain again and fry a rich brown in sweet butter. Sprinkle powdered sugar and cinnamon over slices and serve hot.

This is a more exciting matter than the similar French Toast because the bread is dipped in wine instead of milk.

BRAZILIAN SWEETS

ALMOND CAKE
Bolo com Amendõas

6 egg yolks	1 cup granulated sugar
1 cup blanched almonds, ground	Juice of 4 oranges
	6 egg whites
1 teaspoon grated orange rind	¼ pound potato flour
	Apricot jam
Orange icing	

Beat egg yolks with sugar until light and creamy. Add ground almonds, orange rind and juice. Beat egg whites to a stiff froth and beat in, alternately with potato flour. Pour mixture about 1 inch thick into a greased and floured baking sheet. Bake in moderate oven, 350°. When cool cover with a thin layer of apricot jam and ice with orange-flavored icing.

CAKES TO EAT WITH WINE
Bolo para Vinho

½ cup butter	9 egg yolks
1 cup granulated sugar	5 egg whites
2 cups cake flour, sifted 4 times	1 teaspoon grated orange rind
A pinch of cinnamon	

Cream butter and sugar. Add egg yolks and beat until all are light and creamy. Beat egg whites until stiff but not dry and add to batter, a little at a time, continually beating. Add flour gradually, also the cinnamon and orange rind. Butter a shallow baking tin. Line bottom with oiled paper. Put in batter and bake in moderate oven, 350°. When cold slice cake and toast slices on both sides. Serve cold.

FRIED CREAM
Torrijas de Nata

3 egg yolks	Butter
1 cup whipping cream	Powdered sugar
1 whole egg, beaten	Cinnamon

Beat egg yolks lightly and whip into cream. Spread not more than ½ inch thick in a greased pan. Place over a very low flame and cook slowly. Cool and cut in small pieces. Take up with spatula. Brush lightly with beaten egg and fry in butter. Sprinkle with powdered sugar and cinnamon. Serve hot.

Brazilian desserts are seldom the feature of the meal, because sweets are not craved after copious wining and dining; so a plain pudding or caramel custard is the standard *sobremesa*, or fruits and cheese.

MAIDEN'S KISSES
Beijinhos de Moça

2½ cups granulated sugar	3 egg yolks, well beaten
¾ cup water	1 cup grated cheese
½ coconut, freshly grated	Flour

Cook sugar with water until it forms a firm ball in cold water. Remove from fire. Add coconut and cool. Mix in beaten yolks. Return to fire and stir until mixture begins to boil. Turn into a bowl and leave until following day. Mix in grated cheese and sufficient flour to make a paste. Put in buttered patty pans or small forms and bake in moderately hot oven, 375°.

TINDERBOXES
Petiscos

1 cup grated hard cheese	½ cup granulated sugar
1 tablespoon butter	12 egg yolks
½ cup flour	Juice of 1 lemon

Mix all ingredients thoroughly together. When they are well blended put in small oblong forms, the size and shape of tinder-boxes, from which this old reliable recipe gets its name. Bake about 10 minutes in hot oven, 400°.

DREAMS
Sonhos

1 cup hot milk	1 cup flour
A few grains salt	4 eggs
1 tablespoon granulated	Powdered sugar
sugar	Cinnamon

Bring milk, salt and sugar to boiling point. Drop in flour all at once and stir vigorously until dough is a smooth ball in pan. Remove from fire and add eggs, 1 at a time, beating thoroughly after each addition. Drop mixture by dessert spoonfuls into deep hot fat, a few at a time. Take out when a rich brown. Drain and sprinkle with powdered sugar and cinnamon.

These puffs are served with coffee, that is, Brazilian coffee, as rich and heavy as a liqueur.

HEAVENLY "BACON"

12 egg yolks	2 tablespoons caramel
3 cups granulated sugar	1 inch stick cinnamon
2 cups water	2–3 strips lemon rind

Beat egg yolks until thick and lemon colored. Grease a pudding dish with sweet butter and pour in mixture. Place in steamer over hot water and cook gently until eggs are jelly-like, but firm. Remove. Let cool, then cut in slices. Mix sugar, water and caramel in saucepan. Add cinnamon and lemon rind. Place over fire and boil 5 minutes. Put in egg slices. Let simmer until slices are well soaked. Then remove and arrange them on a dessert plate. Remove cinnamon and lemon and pour syrup over. Serve cold.

The pet name of this popular sweet, *Toucinho do Ceo*, translates literally "Bacon of Heaven," and heavenly bacon means much to a Portuguese or Brazilian, for it is his favorite seasoning and goes into all stews. Bacon to him symbolizes good living, the fat of the land. (From the Portuguese section of *The European Cookbook*, by the Browns.

A lady who eats enough of these will doubtless be rewarded with one of the highest of Brazilian compliments: "A Senhora e sempre mais gorda e bonita."—"Your ladyship is always fatter and prettier." Fat and beauty are synonymous when it comes to judging feminine pulchritude in Brazil.

BLESSED MOTHERS
Mãe Bentos

A scant cup butter   ½ cup coconut milk
A scant cup sugar   2 cups rice flour (about)
6 egg yolks, beaten thick   3 egg whites, beaten stiff
            ½ cup grated coconut

Grate ½ of a fresh coconut. Reserve ½ cup of gratings. Add 2–3 tablespoons of water to remainder. Place over slow fire. Stir continually until hot and press out milk at once through a firm cloth. Cream butter and sugar. Add beaten egg yolks. Continue beating and add coconut milk and rice flour. Beat 5 minutes. Fold in beaten whites and lastly the grated coconut. Bake in paper forms in hot oven, 400°. When cakes start to rise (about 6 minutes) open oven door for 1 minute. This will cause them to crack in center. Repeat process once before tops brown. The expert will have 2 cracks in shape of a cross on her cakes, hence the holy name. The forms are usually lined with banana leaf to impart its slight flavor while baking.

KISSES OF THE FARMER'S DAUGHTER
Beijos de Cabocla

Grate 1 large fresh coconut finely. Put gratings in a cloth and squeeze out all of the milk and save. Prepare a syrup with

1½ cups sugar and ½ cup water. Boil until it threads from spoon. Let cool a little, then stir in 6 tablespoons sweet butter, 4 tablespoons flour, 6 beaten egg whites. Add coconut milk and beat thoroughly. Place in small buttered pans and bake in moderate oven.

This only goes to show that the kisses of a farmer's daughter in Brazil are quite as sweet as anywhere else.

BRAZILIAN LONGINGS
Saudades

Lightly beat 5 egg yolks with 1 cup sugar and knead in enough sifted *polvinho* to mold into small balls. Place these on an oiled board and bake until dry in a cool oven.

Saudades is a word often heard in Brazil. It covers a whole lot of emotions, all the way from homesickness to a vague longing for sweets like these.

EYE OF THE MOTHER–IN–LAW
Olha de Sogra

Large prunes, pitted   Confectioners' sugar
Eggs, separated   Flavoring

Beat egg yolks with sufficient confectioners' sugar to mold into small balls for "eye" pupils. Add flavoring to egg whites and mix with sufficient sugar to mold into almond shapes for whites of "eye." The eyes are molded and inserted into the prunes quite realistically.

This Brazilian specialty is popular in all the sweetshops where large families, including mothers-in-law, gather for afternoon tea. The yellow pupil of the eye gives it a droll, jaundiced leer which, happily, does not detract from its edibility.

LITTLE MOTHER–IN–LAW KISSES
Beijinhos de Ya-ya

Beat 2 eggs with 1 cup sugar until creamy. Add 1 teaspoon lemon juice and beat 2 minutes. Sprinkle 1 cup freshly grated coconut with 1 tablespoon flour and 1 teaspoon grated lemon rind. Add to mixture and beat until well blended. Use 2 tablespoons to shape and drop little eggs of the mixture on a buttered cookie tin. Bake light yellow in moderate oven.

Ya-ya is an effectionate term for mother-in-law that's much less formal than *sogra*.

These Little Mother-in-Law Kisses give us a chance to carry out the biblical admonition to Ruth: "Go not empty unto thy mother-in-law."

SWEET GIRL
Moça Doce

2 cups manioc meal	1 cup ground peanuts
1 cup rice flour	2 cups brown sugar

Eggs

Mix meal and flour together. Take 1½ cups of mixture and mix well with finely ground peanuts.

Make a thick hot syrup of brown sugar and add ½ of it to remaining 1½ cups of the meal-flour mixture, stirring to a paste. When cold add to nut mixture. Drop in as many eggs as are necessary to moisten for molding into loaves. Bake in moderate oven. While loaves are still warm cover with remaining ½ of the brown sugar syrup.

Alzira, a beautiful Brazilian lady who cooked for us for a year in Rio de Janeiro, gave us this recipe from memory, but instead of cup measurements she used plates—2 plates of manioc meal, 1 plate of peanuts, etc. Cups, of course, outside of the common white china demitasse, are little used in this coffee country where tea is considered a medicine and never drunk for pleasure. So with nothing more practical than a half-size coffee cup or an off-size teacup the best standard measurement is a dinner plate, and no cook would think of specifying whether it be level or full, since her own eye is the best judge of all such matters.

SPONGECAKE
Pão de Lo

This cake is as popular in Brazil as it is in the United States, both countries having borrowed it from Europe.

PIO NONOS

These are slices of freshly made spongecake spread with Brazilian *guava* or quince paste and heavily powdered with sugar. Named "Pious Ninths" in honor of some religious feast.

DESSERTS, FRUITS AND NUTS

RICE DESSERT
Dulce de Arroz

Wash 1 cup of rice through several waters and soak 3 hours in 1½ pints milk, seasoned with scant teaspoon of salt. Heat in double boiler until rice is nearly soft, then add ½ cup sugar with ½ cup ground almonds and carefully stir in the beaten yolks of 2 eggs. Cook about 15 minutes more but do not allow rice to become mushy. Turn out in glass dish. Sprinkle with cinnamon and serve cold.

BIEN–ME–SABE

Since *bien me sabe* translates into English "I know it well," the name may be applied to any cook's most familiar dishes. Actually it is restricted to simple sweets in an array that is confusing to the foreigner who never savvys just what he is going to get when he orders *Bien-Me-Sabe* from a menu. It may turn out to be some species of *dulce de leche* to spread over a slice of cake, or a sticky coconut custard, a cornstarch pudding, maybe even a tamale with something like marzipan in the center of it, just to mention a few of the chances he takes according to the hostelry and the country he happens to be in. Of a score or more recipes the following serves as a sample:

BIEN–ME–SABE OF YELLOW SWEET POTATO
Bien-Me-Sabe de Camote Amarillo

1 quart milk, scalded	1 medium sweet potato,
4 teaspoons rice	grated
2 tablespoons cornstarch	6 almonds, blanched, peeled
2 cups sugar	and pounded

¼ teaspoon salt

Cook rice in milk until very soft. Mix cornstarch, sugar and salt and stir into rice gradually. Add sweet potato and almonds and simmer, stirring constantly, until quite thick.

ECUADORIAN BLANCMANGE
Manjar Blanco

3 cups milk	1 tablespoon cornstarch
1 cup sugar	¼ teaspoon salt
	1 teaspoon vanilla

Mix all ingredients except vanilla. Stir until sugar dissolves. Cook 15 minutes in double boiler while continuously stirring. Add vanilla and serve.

This is really a dessert cream and is served as such, eaten with or spread on crackers or cake.

BOLIVIAN BLANCMANGE

Put 1 quart of milk with a stick of cinnamon into saucepan. Slowly bring to boiling point and stir in 2 cups sugar. Cook slowly, stirring continuously with a wooden spoon until mixture will "hair" from spoon. Then remove at once. It will harden when cool and is not unlike fudge.

All sorts of similar creams, custards and flans are favored desserts throughout Latin America. Blancmange is French, of course, for "white food," and the Brazilians have a specialty they call simply:

BRAZILIAN FOOD
Manjar a Brazileira

Sift together 1½ cups rice flour, 1 cup sugar and ½ teaspoon salt. Stir into 1 quart scalded milk and cook 20 minutes in double boiler. Butter a pudding dish and fill it with oval spoonfuls of the rice and milk mixture. Brown well in oven. Sprinkle with powdered sugar and cinnamon and serve.

CHILEAN YELLOW FOOD
Manjar Amarillo

1 tablespoon gelatine
1 cup water
Juice of 1 orange

Juice of 1 lemon
2 egg yolks, well beaten
Sugar to taste

Soften gelatine in cold water. Add everything else. Strain into double boiler and stir mixture until hot. Let it cool. Turn into mold and keep on ice until needed.

SPANISH CREAM
Crema Española

2 tablespoons gelatine
1 quart milk
3 egg yolks

6 tablespoons sugar
3 egg whites
1 tablespoon vanilla

Stir gelatine in milk and cook until dissolved. Beat egg yolks with 3 tablespoons sugar and add. Stir well and bring to boiling point. Beat whites with remaining 3 tablespoons sugar. Pour boiling milk mixture over them. Beat briskly and thoroughly. Turn out into large mold or individual cups and serve ice cold.

COLOMBIAN QUIMBO EGGS

Beat 6 egg yolks stiff. Put in buttered baking dish and cook 30 minutes in medium oven. Let cool. Cut into fancy shapes. Cover with 2 cups thin sugar syrup and let stand 6–8 hours before serving.

This is a sort of *baba au rhum* without the rum, and there would be no harm in adding a little of that to flavor the syrup. The name comes from Quimbaya, an extinct tribe of Colombian Indians who were skilled workers in gold.

BRAZILIAN CUSTARD
Caramela

3 cups milk   6 tablespoons sugar
6 egg yolks   ¼ teaspoon salt

Mix together milk, eggs, 2 tablespoons sugar and salt, and strain. Use 12 small metal custard cups, each easily accommodating ⅓ cup liquid. Place 1 teaspoon sugar in each cup and heat until sugar caramels, being careful it does not burn. Let cool. Pour ⅓ cup custard mixture into each cup. Set cups into pan of hot water and bake in moderate oven until firm. Test by inserting silver knife previously wet in cold water. If it comes out clean the custard is done. Do not overbake. Remove cups and cool.

When unmolded the liquefied caramel will run over custard in a brown sauce.

The same recipe is made in one large mold, and bits of vanilla bean are often added for flavoring.

Caramela, made according to this old French recipe, is one of Brazil's most popular desserts and appears as often on the family table as do pies in the United States, besides being sold in every *leiteria* (milk shop) where busy folk drop in for a quick snack of one of these little custards and a glass of milk, much as we stop at a soda fountain.

CUBAN MAJARETE
Green Corn Dessert

1 dozen ears green corn   2 sticks cinnamon
4 cups milk   ¼ teaspoon salt
2 cups sugar   Ground cinnamon

Grate well-developed, slightly hardened corn. Mix with milk, sugar, stick cinnamon and salt and stir over low heat until a thick mush is formed. Turn out into a shallow mold. Sprinkle with powdered cinnamon and let stand until cold. Eat like blancmange.

ARGENTINE DULCE DE LECHE

3 quarts milk   2 pounds sugar
2-inch length of vanilla bean

Cook ingredients together rather rapidly, stirring occasionally to prevent scorching, until mixture begins to thicken. Then reduce heat and stir continuously until a spoonful dropped into cold water forms a very soft ball. Add a good dash of hot water. Remove from heat and stir vigorously while *dulce* is cooling. Cooking time is about 1½ hours. When cold use as a sauce over puddings, as a spread on cake or bread, or just eat plain with a spoon.

Dulce de Leche is always on hand in the Argentine household, since a considerable quantity is made at one time and it keeps indefinitely. The faintly grainy but fluid consistency suits it to many purposes, and its use is so much a habit in this cattle and dairy country that it is now put up commercially in tins. The flavor is occasionally varied by the addition of cinnamon, lemon peel or ground almonds.

SWEET–POTATO PONE

4 cups sweet potatoes, peeled and grated
2¼ cups West Indian molasses
1½ cups butter, softened
¾ cup preserved ginger

¾ cup preserved orange peel
¾ teaspoon salt
¾ teaspoon preserved ginger
2 teaspoons cinnamon
1 teaspoon cloves
1 teaspoon mace

Have butter softened but not melted. Chop preserved orange peel and ginger very fine. Mix and beat ingredients until thoroughly blended. Pour into greased pan and bake in moderately hot oven, 375°, until an inserted broomcorn will come out clean.

PUERTO RICAN SWEET–POTATO SOUFFLÉ

Peel, boil and mash 1 pound of sweet potatoes. Cut 6 marsh-mallows in pieces and add to the hot mashed potatoes. Add a little milk, butter and cinnamon. Put in a casserole. Cut up a few marshmallows over the top and bake in the oven until brown.

The influence of the United States in Puerto Rican cooking is evidenced in the adoption of such specialties as marshmallows and "American" cheese, which are not so common in the cuisine of countries farther south.

SWEET–POTATO SWEET
Dulce de Camote

2 cups mashed sweet potatoes	½ teaspoon salt
	2 cups brown sugar
1 cup grated pineapple, with juice	¼ teaspoon cream of tartar
	⅔ cup hot water
1 cup nutmeats	

Select yellow sweet potatoes, or yams. Boil in jackets. Peel and mash while hot. Let partially cool and mix with pineapple. Add 4–5 tablespoons warm water. Put over slow fire and sim-mer, stirring continuously until somewhat thickened. Dissolve salt, sugar and cream of tartar in water. Add to mixture and cook until it will form a soft ball when dropped in cold water. Remove and beat like fudge. Add nutmeats just before drop-ping by spoonfuls on a buttered platter.

A cheap and popular sweet in many parts of South America.

WEST INDIAN SWEET–POTATO CAKES

1 pound sweet potatoes	1 cup milk
2 eggs	2 tablespoons butter
1 cup sugar	Nutmeg
	Cinnamon

Grate raw sweet potatoes. Mix with eggs, sugar, milk, butter, a little grated nutmeg and powdered cinnamon. Fry in hot butter or lard and serve as a sweet after dusting well with sugar and cinnamon.

HAITIAN SWEET–POTATO "BREAD"
Pain Patate

12 medium-sized sweet
  potatoes
2 ripe bananas, crushed
2 cups very hot milk
1 tablespoon butter
1 tablespoon lard

1 teaspoon olive oil
2 cups syrup
Cinnamon
Nutmeg
A pinch of black pepper and
  salt

½ teaspoon vanilla

Wash, peel and grate sweet potatoes. Add crushed bananas, hot milk, butter, lard, olive oil, syrup, spices, vanilla. Grease a pan well. Pour in mixture. Bake in moderate oven. Stick in a knife, and when it comes out clean your cakelike "bread" is done, with a golden crust on top.

This sweet may be served hot or cold, with or without rum sauce.

Haitians use a very sweet pure-cane syrup. If maple syrup is substituted perhaps more syrup should be used since it is not so sweet.

WEST INDIAN YAM PUDDING

3 cups mashed yams
2 tablespoons melted butter
2 eggs, well beaten
¼ cup milk

¼ teaspoon salt
¼ teaspoon cinnamon
¼ teaspoon nutmeg
1 teaspoon rose water

¼ cup sugar

Have yams freshly boiled and hot. Mash and add remaining ingredients, reserving 1 tablespoon sugar. Place in buttered baking dish. Sprinkle reserved sugar on top and brown in oven.

ICE CREAMS

BRAZILIAN COCONUT ICE CREAM
Coco Gelado

1 ripe coconut	1 tablespoon flour
3 cups milk	¼ teaspoon salt
¾ cups sugar	3 egg yolks, slightly beaten
1 cup whipped cream	

Open coconut as directed under recipe for Coconut Cream, saving coconut water. Place grated coconut in top of double boiler. Add milk and warm over low heat until just hot enough to handle. Strain through strong thin cloth and wring grated coconut until it is dry as sawdust. Return liquid to pan, adding reserved coconut water, and heat to near boiling point. Sift sugar, flour and salt together. Add hot-milk mixture, stirring constantly. Cook and stir over boiling water 10 minutes. Pour hot mixture over egg yolks. Cool and chill. Freeze. When mixture begins to congeal stir in whipped cream and finish freezing.

BRAZILIAN AVOCADO ICE CREAM
Gelado do Abacate

3 pints milk	½ pint cream
1 cup sugar	3 ripe avocados
1 tablespoon cornstarch	Juice of 1 lime, or ½ lemon
3 eggs	4 tablespoons sugar

Cook milk and sugar together to boiling point. Add cornstarch dissolved in a little water. Boil 3 minutes, stirring constantly, then remove from heat and let stand 3 minutes.

Beat eggs slightly. Pour milk mixture over them, beating steadily, and let cool. Then add cream and the pulp of ripe avocados mashed to a smooth, velvety cream with lime juice and powdered sugar. Stir thoroughly and freeze.

This makes an ideal dessert in any man's land.

Besides Avocado Ice Cream, Pineapple Ice is another Brazilian cooler that's in demand both day and night. The nights of Rio de Janeiro are made melodious by street vendors of it singing "¡*Abacaxi!* ¡Aaa-baaaa-caaaa-she! ¡A-backa-she!" And this is reminiscent of the hot-tamale sellers whose musical cries are heard at midnight in every Mexican border town.

HAITIAN PAPAYA ICE CREAM

Press papaya flesh through sieve and to the juice add small pieces of very ripe papaya and a few crushed papaya seeds. Make as you would peach ice cream, which it somewhat resembles, although it has a tang of its own and a "fainty" flavor of pepsin from the seeds. West Indians are so accustomed to full-flavored tropical fruits that on the English-speaking islands they've coined the word "fainty" to cover those of faint flavor.

DOMINICAN COCONUT ICE CREAM

Crack open a couple of coconuts and grate the flesh fresh. Scald 3 cups milk in double boiler and stir in coconut. Keep stirring without flagging for fully half an hour, then add sugar to taste. Stir some more. Remove from heat and let cool. Strain through linen and squeeze as in making coconut "milk." Freeze like any ice cream.

CUBAN BANANA ICE CREAM

Pour 1 cup powdered sugar over half a dozen bananas, thinly sliced, and set aside for 30 minutes. Then dissolve sugar with 1 quart water. Add grated peel of ½ lemon and freeze.

ORGEAT ICE
Horchata Nevada, or Helado de Horchata

Grind in a mortar or pound together 1 cup melon or cantaloupe seeds and ½ cup almonds, skins and all, adding a little water occasionally to prevent oiling. When ground very fine stir in 3 pints water. Strain through cloth and squeeze out all milky juice. Add ¼ cup sugar and a little grated lemon peel. Stir well and let infuse ½ hour. Then freeze.

ICE OF THE FOUR SEEDS
Helado de las Cuatro Simientes

Grind in a mortar or pound together ⅔ cup sweet almonds and ¼ cup each of cantaloupe, watermelon, squash and cucumber seeds (shells of seeds and skins of almonds included). Add a little water occasionally to keep nuts from oiling. When ground very fine stir in 1 quart water. Strain through cloth and squeeze out all milky juice. Add ⅔ cup sugar and a little lemon peel. Stir well. Let stand ½ hour. Stir again and freeze.

These *helados* (ices) might also be called *sorbetes* (sherbets), and both words are used for ice cream as well.

COCONUT SPECIALTIES

MILK OF COCONUT

By milk of coconut Latin Americans mean the milky colored liquid that can be expressed from the coconut meat, and not, of course, the coconut water. It is prepared as follows: The coconut is first grated on the finest grater. The gratings are then spread in a shallow pan, sprinkled with a bit of the water from inside the coconut, and set in a warm, not hot, oven for a few moments to loosen up the oils of the nut. It must by no means become hot, only slightly warmed. It is then put in a strong, loose-woven cloth and wrung hard over a dish until all the milk is wrung out. What remains in the cloth resembles dry sawdust and is thrown away.

A less effective but sometimes necessary method of producing the coco milk called for in so many tropical recipes is used only where whole coconuts aren't to be had: Place in a deep bowl a cupful of prepared and grated coconut from a package. Pour over it 1 cup boiling water. Cover with a plate and let cool. Then place in a cloth and wring as you would fresh coconut.

COCONUT DESSERT
Postre de Coco

2 cups sugar
1 cup water
Juice of 1 lemon
1 fresh coconut, grated
4 egg yolks, beaten

½ cup seeded raisins, previously soaked and seeded
4 egg whites, beaten stiff with 2 tablespoons sugar
½ teaspoon vanilla

Boil sugar and water until it threads. Add lemon juice and grated coconut. Cook gently 15 minutes and remove from heat. Slowly stir in beaten egg yolks, keeping mixture creamy, and add raisins. Put in buttered baking dish. Cover with meringue made with egg whites, sugar and vanilla. Put in oven until meringue is a golden brown.

BRAZILIAN COCONUT CREAM
Creme de Coco

1 ripe coconut
Milk (about 1 pint)

3 tablespoons cornstarch
2 tablespoons sugar

Select a heavy ripe coconut, shaking it to make sure it is full of liquid. Punch open two of the eyes with an ice pick to let in air so liquid will flow. Pour liquid out into a dish and reserve it. Split nut by inserting a dull butcher knife into an open eye and tapping with a hammer. Break into pieces of convenient size and pry meat away from shell. Pare off brown skin.

Grate coconut meat on fine grater. Spread in baking pan. Sprinkle with a little of the reserved coconut liquid and warm in open oven. Then place in strong cloth and wring until no "milk" is left in grated meat. Save every drop of this "milk" and add to coconut liquid. Measure out enough cow's milk to make 1 quart with coconut liquid, keeping cow's milk separate. Heat cow's milk to boiling point. Work cornstarch smooth in a little water. Add coconut liquid and sugar and stir slowly into hot cow's milk. Let mixture come to boiling point, stirring constantly. Pour into mold previously wet with cold water. Cool and slightly chill. Unmold on platter and serve with cream or cream sauce.

The texture should be very tender, and the flavor is surprisingly delicious if the coconut is ripe.

Brazilians also serve *Creme de Coco* with slightly thickened raspberry or cherry sauce.

BRAZILIAN CHEESE AND COCONUT PUDDING

Drop a dozen egg yolks into 2 cups sugar and mix until sugar melts. Then beat well and add ¼ pound butter, ½ fresh coconut, grated, 1 tablespoon flour, ¼ pound grated cheese, raisins, cinnamon, cloves, citron and a dash of orange flower water. Bake until golden.

BAHIAN COCONUT FOAM
Espumas de Coco Bahianas

6 egg yolks	2 cups boiling milk
4 tablespoons sugar	2 egg whites
½ coconut, grated	2 tablespoons powdered sugar

Beat egg yolks. Add sugar and beat until light. Pour boiling milk over coconut. Let stand until slightly cooled. Strain through cloth and wring dry, saving liquid. Reheat to near boiling point. Combine with egg yolks. Pour into baking dish. Set in pan of hot water and bake in medium oven until firm. Remove from oven and cool. Beat egg whites until stiff but still moist. Beat in powdered sugar gradually until of meringue consistency. Spread over pudding. Set in slow oven, 300°, and bake until lightly browned.

COLOMBIAN COCONUT IN PASTRY SHELLS
Canastas de Coco

Put over heat in double boiler 1 cup milk, ½ cup sugar, 2 tablespoons butter, 3 beaten eggs and 1 peeled and grated coconut. As soon as mixture reaches boiling point stir in 2 tablespoons cornstarch dissolved in a little cold milk and cook until smooth and thickened. Remove from heat. Stir in 1 cup wine and fill mixture into patty shells. Cover with a meringue. Powder with a little cinnamon. Dot center with a candied cherry and brown lightly in oven.

PUERTO RICAN FRESH COCONUT PIE

Filling:

¾ cup sugar	2 egg yolks
3 tablespoons cornstarch	1 teaspoon vanilla
2 cups milk	1 coconut, grated

Peel of 1 lime, cut in 1 piece

Meringue:

2 egg whites	2 tablespoons sugar

Mix sugar and cornstarch. Add milk, egg yolks, grated coconut and lime peel. Cook until mixture thickens. Remove lime peel. Add vanilla and put the filling in a previously baked pie shell.

For the meringue, beat egg whites stiff and beat in sugar. Cover pie with meringue and bake light brown.

Once you've set your teeth in such a fresh pie you'll grate your own coconut forever afterward.

DOMINICAN COCONUT TARTS

2 eggs, slightly beaten	¼ cup sugar
1½ cups scalded milk	½ cup grated coconut
½ cup cottage cheese	Patty shells

Stir milk into eggs. Add cheese, sugar and coconut. Cool and bake in patty shells in medium oven.

Although the usual dessert throughout the West Indies is guava or other fruit paste and cheese, coconut plays a prominent part in the list of sweets which are consumed as confections, rather than desserts. *Dulce de Coco* is a tropical favorite easily made by boiling coarsely shredded coconut in locally made molasses until it takes on a candied consistency.

A similar specialty of the Dominican Republic is *Coconete*—coconut cooked, thickened with flour and sweetened heavily.

"BRAZILIANS"
Brazileiras

2½ cups sugar	1 cup fresh grated coconut
¾ cup water	5 egg yolks
	1 egg white

Cook sugar and water until syrup threads from spoon. Add coconut. Beat egg yolks and white and whip them in. Put over heat and cook slowly until mixture thickens a little. Then remove and let cool. Make into little balls and put into slow oven, 250°, to lightly brown and crisp.

The proof of the national popularity of this sweet lies in its patriotic name, "Brazilians."

CANDIES

COCONUT AND ALMOND CANDY

2 cups sugar	1 cup almonds, chopped
1 cup hot milk	1 small coconut, grated
	6 egg yolks

Mix sugar and hot milk and stir over low heat to boiling point. Add almonds, stirring constantly until mixture thickens but does not reach soft-ball stage. Then add coconut and egg yolks, lightly beaten. Cook gently and stir until mixture is ready to cream. Let stand overnight and mold next day.

PUERTO RICAN FRESH COCONUT CANDY

Coconut, sugar, water.

Remove brown skin from meat of coconut and grate the meat. For each cup of grated coconut use 1 cup of sugar, either brown or white. Add enough water to sugar to melt or partially dissolve it, and let it boil up well. Then add the fresh coconut meat and boil slowly until it is well soaked in the sugar. Take a little out in a bowl. Beat for a few minutes and drop onto buttered paper. If it spreads and looks watery it is not done. It should hold its shape and harden into cakes when properly cooked. Do not try to drop the mass from the kettle but beat a little at a time in a bowl while the kettle is kept on the back of the stove.

BRAZILIAN CHESTNUT SWEET
Doce de Castanhas

Make a plain syrup with 2 cups sugar and put in it as many peeled and blanched chestnuts as it will take care of. Boil until it forms a soft ball in cold water (like fudge), but before it quite reaches this point add beaten yolks of 2 eggs. Sprinkle with cinnamon and serve with cheese.

NOUGAT
Turrón

A Latin-American Christmas specialty is *turrón*, the Spanish nougat made of sugar boiled with honey, beaten light with whipped egg whites, and wonderfully enriched with almonds. Sometimes the almonds are merely blanched and peeled; again they are toasted, or ground to paste, and often used in all three of these forms. After being worked to a smooth and rich nougat the *turrones* are molded—either into balls or bars—and wrapped in paraffin paper to keep them moist and fresh until eaten.

Turrón means Christmas to Spanish-speaking people all over the Americas, just as marzipan does to German-Americans. The original nougat can be bought specially imported from Spain, but it's also made locally with variations to conform with native products. *Turrones* as made in the Mexican state of Oaxaca, for example, include in addition to the traditional imported almonds a number of other nuts, hazel, walnuts and pine nuts, as well as sesame seed (*ajonjoli*).

MEXICAN PANOCHA
Brown-Sugar Candy

½ square unsweetened   1 cup milk
   chocolate   1 tablespoon butter
3 cups dark brown sugar   1 piece vanilla bean
          1½ cups chopped nuts

Melt chocolate and boil with sugar and milk. Add butter and 1-inch length of vanilla bean slit so seeds will drop out. Stir patiently until candy reaches soft-ball stage. Then remove from heat. Add nuts, mixing them in thoroughly and beating until candy begins to harden. Turn out in buttered tin.

Dulce de Panocha is characteristically Mexican, but we sweet-toothed North Americans have taken it over enthusiastically and so much of it is seen in New Orleans, for instance, that many people think it is a Creole confection.

Nut clusters cooked with dark brown sugar also are called *Panocha*, and the above recipe is usually distinguished by the name Maria Luisa. It is made, too, without the chocolate and butter and in that case ½ cup cream is used with ½ cup milk.

TROPICAL FRUITS

Many North Americans have never tasted a really ripe banana, while most people in the West Indies, Central America and tropical South America have never eaten an unripe one.

Once we watched a six-foot stem ripen on a sturdy palm in the back yard down in Petropolis, beneath our own orchids, vine and fig tree. The green fruit plumped out day by day and became more yellow. We were only waiting for the sun to bring out the little brown sugar freckles to announce that the fruit was ready to eat when one morning we looked out and found it had disappeared during the night. Then we remem-mered that stranger who'd glanced at it several times in the past week and realized that he'd been waiting for it to ripen, too.

Yet it isn't true that fruit can be had so easily in the tropics, or that anything but guavas, which are a pest in some parts, fall right into the mouths of *tierra caliente*, Americans stretched at full length on their backs under the trees. Yet tropical fruit is cheaper and riper than it is farther north, except in Florida and California.

In Cuba bananas are the staff of life (Even roast pigs are stuffed with them.), and a foreigner who has spent a year or so in the country, becoming at last accustomed to the ways and diet, is said to be *abananada*—well bananaed, or acclimatized.

In Brazil and other citrus centers oranges are so plentiful that their juice is used in place of water for cooking. (See *Feijoada.*) And any Brazilian can tell you that the sweetest half of an orange is the top where most of the juice has settled while hanging on the tree, and that Bahia is the place where the first navel orange was developed. It was transplanted to California, but didn't do so well as at home, although it's still the best navel orange we produce. In Washington, D.C., there's what's supposed to be the first orange tree from Brazil, planted in 1872.

The finest oranges we've eaten are those of Brazil and the

Dominican Republic. The best way to enjoy the juice is to impale an orange on a fork, cut off all the skin with a sharp knife, except a little shield above the fork prongs, and just chew your way around. There are twenty-one distinctive ways of eating oranges in places where they abound, all of which we've described already in our *Most for Your Money Cookbook*, so we won't go into it here.

Peru produces the biggest, sweetest strawberries in the whole wide world, even larger and finer in flavor than those monsters the English dip in Devonshire cream and sugar. Both Chile and Colombia are celebrated for light straw-colored strawberries called *frutillas*—yellow rather than red berries that have a wild tang. In Colombia, too, blackberries grow as big as your two thumbs and are noted for their flavor, while in Chile raspberry bushes grow into trees that become forests, and muskmelons weigh up to twenty pounds.

There's no end to the luscious pineapples of many kinds you'll find in all the colorful ports, from Jamaica's Hallelujia market to Bahia's bursting one, in both of which women walk with stately mien, balancing heaping baskets of fruit on their heads. And the pineapple has been accepted everywhere as a symbol of friendship since first it was hung outside the doors of Caribbean homes as a sign of welcome.

Anyone who has munched his way around the huge hairy clingstone of a dead-ripe mango and buttered his ears with its thick golden juice will tell you that's the finest fruit in the whole cornucopia, and we'll agree if you'll let us except the *chirimoya* of Peru, a truly celestial fruit which is called *fruta de conde* and *fruta de condessa* (fruit of the count and fruit of the countess, in Brazil). Its creamy pulp tastes more like a vanilla-pineapple-lemon sundae than anything else.

Then there's the sapid *sapodilla* whose green fruit also yields chicle for our chewing gum (it's called "apple" and "dilly" in the British West Indies), wild plums and cocoa plums, the pinkish-purple custard apple of Guatemala, *jaboticaba*, breadfruit and its big brother, *jaca*, that grows straight out from the bark of the tree without any stem to speak of and often weighs over a hundred pounds. All the sweet sops and sour sops, the papayas and the mameys; tourists call them "papas and mammas," and with reason, since the trees come in both sexes—but only the female bears fruit. Papayas are most familiar to us because they're grown in Florida and well known for the digestive element they contain—*papain*, similar to pepsin.

Granadillas we have, too, and that smaller fruit of the passion flower called maypop, but we have nothing to compare with the *curuba* in Colombia. Neither do our avocados stand up beside those of Ecuador that sometimes weigh eight pounds. But with airplane express supplementing the United Fruit Company's boats we may expect to see some of these perishable wonders in our own markets any day now. For already we are getting our nontropical winter grapes, pears, plums and peaches from the Argentine and Chile after California stops producing, from February to May, and this of course is because the reasons are reversed down there.

TROPICAL FRUITS IN RUM

Puerto Rico is now supplying us with pineapples, mangos, guavas and other tropical fruits, peeled, diced and preserved in rum. So if fresh tropical fruit isn't available you can get it in cans and use it as chutney with meat or fish, spoon it over ice cream or garnish mixed drinks.

GRILLED RED BANANAS

Select fat red bananas of equal size—one for each person. Lay them on a grill and put under a medium flame. After they are hot on one side turn the other cheek and repeat until the skin has turned dark all over, and by pressing with the back of a spoon you can feel that the fruit has softened inside. This will take 15–20 minutes, depending on size.

Put the grilled bananas on a hot platter and hustle them to the table, where the diner opens his own by slitting the blackish skin lengthwise and pushing it back. A tablespoon of fine moist sugar should be sprinkled from end to end of the opened hot fruit and a generous dash of cinnamon added. The rich odor of the steam escaping right under your nostrils adds to the eater's delight.

There are two secrets of success for this dish: (1) The fruit must be served and eaten while piping hot, since grilled bananas collapse and become sodden if they are kept waiting, and their flavor deteriorates rapidly, whether opened or not. Therefore they cannot be reheated with success. (2) The nearest substitute for the tasty South American sugar, which is not so hard and large grained as ours, is "Coffee A" sugar, moist and delicious.

And, by the way, to get the fullest savor from a grilled red banana do it on an outdoor fireplace.

Our national scope for the enjoyment of bananas is much too limited. This delicious fruit comes in every size, from tiny "fig" and "ladyfinger" bananas to long, slim "silver" ones and the toothsome green and starchy plantain, used mostly for frying. In skin color bananas range from pale green and flecked gold to red, almost completing a rainbow. In fact the only thing about them that never changes is their shape.

We have a great deal to learn about this staff of life of all-tropical Latin America. When it first appeared here, more than half a century ago, many people gobbled it, skin and all, and even now it is sold too green and indigestible. The easiest way to overcome this is to wrap a "hand" of bananas in cloth or paper and let them quickly ripen until the little freckles of sugar show on the skin. Then you can enjoy their full perfumy flavor, and then only.

BRAZILIAN BANANA TART
Torta de Banana

4 large bananas	1 tablespoon butter
½ cup sugar	4 tablespoons white wine or
⅛ teaspoon salt	juice of 1 lime
½ teaspoon nutmeg	

Peel bananas and press through sieve. Put pulp into saucepan with sugar, salt and butter. Stir well and cook until mixture starts to boil. Remove from heat and cool. When cold whip in wine and nutmeg and pour into baked pie shell.

PUERTO RICAN BANANA BRAN BREAD

¼ cup shortening	2 teaspoons baking powder
½ cup sugar	½ teaspoon salt
1 egg	½ teaspoon soda
1 cup bran	½ cup nuts
1½ cups mashed bananas	2 tablespoons water
1½ cups flour	1 teaspoon vanilla

Cream sugar and shortening. Add egg and beat. Add bran and mashed bananas. Mix thoroughly. Mix dry ingredients and add, then mix in nuts, water and vanilla. (Raisins may be added if desired.) Bake in a loaf pan for about 1 hour in a moderate oven.

Since products from the United States pay no duty in Puerto Rico many recipes combine imported ingredients, such as All Bran and Crisco with fresh foods and fruits of the island to make truly inter-American dishes.

BANANAS BAKED WITH CHEESE
Bananas Asados con Queso

4 bananas	1 cup thin cream
1 tablespoon melted butter	4 tablespoons sugar
½ cup sugar	1 beaten egg
½ cup grated cheese	Toasted bread crumbs

Peel bananas. Cut in two lengthwise and lay in baking dish. Sprinkle with butter, sugar and grated cheese. Into cream stir sugar and egg and pour over bananas. Dot with toasted bread crumbs and bake 30 minutes in moderate oven.

MEXICAN ORANGES

Slice unpeeled juicy oranges and arrange in layers with plenty of powdered sugar between. Pour over sufficient rum or tequila to wet every slice and dissolve the sugar. Then let it stand awhile. The resulting sweetened syrup heavily flavored with orange peel is delicious. Serve the orange slices with spoonfuls of the syrup poured over. Have a sharp fruit knife at each place to help remove orange peel before eating, although your own fingers will suffice.

Mexicans have many interesting ways with the excellent oranges from their *tierra caliente*. The most curious, perhaps, for foreign taste are juicy oranges cut in halves and thickly sprinkled with finely minced and sifted dry red chilies. In the markets and plazas of tropical towns vendors carry about trays of these biting-hot oranges all ready to eat, and if you like bitter-sweet contrasts you'll find them surprisingly good.

LITTLE BASKETS OF MANGO
Canastillas de Mango

Peel and slice thin 4 mangoes. Put over heat in casserole with 1 cup sugar and ½ cup water. When sauce has cooked 15 minutes add 1 teaspoon cornstarch which has been dissolved in a little cold water and mixed with 2 beaten egg yolks. Let cook 2 or 3 minutes, stirring constantly until thick and smooth. Remove from heat. Stir in 1 teaspoon cinnamon and 2 tablespoons butter and fill into patty shells.

This is a specialty of Colombia where mangoes are prime.

PRUNES, BRAZILIAN STYLE
Compote de Ameixas

Wash ½ pound of fine French prunes. Cover with 1 pint hot water and let stand until prunes are full size. Cook in same

water, adding ½ inch of vanilla bean, juice and rind of ¼
lemon and 1 cup sugar.

The excellence of this depends upon the fine quality of the
imported prunes and the use of true vanilla bean instead of the
comparatively tasteless extract.

BRAZILIAN MARMELADA AND GOIABADA

These celestial and wholesome fruit pastes are part of the
daily fare in a number of Latin-American countries and appear
with equal frequency in homes of rich and poor Brazilians,
either eaten with a buttered roll and *café com leite* (coffee with
hot milk) in the early morning, or served as the simplest of
desserts accompanied by a slice of cheese, usually a curdy type
called Minas after the states of Minas Geraes. They are usually
supplied by modern sanitary jam factories, packed in round
tins about 2½ inches high, holding about 2 pounds, and in this
form are imported into the United States to be sold in fancy
groceries and Spanish stores.

Or they are made at home as follows:

QUINCE PASTE
Marmelada

Wash 12 large quinces. Peel; core and put into kettle with
cold water to cover. Squeeze in juice of 2 lemons. Cover kettle
and cook gently until quinces are soft, then press through purée
sieve. Have quince seed soaking in a little cold water. Weigh
quince pulp, and to each pound of fruit add 1½ pounds sugar,
also water strained from seeds. Stir thoroughly and allow mixture to simmer until it makes a soft ball when tried in cold
water. At this point take from fire and beat 10 minutes. Put in
shallow pan to cool. Paste may be sliced, dried in sun and eaten

like candy. Any left over will keep indefinitely if pieces are wrapped in paraffin paper.

Goiabada (guava paste) is made in same way, substituting guavas for quinces in above recipe.

GUAVA WHIP

Press ripe guavas through purée sieve. To 1 rounding cup of fruit pulp add 1 cup powdered sugar and 1 egg white. Beat together until stiff enough to hold shape. Pile lightly on serving dish and chill.

WHIPPED AVOCADO

Throughout Latin America avocados appear with any course or, indeed, in lieu of almost any course from appetizers, through soups and salads, to sweets. And one of the best desserts we know is Whipped Avocado.

Cut avocado in half. Remove pulp, keeping skin intact. Whip pulp to smooth, velvety cream with powdered sugar and lime juice, just as in preparing Avocado Ice Cream, but instead of freezing it pile it back into the skins for succulent spooning out.

NUTS

"Brazil, where the nuts come from" is a bit of slang that pretty well covers cashews, paradise or cream nuts, peanuts, which are supposed to have originated there, and the ubiquitous Brazil nut itself that's locally known as "Para chestnut."

But the biggest and finest nut in the world is found in the Guianas. It's called the South American butternut or *souri*, and in size compares to the Brazil nut as a walnut to a hazel nut. Its meat is much the same, although richer. If you can get hold of any, which is doubtful, for they're not shipped commercially on account of uncertain supply; just slice them wafer thin and sprinkle with freshly shredded coconut as they do in the Guianas.

Chile has the biggest and finest pine nut in all Christendom. It's as big as a pecan and as full flavored in its way.

While cashew nuts were first roasted in South America the bulk of them are now shipped from India. Everybody who has traveled, in the West Indies has seen in the souvenir shops the roasted nut carved and painted with a monkey face to uphold its local nickname, "monkey nut," which it shares with our pet name for the peanut, but few tourists have time to get acquainted with the unroasted cashew. It grows at the tip end of that excellent tropical fruit, *caju,* and before it's roasted contains a burning acid from which indelible ink is made. We had a cook, Eugenia, who was always telling our children to beware of the nut when green, and one day to demonstrate the effect of its juice she broke one in half and rubbed it on her cheek. It left a mark on her skin, as though it had been seared with a poker, that stayed there for weeks.

It would be carrying coals to Newcastle to give recipes for use in our own country which is quite nutty enough. Latin Americans use their nuts in cooking in just the same ways that we do. Peanut sauce is as popular in Mexico as it is in our Southern states, and about the only appetite in this line we haven't acquired is the use of seeds as nuts. In Peru or Yucatan, for example, roast pumpkin seeds are as popular as peanuts here. Our own New Englanders learned to like squash, pumpkin and sunflower seeds from the Indians they found in residence when they came, but the use of seeds as nuts has never spread, although in cities like New York they're sold in penny packets in candy stores, every fifth or sixth one salted.

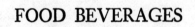

FOOD BEVERAGES

COFFEE

The best cup of coffee in South America can be had in Brazil or Colombia. Brazil grows four fifths of the world's supply, but Colombia produces an exceptionally flavorsome bean at a high altitude, and many coffee tasters say that a judicious mixture of the two makes the finest blend.

In such coffee-conscious cities as Santos, São Paulo and Rio de Janeiro you'll see shiny metal trays set with tin-white porcelain cups and saucers, bowls of heavy, dampish sugar, and little steaming coffeepots being carried about in offices, homes and the streets at all times of day and night. In every factory and workshop, indeed, apprentices are kept busy brewing the national drink or running out for it to the nearest sidewalk cafés which are set with tables for coffee topers, some of whom think nothing of downing 30–40 cups a day.

Coffee in Brazil is always made fresh and, except at breakfast time, drunk jet black from demitasses first filled almost to the brim with the characteristic moist, soft coffee sugar of the country that melts five times as fast as our hard granulated. For breakfast larger cups are used, and they're more than half filled with hot milk, not cream. This *café com leite* doesn't require so much sugar as *café preto*—black coffee.

Every Brazilian household takes a great interest in new coffee-making devices, both imported and domestic, tries them out and then goes back to the time-honored method of the cotton bag. (A clean white sock will do in a pinch.) The bag produces the best results after it has been used a number of times, and Brazilians insist that nothing else will bring out the full, rich coffee flavor. Made of a special fabric, cut or woven in cornucopia shape, the bag has a wire run through its hem to hold it open in a wide circle.

You can fashion one yourself by cutting 2 isosceles triangles from Canton flannel, 9 inches long, or high, and 8½ inches across the base. Sew the long edges of the two pieces together with a double seam, making a pointed bag. At the top run a narrow hem to put the wire through, bending it into a circle. Scald or boil the bag to take out the cottony taste.

Real Brazilian coffee is usually made from the best grade of "Santos" and is always "high roast," roasted until it's dark brown, then ground to the fineness of granulated sugar. Put into the bag 1 tablespoon for each cup and 1 extra for the pot. Have water freshly boiling. Hang bag down inside a coffeepot or over a small-mouth pitcher. Pour in slowly the number of cups of boiling water you want of coffee and a little extra to allow for what's absorbed by bag and grounds.

Do not pour it through more than once, and be sure to pour it slowly, according to the New Orleans Creole saying: "If you can hear it dripping, honey, it's dripping too fast."

If your taste for coffee is highly developed you'll be delighted with the result.

The bag should be kept in cold fresh water after using and must be boiled and hung in the sun two or three times a week.

Coffee made in Brazilian style is so good that even the family parrot goes for it, so you mustn't be surprised if when having breakfast in Santos or Rio you see a green or golden head dipping into your cup. European zoo keepers have found coffee so essential to the diet of Latin-American parrots that they fill the birds' drinking cups with good strong coffee several times a day.

You may not have heard about painted coffee, but Brazil dyes the unroasted beans with several colors of painted earth to please the eye of customers in different countries—Africans, for instance, insist on bright red beans. There's no harm in this, of course, since the paint is roasted away and the beans cleaned before being ground.

MARTINIQUE CAFÉ DIABLE

Per person:
2 tablespoons fine coffee of high roast, freshly ground
¾ cup water
Juice of ½ orange (Save the half-orange skin, scooped clean
    and dry.)
Add pinches of cloves, vanilla bean, lemon peel and stick cin-
    namon to taste.

Boil all together as you would make plain coffee. Heat 2–3
tablespoons of cognac per person. Rub rim of empty half-
orange skin in sugar. Place in cup snugly and pour your spiced
coffee into this to drink it from the sugar orange skin, after
sweetening to taste.

Float in hot brandy on the back of a spoon, making sure that
it remains on top and comes level with the sugared rim. Then
light it and begin to sip as soon as the flame dies down. Vanilla
bean and cinnamon in the stick should always be used in preference to powdered or insipid liquid extracts.

If the cognac is of the quality called Fine Champagne, so
much the tastier, although Grande Champagne would be
wasted on it.

Café Diable probably got its name from being devilish fine
besides being fiery. In Paris it's called *Café Brulot*, but when
the French brought it to their colonies in Martinique, Haiti,
Guiana and Louisiana its name was changed to *Diable*. You can
get it made to perfection in New Orleans.

CENTRAL AMERICAN COFFEE ESSENCE

Throughout Central America and Mexico coffee is not
brewed fresh for the table but is made by pouring cold, bottled
cooked black coffee into the cup and then adding hot milk to
the extract or essence, or hot water for black coffee. Coffee
Essence is brewed in any of the common ways, by dripping,
percolating or boiling, but about 3 or 4 times as much coffee

is used with the same amount of water, making an extract just that much stronger than ours and impossible to drink without diluting.

And once you get used to having your coffee in this handy fashion you'll find it just as good and a whole lot less bother. (The method isn't at all strange when we realize that many tea tipplers in England and Russia prefer to make a strong infusion first and use it in the same way, adding hot water for hot tea or ice water for iced tea. But our familiar oriental tea is little used in any form in Latin America where it's still looked upon as a medicine and drunk chiefly as a headache cure, except in the tourist hotels.)

CENTRAL AMERICAN BROWN-SUGAR COFFEE
Café de Pilón

Dissolve ½ cup dark brown sugar by simmering in 1 quart water. Add 4 tablespoons pulverized coffee and cook only 1 minute before setting it in a warm place for coffee to settle.

In the tropics where brown sugar is eaten every day in every way this *Café de Pilón* is looked upon as both food and drink. Its high sugar content, indeed, is more stimulating than the coffee itself.

In the West Indies where coconuts are more common than cows coconut milk is used in place of any other in the morning coffee.

YERBA MATÉ

Yerba Maté, or Paraguay tea as the English call it, is drunk by 30,000,000 South Americans every day, and nearly all day. Brazil, Argentina, Uruguay, Paraguay and Chile supply most of the drinkers, and with many of them it is the sole liquid refreshment from breakfast to nightcap. It is supposed to possess miraculous virtues but probably isn't any healthier a beverage than coffee or other tea.

Early Spanish settlers in Paraguay learned to drink it from

the Indians who still gather it from a kind of holly tree. The leaves are either crushed coarsely with some of the stems in the style called *Gaucho* (which we like best) or ground more finely for better grades.

It is not made in a pot like oriental tea, but in a gourd or *maté* the size of a man's fist and often beautifully decorated, mounted in silver. There's a small hole in the top or stem end of the gourd through which about 2 heaping teaspoons of the crushed leaves are poured, together with sugar to taste (or none), and often that half fills the gourd, then hot water, but not boiling hot. You hold it in your hand while it seeps a little, then insert a silver tube called *bombilla* and suck as you would cider through a straw. The *bombilla* stem is the size of a straw and has a hollow ball at the end that rests in the bottom of the *maté*, pierced with fine holes so none of the herb (*yerba*) will be sucked up. *Maté* fanciers are so fond of this little pump (*bombilla*) and gourd (*maté*) outfit that they collect beautifully decorated antique ones, sometimes made of gold, and the hard egg shell of the Argentine rhea is often mounted to serve as a *maté* cup, usually with tripod legs to rest it on, although most *yerba* gourds cannot be set down and have to be held cupped in the hands, which helps to warm things up on chilly mornings.

COLD MATÉ
Tetre

Plainsmen and travelers drink their *maté* cold when hot water is not available. This is called *tetre*, and in the rural districts you'll find many people whose devotion to it is constant and keen. Very often it's a long drink prepared in a polished and decorated cow's horn, often bound with silver.

Although usually drunk plain, both cold and hot *maté* is occasionally spiked with rum or curaçao, and the Germans put up the herb for use in Germany, already mixed with alcoholic flavors, which to our way of thinking doesn't add anything.

Maté is sold in leading North American groceries and specialty shops now, and it's best and cheapest to buy the brands packed in Paraguay, not those shipped here in bulk and put up in fancy, expensive packages.

MEXICAN ATOLES

Atole is a gruel made in most cases from tortilla dough boiled with plenty of water and a variety of seasonings. It is served in cups with meals, as we serve cocoa, and is a favorite refreshment sent hot to workers in the fields or soldiers on duty.

Sometimes it is simply flavored with a kind of wild sage called *chia*, again it will be made with fruit juice and brown sugar or honey. An *atole* flavored generously with chocolate is often served for breakfast with a roll and butter beside it, and from this thick Mexican chocolate the Spanish got the idea of making chocolate with cornstarch, a drink so thick the spoon will stand up by itself in a cup of it. This is called *Atole Champurrado*, from *champurrar*—to mix one drink with another.

A nourishing *atole* has a purée of cooked beans beaten up in it. Another is mixed with the usual Mexican cooking sauce made of chilies, tomato and onion.

In houses of the well to do a purée of rice or of plain wheat flour is sometimes substituted for the tortilla dough.

CHOCOLATE ATOLE
Atole Champurrado

Grind tortilla dough well. Whip it up with some water and pour into an earthen pot. Boil it down until it's thick. Then add chocolate, sugar and much water. When chocolate is cooked beat the drink well and serve steaming hot and frothing.

BEAN ATOLE
Atole de Frijol

Prepare tortilla dough as above, but cook it with beans previously boiled with saltpeter and finish in the same way as Chocolate Atole.

MEXICAN SOFT DRINKS

Mexico is the land of strange drinks. Besides the enormous consumption of pulque, which is the sap of the maguey plant fermented in a fresh cowhide, and the potent tequila distilled from it, Mexicans are always downing one or another of their many unintoxicating beverages, many of which are delicious.

They make a pleasant tea from fresh or dried leaves of the orange tree. And their cold fresh fruit-juice drinks are legion. An unusual one is called *colonche*. It is made of the juice of the prickly pear, sweetened with honey and allowed to stand 24 hours to improve its flavor.

Milk is plentiful in some sections. For adults it is always sweetened slightly, and when served hot a dash of nutmeg or cinnamon is sprinkled on top. Many foreigners who do not like milk find that this addition makes it very palatable.

Chocolate, which is native, is often served very thick in the Spanish fashion and taken instead of coffee in the early morning. (See recipes.)

But the national soft drink is *atole*, of which there are many kinds, flavored with all sorts of things from beans to plums.

RICE ATOLE
Atole de Arroz

Cook 1 cup rice without salt in boiling water until soft. Press through a sieve. Add 1 quart of hot, not boiling, milk to the rice mush. Put in a double boiler to cook until rice and milk blend. Serve hot, like chocolate, with a dash of cinnamon or nutmeg or vanilla. Each cup may be topped with whipped cream if desired, but that wouldn't be exactly Mexican, for they put their hot drinks, especially chocolate, in a tall narrow pot with a hole in the cover to accommodate the handle of a beater which is twirled so fast between the palms that the drink froths up as thick as whipped cream itself.

And here's a little story a Mexican farmer told us to illustrate the homely attributes of *atole* which is both the drink and the food of the people: A neighbor's son went away to school for two years in the United States and then returned to the home hacienda with much grandeur. The first night at home he sat down to supper with all the family.

"¿Qui es este, mama [What's this]?" he asked, picking up his bowl and turning it around and around.

"*Atole—atole*," absent-mindedly answered his mother.

"¿Que es atole, mama [And what's *atole*]?" Then his mother looked at him, watching him critically while he kept turning the bowl rhythmically in his hands.

"¿Come se te olvida el atole, pero no se te olvida el movimento [How is it that you have forgotten the *atole* but haven't forgotten the movement]?" she asked him sarcastically.

MEXICAN CHOCOLATE
Aztec Chocolatl

2 squares unsweetened chocolate	½ cup water
	1½ cups milk
2 tablespoons sugar	

Melt and cook chocolate in water and when it thickens add milk and sugar, bring to boiling point and beat to a stiff froth.

The secret of making fine Mexican chocolate is in the strenuous beating thereof. For this purpose the Aztecs of old invented a hand chocolate mill, consisting of a pot holding 2 or 3 cups, a tight-fitting cover with a hole in the middle to accommodate a wooden plunger or swizzle stick equipped with paddles. The handle is rotated rapidly between the palms until the drink foams over.

When Cortez took one back to Spain together with the Aztec's *chocolatl*, the chocolate pot and plunger was named *molinillo* (little mill) by the Spaniards who adopted the new beverage with enthusiasm—but later ruined it by making it too thick with cornstarch in an effort to imitate Mexican *Atole Champurrado*. (See recipe.)

If you ever get used to making chocolate in a *molinillo* you'll never like it half so well in any other way. We have a battered antique one of silver we picked up in Guadalajara twenty years ago, and it's as indispensable as our French pepper grinder which, by the way, we bought in Rio de Janeiro. *Molinillos* are made of all sorts of materials and come in beautiful shapes with richly embossed or colored decorations, and they're collected as enthusiastically by chocolate topers as *yerba maté* addicts gather in the artistic drinking gourds and *bombillas* of Paraguay and the Argentine. The great Montezuma, who drank fifty cups of chocolate a day, had it all made in a *molinillo* of gold, and chocolate was so highly esteemed then that the *cacao* seeds of which it is made were used as money. (*Cacao* has been senselessly Anglicized to "cocoa.")

Mexicans often make their mulled or milled chocolate with honey in place of sugar, and it was from this thick sweet mixture that Antonio Carletti, pastry chef to the king of Spain got the idea of making the first chocolate candy in 1662.

GUATEMALAN CHOCOLATE

2 squares unsweetened chocolate	2 cups black coffee
½ cup sugar	1 tablespoon cinnamon
1 tablespoon cornstarch	1 piece vanilla bean
	1 salt spoon salt
3 cups hot milk	

Melt chocolate with a little water in double boiler over low flame. Add sugar and cornstarch mixed together, then the coffee, and stir until smooth. Simmer 5 minutes. Add cinnamon, vanilla bean and hot milk. Cook 30 minutes. Whip to a froth. Remove vanilla bean and serve.

In Guatemala, as in Mexico, coffee isn't brewed fresh each time it's wanted. A strong essence is made in quantity and bottled for use; by adding hot milk or milk and water to the cold essence you get a good cup of coffee.

The use of vanilla bean instead of extract gives added flavor to this chocolate-coffee combination. A piece a little over an inch long, slit so the seeds will drop out in cooking, is sufficient; or the segment of bean may be mashed·with a spoon so all the flavor will go into the drink.

Like most chocolate in Spain, this is thickened with cornstarch and is so popular in the mother country that it's known as Granada Chocolate, after the city of that name. It might as well be named for the smaller city of Granada in Nicaragua, however, for such coffee and chocolate foody beverages are popular throughout Central America.

Technically, Guatemalan Chocolate is a *champurrado*, the Spanish word for any beverage made by mixing one kind of drink with another. (See *Mexican Atole Champurrado*.)

SPANISH EGG CHOCOLATE

2 squares unsweetened chocolate	½ cup sugar
	½ tablespoon cinnamon
2 cups milk	1 teaspoon vanilla extract

In double boiler cook chocolate and milk together to velvety consistency. Keep stirring as you add salt and sugar, then cinnamon and vanilla at the finish. Beat an egg in the bottom of a pitcher or *molinillo* and pour hot chocolate over. Froth it well and serve.

In Mexico, chocolate's homeland, the type called Spanish is very different from this, for it is made without sugar and not beaten foamy in the national mulling pot—*molinillo*. And like most other Spanish chocolate it's so thick a spoon will stand up alone in it. In Spain the thickening is more often cornstarch than egg, but both methods are used in some Latin-American places where the food and drink is still almost wholly Spanish.

If a piece of real vanilla bean is used in place of the extract it will be more flavorsome, for a lot of vanilla extracts are made of coal tar and other cheap substitutes. Also, in our experience, Baker's unsweetened chocolate makes the best brew, although there are many other brands to choose from. In Spain chocolate bars usually are sweetened and adulterated with cornstarch.

TISTE–NICARAGUA'S NATIONAL DRINK

Roast 1 quart dried corn and grind it fine. Mix with ½ pound roasted cocoa beans, also ground fine, and ½ ounce cinnamon stick, powdered. Stir into 3 quarts water. Let stand 2 hours, stirring occasionally. Then strain through cloth, squeezing out "milk" of corn and cocoa beans. Sugar to taste and drink with plenty of ice.

All Central Americans use spices in their natural state and powder them as needed.

GUARANA

Brazilian *guarana* is one of the nicest drinks we know. It's sold already mixed in Brazil as commonly as Coca-Cola is dispensed here, and there have been attempts to put it on the North American market which have failed because of the millions needed to advertise a new drink.

You can buy the outfit for making *guarana*, however, in some specialty shops, and it consists of a chocolate-colored roll, about the size and shape of a thinnish banana made of *guarana* berries crushed to powder, dried and pressed. With it comes a dried shark's palate you use, exactly as the Amazon Indians have done for centuries, to scrape off about a tablespoon of powdered *guarana*. Simply mix this with sugar and water, preferably sparkling water, and you've got something.

When lemon juice is added you have a delightful *Limonada de Guarana*.

As with *maté*, there's a lot of ballyhoo about *guarana* arresting hunger and being a healthier stimulant than coffee or tea, but it contains caffeine, too, and all we can say is that it's about the most potable soft beverage we ever set lip to.

HAVANA ALMOND DRINK
Amande

20 sweet almonds   1 quart milk
2 bitter almonds   1-inch piece vanilla bean
1 cup sugar

Parboil almonds to remove skins easily, then pound nuts to pulp and boil slowly in milk. Slit vanilla bean so seeds will spice the drink and add with sugar. Stir; heat again, and your drink's done. But you must strain it, cool it and then drink with plenty of ice.

Such almond refreshers, originally from Spain, are standard cooler-offers throughout the Spanish-drinking world.

ORGEAT
Horchata

Horchata is Spanish for orgeat, originally a refreshing barley water which the French changed by making it with almonds. But Spaniards and Mexicans who have more melons than almonds substitute cantaloupe, watermelon, cucumber and pumpkin seeds for the original. So today in Mexico you will get a fine cooler made of any of these seeds or all of them put together.

MELON SEED HORCHATA

2 cups melon seeds   ½ cup sugar
1 quart water   2 teaspoons cinnamon

Wash seeds thoroughly and grind them fine, shells and all. Stir in water with sugar and cinnamon. Let stand in refrigera-

tor, stirring occasionally, and when all of the succulent seed
flavor has gone into the water strain through hair sieve. Add
ice and serve.

HORCHATA OF THE FOUR SEEDS

½ cup cantaloupe seeds	1 quart water
½ cup watermelon seeds	½ cup sugar
½ cup squash seeds	A dash of orange flower water
½ cup cucumber seeds	2 teaspoons cinnamon

Make as above.

A dash of lime or any other citrous juice may take the place
of orange flower water. Kumquat peel adds bouquet, too. If
fresh seeds are used, taken from the ripe melons themselves,
your *horchata* is all the better for it, and it doesn't take nearly
so long to make.

(See recipe for *Helado de las Cuatro Simientes,* among the
Desserts.)

ALMOND HORCHATA

1 pound sweet Jordan al- monds	2 cups powdered sugar
	2 quarts water
20 bitter almonds	

Soak skins off by scalding with hot water. Then let the
blanched kernels lie 2 hours in cold water. Mash them to
creamy paste with sugar. Stir into water and bottle.

This makes a strong almond essence which has to be diluted
with 3–4 times as much water when you're ready to drink it.
It's fine, too, for putting flavor into wine cups or mixing with
fresh juice squeezed by hand from big white grapes like those
of Mendoza, as we learned to do in Buenos Aires.

Horchata is bottled under its Spanish name, *Orgeat,* and sold
commonly in Spanish-American cities. You can get it ready
made in Spanish sections of North American towns, too.

Bitter almonds are essential for imparting that bittersweet tang, and a few dashes of orange flower water give contrasting zest to please the tongue.

This Almond *Horchata* is made into a syrup, with lemon juice, in Mexico where a popular ice is called *Horchata Nevada* (snow) or *Helado de Horchata*. (See recipe.)

MILK

Tropical countries have more coconut milk than cow's milk. Goat's milk is more common and is very good when poured hot into coffee. An even richer milk is used in Ecuador and Peru from the lady donkey. It is supposed to have medicinal value. In Brazil milk comes from zebu-humped cattle imported from East India. But the Argentine and Chile have extra good cow juice for drinking.

FRUIT JUICES

Where all sorts of tropical fruits are picked sun ripened off the tree all the year around it's not necessary to tell the children, "Now drink your orange juice," for they go around sucking oranges, custard apples, chunks of pineapple and sugar cane all day long.

It's not surprising that tropical Americans are more fruit and fruit-juice conscious than we Northerners. Their word for juice is *succo* in Spanish, *jugo* in Portuguese, and wherever these languages flow the familiar word is used more commonly than here. For instance, in Brazil, when you wish to express your delight with anything you exclaim "¡E succo de uva [It's the juice of the grape]!" There can be no higher approval than that, and they mean unfermented grape juice, not wine, for in such hot places alcoholic drinks aren't so suitable.

The juice of cane is likewise appreciated when bubbling fresh as our cider from the press, so wherever sugar is made you'll find miniature presses in the towns grinding out the juice at so much a glass.

In many tropical and desert sections water is either scarce or dangerous to drink, so fruit juice quenches the thirst instead. In Mexico the juice of the barrel cactus comes in handy on the desert, and the fresh juice of the maguey, a kind of cactus or century plant, is as much in demand as cane juice in other parts. It's sold in the stores or delivered to your door more often than milk.

When such juices are not taken in their natural undiluted form they are mixed with water and sugar into cooling *refrescos*, of which there are as many as there are different kinds of fruits. As with us, lemonade leads the list, and besides being made plain it is mixed with juices of pineapple, oranges, limes, *cajus*, etc.

REFRESCOS

Wherever coconuts are common everybody goes for *refresco de coco*, made of the "milk" squeezed from fresh coconut meat and frothed up with sugar and water. Sometimes it's pleasantly colored with grenadine or fresh pomegranate juice.

In Haiti on a hot afternoon the proper thing is to break out the old punch bowl and dice up a few watermelon hearts in it, without letting a single drop of the juice get away. Use plenty of cracked ice in place of water. Sweeten it a little with red grenadine and give it bouquet with *eau d'oranger*, orange flower water. And what you don't eat you can drink.

Other Haitian *refrescos* are made with papaya juice (locally called *papaye*) and fruits unknown to us, such as *corosole* and *caimites*.

MEXICAN LEMON DRINK
Chicha de Limón

Crush 3 pineapples, skin and all. Add juice of 24 lemons, 2 pounds sugar, 1 tablespoon cinnamon and a pinch of cloves. Stir well. Let stand overnight, and next day add more sugar to taste. Color pink with pomegranates, currant or grape juice. Ice and serve.

Mexicans are as fond of pink lemonades as we are, especially at fiestas and circuses. Pomegranate juice is used to color fruit drinks all along the West coast to Chile. Xochimilco, the floating gardens near Mexico City, has a specialty of pulque, colored with pomegranate juice which is most palatable.

Chicha usually is a fermented drink, which this will become if allowed to stand long enough in a warm place.

PINEAPPLE REFRESHER
Refresco de Ananas

Peel a pineapple. Cut in pieces and crush with 1 pound sugar. Pour in ½ cup white wine, juice of 1 lemon and let stand 30 minutes. Then strain. Fill with enough water and ice to make 12 glasses.

CHILEAN ORANGE LEAF TEA
Te de Naranja

Lightly bruise freshly gathered baby leaves from an orange tree. Put half a dozen in each cup. Add lump sugar browned or burnt on all sides under broiler and boiling water.

This is used as a nightcap and is a soothing draught.

ALCOHOLIC DRINKS

WEST INDIAN RUMS

Jamaica rum is fullest flavored of all West Indian rums. You can get it heavy or light bodied, and it's easy to recognize by its fragrance and typical rummy taste.

Cuban rum, of which Bacardi is best known, is milder in flavor but sharper in smell. Bacardi is lighter in body, taste and aroma. Martinique rum is a light type, too. Good in long, cold drinks. Puerto Rican, also light. Virgin Island, full flavored and fine for hot drinks.

BACARDI COCKTAIL

1 jigger Bacardi rum   ½ pony grenadine
2 dashes lime juice

DAIQUIRI COCKTAIL

⅔ Bacardi rum   ⅙ lime juice
⅙ simple syrup, or sugar

Some people claim that this is the great-granddaddy of all cocktails.

RUM HIGHBALL

Wherever rum takes the place of whisky, as in the West Indies, many wise drinkers prefer it well diluted in a highball. So Rum Highball is simply a tot of the native firewater poured into a tall glass, partly filled with cracked ice and then deluged with seltzer or any fizzy water.

CUBA LIBRE

This is simply a Rum Highball made with Coca-Cola in place of water. The novelty of it has blazed its reputation throughout the West Indies. The valiant name "Free Cuba" attracts tourists, only to let down us North Americans when we hear about the coke.

It is interesting to note that all Cubans who can afford it drink French or Spanish wine for Christmas and other holidays in preference to their own rum. But the North American invasion has popularized such novelties as Cuba Libre among people who formerly drank their rum straight. Rum was never indulged in by the Cuban family, but only by men, in the many little bars, such as Sloppy Joe's in Havana, which became as internationally famous as London's Dirty Dick's.

The British, too, have introduced shandygaff from neighboring Jamaica which furnishes the ginger for the ginger beer that's mixed fifty-fifty with lager beer, supplied by the Cubans themselves.

RUM COLLINS

1½ jiggers rum	2 teaspoons powdered sugar
Juice of 1 lime	3 ice cubes

Put in 12-ounce or half-pint Collins glass. Stir together and fill with iced soda or sparkling water. The chemical action of powdered or confectioners' sugar with the lime juice gives the desired snap.

In some places it's colored pink with grenadine or savored with a dash of curaçao or orange flower water.

MATÉ RUM COLLINS

This is a Rum Collins with cold *maté* (See *Tetre*.) used in place of sparkling water. It has its fans in Paraguay and the Argentine where *maté* is the national soft drink.

PUERTO RICAN PUNCH

A drink as seemingly innocuous as Chilean Grape *Chicha* is now popular in the city clubs of San Juan, Ponce and Mayagüez under the generic name of *Ponche* (Punch). It is made the same as a Rum Highball except that grape juice takes the place of water.

A North American invention, no doubt, since most Latin Americans shiver at the thought of wasting good grape juice by drinking it before it turns to wine.

The innocent sweet juice of the grape camouflages the potence as well as the flavor of the rum and makes it a deceptive beverage all around. When made with white grape juice instead of red it's a little more subtle, but on the whole it would be better if mixed with pineapple juice which has a natural affinity with rum.

WATER COCONUTS

One good reason to take a trip to the tropics is to drink off a whole coconut spiked with rum.

Large green coconuts are heaped up like elongated green cannon balls both on street stands and in bars, ready for the coconut slasher to lop off their topknots with his *machete* and let the customer at the cool sweet and fruity water inside.

Water coconuts are drunk either plain or pepped up with rum. In the latter case a tot of good old Jamaica or almost any good local *aguardiente* is poured through the opening in the coconut, swizzled around a bit and then downed.

Water coconuts provide a long drink and a refreshing one. Unlike the meaty kind they are raised solely for drinking purposes.

MEXICAN ORANGE FLOWER WATER REFRESHER
Refresco Flor de Naranja

Juice of 2 oranges	Powdered sugar
Juice of 1 lime	½ cup Cuban rum
2 tablespoons orange flower water	

Put juices with sugar to taste and rum in cocktail shaker with plenty of ice. Shake a little, then add orange flower water and shake a lot. Serve in wide champagne glasses.

Cuban rum is called *Habanero* in Mexico and neighboring tropics where it is greatly appreciated. The older it is, the better, of course. Gin may be used in place of rum.

Mexicans use flowers for flavoring both drinks and dishes, and among the fragrant blossoms most in demand are orange and lemon blossoms.

A MEXICAN EGGNOG
Ron Pope

2 quarts milk	1 cup sugar
A short stick of cinnamon	18 egg yolks
A long piece of vanilla bean	1½ cups rum or tequila

Boil milk with cinnamon, vanilla and sugar. Beat yolks in a big bowl. Traditionally a special wooden paddle was used for this, but nowadays an electric mixer does the job just as well. Add milk mixture gradually. Whip in tequila last. Let stand in refrigerator to ripen and then drink ad lib.

If there's any leftover *Ron Pope* it will keep well when tightly corked in bottles.

The name *Ron Pope* sounds like rum punch, and the recipe is close to our eggnog, so everybody should be satisfied.

BRAZILIAN BATIDA

1 part honey or simple syrup	3 parts old *cachacha* (Brazilian white rum)
	1 part lime or lemon juice

Shake well with cracked ice and serve in cocktail glasses.

Brazilians like soft drinks, coffee, *maté*, *guarana*, and the countless *refrescos* of fruit juice and water, and this cocktail is the only really Brazilian one that we know of although every sort of North American cocktail is served in the big hotel bars.

The Brazilian white rum called *cachacha*, which is closely related to the Portuguese word *cachacão*, meaning "a cuff on the neck," is, indeed, a paralyzing drink, at least when it is drunk without proper aging. It is distilled from the juice of sugar cane and sometimes buried in casks in the ground for many years, just as Kentucky Bourbon used to be, until the liquor becomes yellow, mellow and equal to the best strong drink of any other country.

The cheapest kinds are distilled from the woody residue of crushed cane, and because of the wood alcohol suspected in them are likely to cause blindness. In any case many habitual drinkers of this *pinga* go blind; but well-made, well-matured *cachacha* is no more harmful than any other fine rum, and if it weren't so scarce nowadays it would be imported into this country as enthusiastically as the West Indian rums.

MEXICAN PINEAPPLE AND TEQUILA MILK

1 large juicy pineapple	3-4 tablespoons honey
1 quart milk	A piece of vanilla bean
	1 cup tequila, well aged

Stir pineapple cut in small pieces into milk with everything else, slitting the piece of vanilla bean, which should be about 1½ inches long, so the seeds will flavor the drink. Mix well and put out of sight and out of mind in refrigerator to ripen 4 hours or more.

Tequila, distilled from the century plant's juice after it is first fermented into pulque, is Mexico's finest firewater. When well aged it is as golden as any country's brandy or whisky and makes as perfect a tipple.

In Mexico a spiked milk punch like the above is delicately referred to as *Leche Preparada*—Prepared Milk—so you can't say you weren't warned.

JAMAICA GLOW COCKTAIL

½ gin   ¼ orange juice
¼ claret   3 dashes Jamaica ginger

Jamaica ginger is an excellent stomachic, whether in ginger ale, cocktail or drugstore bottle. It certainly helps put the glow in this drink, although the name comes from the glowing red imparted by the claret.

JAMAICAN SANTA SHRUB

A refreshing drink named by resident British, perhaps after Santa Claus. It is simply rum with orange, lemon and pineapple juice, sweetened with sugar and diluted with water. Englishmen seldom ice their drinks at home, but as soon as they arrive in the tropics they get the habit, so this calls for plenty of ice.

HAVANA COCKTAIL

½ apricot brandy   ¼ Swedish punch
¼ gin   1 dash lemon juice

To please the tourist trade from North America the bars of Havana go off the deep end when it comes to shaking up fancy cocktails. Probably there are more different kinds compounded here than in New York City, and since many of them are not even made with native or West Indian rum they're hardly typical, although always soothing.

But the weirdest cocktail we ever tasted was compounded by Dr Monday in Mexico City with a touch of oil from worms of maquey macerated in alcohol. (Worms of maguey are popular meat in Mexico and are clean little animals that never leave the heart of the maguey palm until they're popped into the frying pan or stew kettle.)

The origin of the word "cocktail" is variously attributed to an Aztec princess named Xoctl who first served it and to Trinidad planters telling their bar boys to "cork" the "tail" end of a bottle, but both seem very farfetched.

COLOMBIAN MANDARIN CREAM
Crema Mandarina

Sweeten 1 quart milk to taste and add, a little at a time, 1 pint mandarin orange juice. Beat constantly and finish by slowly adding 1 cup white wine. Let it ripen an hour or two in the refrigerator, and before serving beat it so furiously that froth stands in a high collar on top of each cup or glass when served. Sprinkle top with cinnamon and nutmeg.

In Colombia this pleasant beverage is made in a big *molinillo*, the chocolate mill in which Mexicans and most Americans in the tropical *tierra caliente*—hot country—froth their drinks with a swizzle stick much thicker than the kind used in the West Indies.

MARTINIQUE

This drink which takes its name from the French colony in the West Indies is an original and soothing concoction. It's a sort of simplified pousse-café consisting of equal parts of benedictine, kümmel and cream.

Use a large liqueur glass and pour in the gleaming white kümmel first, to fill one third of the glass. Then float on a golden band of benedictine of the same amount and top everything with rich cream. The separate layers are sipped off in succession to give pleasing contrasts to the palate.

CREME DE CACAO

This classic liqueur flavored with cocoa beans, although originating in the West Indies, is drunk more frequently in Paris, London or New York, either plain or with a fleck of whipped cream on top.

CURAÇAO

Curaçao is a triumph of West Indian liqueur making, but since the little island off the coast of Venezuela from which it is named belongs to the Dutch it's not strictly Latin American.

This lovely orange-flavored liqueur was made originally from a peculiar kind of local orange that had to fall from the tree before it was fit for distilling. The peel gave it the unusual flavor, after being soaked in water, then distilled with alcohol and water, flavored with Jamaica rum and sweetened a little or a lot, to make two kinds, a curaçao *sec* and a syrupy sweet tipple. The dry variety is the stronger, with about 40 degrees of alcoholic strength, the sweet kind is milder, with 30 degrees.

But now the bulk of curaçao is manufactured in Holland from almost any kind of orange peel, and the surest place to get the genuine article is in the West Indian island itself, although it is said that the Dutch ship over their own imitations for local consumption.

In Brazil, Paraguay and other Latin-American countries where sweet cordials are enjoyed a kind of curaçao is made at home by steeping thin peels of orange in sugar and water, then in pure alcohol.

MISCELLANEOUS TIPPLES

Asunción, Paraguay, and other South American centers have local cordials, liqueurs, mild and strong tipples of all sorts which can only be had on the spot. And every juicy tropical fruit is turned into wine.

The *chichas* of Chile and Bolivia, made variously from corn, other cereals and grapes, drunk out of polished horns and with a kick like a steer, are made fresh and downed to the last drop on feast days, so there's none left to ship to North America.

The grape brandy of Chile, *pisco*, is exported, however, and it's as fine as Mexico's tequila either for drinking straight or mixing, especially in punch.

SWIZZLES

The West Indies is the home of the swizzle stick, used exclusively in making refreshing drinks called swizzles. The sticks are supplied chiefly from Jamaica where a low bush with four roots thrusting out like tiny fingers makes a natural drink swirler. The stick is about fifteen inches long and the root prongs about one inch. You hold it between the palms and rotate the root end in whatever drink you want to beat to a froth. Usually the drink has an alcoholic "stick" in it besides.

BITTERS SWIZZLE

½ cup brandy   ¼ teaspoon sugar
1 jigger orange bitters   2 cups water

Froth with swizzle stick and serve at once.

Since swizzles were invented before cocktail shakers and by tropical Englishmen who never used ice in their drinks (not even the "ice" cubes made of glass that are sometimes put in to give an illusion of coolness), West Indian swizzles are usually too tepid for North American taste, so ice should be added.

RED SWIZZLE, OR RUM SWIZZLE

½ cup rum   Lime juice
1 pony grenadine   2 cups water

Curaçao and orange flower water are also used in flavoring swizzles, which can be compounded to fancy, just the same as cocktails. There are gin swizzles, green swizzles and fruity swizzles galore.

HOMEMADE LIQUEURS

MILK LIQUEUR

Boil 1 quart milk and cool. Add 3 cups grain alcohol, 2 pounds sugar, 2-inch length of vanilla bean, split, 1 square unsweetened chocolate, grated, and 2 round slices lemon with skin. Let stand 9 days, stirring every day at the same hour. Filter and bottle for use.

CHOCOLATE LIQUEUR

Crush 6 squares unsweetened chocolate and let stand in 3 cups alcohol 6 days. Filter and add 1 quart sugar syrup. Add 2 quarts water and filter again.

ANISE LIQUEUR

Make a syrup of 3 pounds sugar with 1 quart water. Add 30 drops essence of aniseed dissolved in 3 cups alcohol. Filter and add 2–3 tablespoons of magnesium carbonate. Stir; filter again and bottle for use.

Following Spanish custom, millions of Latin Americans enjoy a *copita* of Anise Liqueur with the morning coffee or chocolate.

WEST INDIAN COUPEREE

This is a vanilla ice-cream sundae with a jigger of brandy and a pony of curaçao poured over.

SMOKES

Cuba and Brazil are rivals in cigar making, although the *vuelta baja* tobacco of Cuba is rated as finest in the world. Bahia is Brazil's cigar center, and there you can buy the best, turned out by old Dutch firms such as Suerdick's who have captured much of the European market.

Cuban cigarettes also set the standard for the black tobacco kind preferred in most Latin-American countries and Puerto Rico competes by shipping us her own. But they're too strong for the average North American taste and the thick black or white blotting paper in which Havanas are wrapped makes too much of a smudge, even for mosquitoes.

Straw-wrapped cigarettes in Mexico, Central and South America are better suited to our nose, although usually made from a leaf as black as perique. They are strong, but once you're accustomed to the fragrant corncobby smell you can scarcely do without them. This is specially true of the tiny *Goyanas* of Brazil, shorter than your little finger and only a quarter as big around. Central American cigarettes made long and slim with white paper and milder tobacco are often distinctively flavored with native spices such as cinnamon and vanilla. This may sound sissy, but they've got what it takes.

NOTES ON NATIONAL CUISINES

TWO HAITIAN MENUS

A Haitian family living in the city enjoys this sort of a menu on Sundays and holidays:

Cocktail—made with Haitian rum
Red kidney bean soup
Chicken marinades (*Marinade de Poulet*)
Stuffed eggplant (*Aubergine Farcies*)
Roast turkey
Russian salad
Rice and beans
Fried ripe plantains served with rum sauce
Liqueurs
Demitasse with Haitian coffee

Since the language of Haiti is French, the menus include French dishes and white and red French wines, including champagne, are drunk with gala meals, although only red wine is served at ordinary weekday repasts.

EVERYDAY MENU

Fruit cup
Light soup
Meat balls and green plantains
Rice and beans
Sweet potato cake
Demitasse

Although no other Latin-American country, except neighboring Martinique, enjoys so many French dishes made by the original French recipes, the Everyday Menu shows that Haiti is one of the rice-and-beans republics with simple, substantial tastes.

THE BRAZILIAN CUISINE

Until recently no one in Brazil ever went hungry. The rivers and sea are teeming with fish, the forests with game, sharing with man the countless varieties of nourishing fruits, nuts and roots; bread literally hanging on the breadfruit tree requiring only the effort of climbing for it and afterward roasting it in the ashes of a casual campfire. So rich is this country with its four thousand miles of coast line and twenty-five-hundred-mile width of rich soil that the aborigines had no incentive to develop a culture, but lived under grass shelters, went naked and ate what was nearest at hand.

Before the depression even in Rio, a city of nearly two million inhabitants, those in need of black beans and rice, which are the bread and meat of the people, had only to apply at the nearest kitchen door to receive a portion of each, large enough for a day's living. So one would expect in such a country to find a race which likes to eat well and knows well how to do it.

What first impresses the stranger at the Brazilian table is its prodigality, and the number of persons, large and small, seated around the board, the big and comfortable families always augmented by visiting sisters, brothers, cousins, in-laws and all their children. Course after course appears between the chicken soup (*canja*) and the sweets and fruit and cheese, which invariably end a meal.

Until factories began draining the homes of domestic labor, service was cheap. It still is, in comparison with our pay standards, a good cook costing about twenty dollars a month, from which the scale grades downward to the small apprentices who work for their keep, do the running and carry trays of coffee at all hours.

Usually the day begins with a demitasse of sweet black coffee, served to each member of the family separately, at the bedside, or in the garden or on the terrace, wherever he happens to be in the early tropical dawn. Sometimes it is a cup of *maté* instead of coffee which breaks the night's fast. Coffee with hot milk, crisp rolls and butter with *marmelada* or *guiabada* (quince or guava paste) are served in the same informal fashion after the breadman arrives. The maids attend to this preliminary refreshment, because the cook is already busy with the preparation of the early lunch.

The Germans who have largely settled the Southern states and are sprinkled all over the rest of Brazil, the Italians who have always influenced the culture of the country, and the French have made their contributions to the art of cooking, especially in the sophisticated centers of population. But most of Brazilian dishes are Portuguese in origin, since the country was a colony of Portugal until 1822. The cooks in early times were not Portuguese, but black slaves from Africa. There is a saying, current to this day, "A mais preta a cozinheira, o melhor a comida." (The blacker the cook, the better the food.)

Cooking began to take on from the very first the distinctly national character which it still possesses, keeping its dependence on certain Portuguese products, such as olives, and olive oil, sheep cheese (*traz os montes*) from the old country, port wine and Madeira, salt codfish, almonds, etc., which were forced on the New World in the development of Portuguese export trade. The methods of preserving meats and making sausages are Portuguese, and the plates of hors d'oeuvres, so often served at the beginning of a dinner, always contain several Portuguese specialties, such as sardines, tuna fish, olives and pickles, thin curls of smoked ham (uncooked) and thinly sliced smoked sausages resembling bologna and salami.

No country has so many preserved meats. Whole stores are devoted to their sale, and supply pantries are always stocked with them since they do not spoil and are in constant use. Every part of the pig is pickled, or smoked or put up in cases. But the main stand-by is *carne secca*, the kitchen name for *Xarque* (pronounced sharkey), the side and under part of the beef minus the rib bones which has been preserved in a pickling bath and hung in the hot sun to dry. It is similar to the jerked beef of Texas which originated in Mexico, sublimely made in enormous quantities. *Xarque* is a part of the daily diet, enters into all boiled dinners and is the main meat ingredient of *Feijoada*, the national dish.

The possibilities of the Brazilian larder are infinite, with fine dishes made of the squashlike *xu-xu* (pronounced shoo-shoo), the seedy *quiabo* or okra and the bitter *gilo*, many varieties of squashes, pumpkins and pumpkinlike squashes whose tendrils, flowers and seeds have a delicious succulence. The unopened fronds of the bracken fern are also relished. There are countless varieties of the orange, banana, mango, custard apple, papaya, alligator pear, tamarind, breadfruit and others which have no English names—such as *guarana, sapoti, carambola* (whose slices are five-pointed stars). That delicious jelly-making *jabotacabo* whose fruit stems straight out from the bark, and the *jaca* which grows to watermelon size right out of the trunk of the tree. All of these are used for making cool drinks (*refrescos*) or sweets (*doces*) and are also eaten raw.

Farinha, the snowy white grated and toasted meal of manioc is ever present alongside the sugar bowl in a wooden dish accompanied by a wooden spoon. It is sprinkled at will over meats and vegetables and served up cooked in a hundred ways. But manioc is only one of many roots whose use would enrich our cuisine, although thus far they're unknown in colder climes.

One's approach to the equator is measured by the increase of spiciness in the food. But peppercorns, freshly ground or pounded, little pepper pods, either green or ripe red, pepper sauce made of pepper pods mashed in lime juice, grow fainter in Brazil as one travels southward toward cooler sections, while bay leaf, thyme, garlic, onion and a number of indigenous herbs stay with the meats and vegetables and impart the high flavors associated with tropical cooking, giving it the character so intriguing to our Northern palates.

BRAZILIAN TABLE DECORATIONS
AND MENUS

Flowers play a large part in the social and domestic life of Brazil, where even the humblest restaurants and pensions have a vase of blossoms on every table. Sometimes the food itself is decorated. A roast suckling pig will have a rose in its mouth, or a cake will be set in a wreath of flowers and leaves. There is also a lovely fashion of setting the stem of a liqueur glass on a circle of rose petals arranged on a tiny plate, the petals curling up around the base of the glass in a most inviting way.

MENUS
City Meals

Canja	*Fejoiada completa*
Peixe com molho do mar	*Caramella*
Quiabos com tomato	Cheese with *goiabada*
Pudim de banana	Coffee
Cheese	
Coffee	

Cozido	*Bouquet do mar*
Creme de coco	*Ovos Portuguezes*
Cheese with *marmelada*	*Pudim de coco,* or
Coffee	*Creme de laranjas*
	Coffee

Country Meals

Cabrito	*Caldo*
Abobereira no forno	*Peixe recheado*
Banana asada	*Arroz com palmito*
Cheese with *goiabada*	Oranges cut up as for
Coffee	*fejoiada* and sugared
	Coffee

Country Meals—*Continued:*

Pato com olivos

Abobereira no forno

Lettuce salad

Cheese with *marmelada*

Coffee

Cuelho Bahiano

Alface Romano

Salad *de abacate*

Cangica, or *Creme do milho verde*

Coffee

Unusual measures used in Brazilian kitchens:

A plateful: a dinner plate is a common measure in the Brazilian kitchen for dry materials. It is neither heaped nor level. The cook dips it into the sugar bucket or flour bin and shakes it back and forth a few times until its contents are slightly rounded.

A saucerful: a saucer used in the same manner.

A bottle: a pint and a half (3 cups).

A glassful: about 1 cup.

A fistful: about ⅓ cup.

When confronted with a Brazilian recipe requiring a plateful of flour, a saucerful of sugar, a half bottle of liquid and a fistful of raisins any North American breathes a sigh of relief when she comes to so-many eggs in the strange list of ingredients— at last a definite quantity, something she is sure of. But here her troubles are just beginning, for the average Brazilian cook seldom counts the eggs exactly, but has a technique just as baffling for making such things as spongecake. She piles the sugar and flour in a heap on a bread board, makes a hole in the center with her hand and breaks eggs into the hole until she thinks she has enough. Whereupon she begins to work the dry ingredients from the outside into the hole with her hand until the mass is wet enough, adding another egg or two as she sees fit, for the more eggs the better and lighter the cake that has no baking powder to make it rise. One of our cooks who boasted she carried over 300 recipes in her head was always talking about a cake which called for 60 eggs. We never encouraged her to try that one, but her others were excellent. A number of them were out of a book she called "Royal," a

Portuguese translation of the Royal Baking Powder pamphlet of recipes, all of which called for *fermento de po*, literally "yeast powder," sometimes briefly called "Royal," no matter what the brand, but she never entirely trusted them as she did her rule-of-thumb proportions and methods.

HORS D'OEUVRES IN RIO DE JANEIRO

In most of Latin America hors d'oeuvres are sketchy at best. One may receive a little meat pie to nibble at, or a piece of fish *escabeche* with olives and radishes to pass the time while the chef is putting on the individual touches that will make the meal personal. But Rio is the glamorous exception, especially if one eats at the Copacabana Hotel, perhaps the best in South America, or at the Jockey Club, where the hors d'oeuvre tables groan louder than anywhere else in the world except in Sweden, Denmark and a few Paris restaurants. Every guest makes at least one circle of this spread, gazing with rapt eyes at the great fish masked in mayonnaise, the hams, game, sausages and uncountable tidbits in amazing array while the headwaiter stands beaming at the parade. Service that follows the choice is formal and exquisite, and perhaps the headwaiter himself will carry the plate to the table if the guest is sufficiently distinguished.

Incidentally, the Jockey Club in Rio and the Jockey Club in Buenos Aires boast the finest wine cellars in Latin America.

FAVORITE CUBAN DISHES

The two most important dishes of every Cuban household, one of which is served every day, are *Arroz con Pollo*, and *Arroz con Frijoles*. With these fried plantains (*platanos verdes fritos*) are always served, and the commonest dessert that follows is guava paste (*dulce de guayaba*) with a tiny portion of cheese. Black coffee follows, Cuban coffee, strong and roasted to a dark brown. If there is one thing that Cubans miss on trips to this country, it is their own distinctive coffee. Their complaint is that our coffee is never sufficiently roasted and is made too weak, our idea being a thin brew with a very little thin cream, and theirs being a heavy dark infusion, taken without milk or cream for dinner or luncheon and mixed with at least half hot milk for breakfast. This is the invariable practice in all the Americas where coffee is raised.

Another very homely Cuban meal consists of fried green plantains, plain boiled rice, eggs fried soft and *picadello*. Now *picadello* is a very tasty little fry made of leftover meat, usually boiled beef, chopped quite fine (never ground), well seasoned and browned in lard with a minced onion, a bit of minced garlic and any handy herb. Eggs, rice and *picadello* are all mixed together on the plate, an intimate family custom not practiced on formal occasions or in public restaurants—a truly delicious combination and a well-balanced meal, with the fruity plantains to furnish vitamins.

Although *dulce de guayaba* is the ever-present sweet, there is no end of other confections and desserts, many of them heavy and rich with egg yolks and coconut. But best of all to finish a meal is an endless variety of fruits and ices made from their juices, fruits with no English names, like the *zapote*, *mamey*, *guanabana* and mango. (Of the last there is a new one introduced from the Philippines, called *Filipino*, with a very small flat seed which makes it easier to eat than the usual varieties.) Papaya ice, popularized originally for American tourists, is being made in many Cuban households.

The great Christmas dish is roast suckling pig (*lechon asado*), cooked in the oven, or preferably on a spit over live coals. The ubiquitous rice and beans are used for stuffing the little pig, but they are cooked together for this especial occasion with bits of guava paste scattered through to give that fruity flavor Northerners obtain by using apples, prunes, raisins, etc. Naturally this piggy has no red apple in his mouth, after the European fashion followed in the United States, for apples have no affinity with tropical climes.

PARAGUAYAN SPECIALTIES

Land-locked Paraguay is so peculiarly situated that communication with the outside world is had chiefly by the magnificent waterways of the Paraguay and Paraná rivers emptying into the Río de la Plata and connecting the country culturally with Buenos Aires. But unlike the Argentine, Paraguay straddles the Tropic of Capricorn, and half of it lies within the Torrid Zone, so it shares tropical food products, flora and fauna with Rio de Janeiro in the same latitude.

This republic is one vast orange grove, due not only to the climate but to the fact that at one time every homeowner was required by law to plant orange trees in his garden. Thus, too, the national diet is marked by the devotion to cassava or manioc, as is brought out in the following brief summary made for us by Sr. P. M. Ynsfran, counselor at the Paraguayan legation in Washington.

In the towns: The town dwellers' food in Paraguay is strongly influenced by both French and Italian cookery, although they still retain the old River Plate dish known as *Puchero* (See recipes.), which consists of beef, some bacon and several vegetables (cabbage, carrots, onions and sweet potatoes) all boiled together with rice or noodles. In Paraguay we add the manioc, which is a root gathered in tropical and subtropical countries, and is widely used in native cooking. Italian spaghetti or Italian ravioli are the outstanding features on holidays or fiestas. These are prepared exactly after the Italian fashion. It is worth noting that people of Italian descent make up a high percentage of the Paraguayan population.

Another native dish is turkey, prepared in the same manner as the North American Thanksgiving turkey.

As to drinking, the usual beverages are wine and beer. Paraguayans just drink coffee (black coffee, or with milk) or *yerba maté* for breakfast. Breakfast is served early in the morning between six and seven-thirty. Luncheon is served at twelve noon and is the main meal of the day. Well-to-do classes have tea with biscuits and cakes at five in the afternoon, after the English fashion. Dinner is served at eight in the evening.

In the country: People in the countryside have *yerba maté* early in the morning as soon as they get up and continue drinking it all during the day at various intervals. On the ranches they have luncheon about noon. This meal usually is a stew of beef and black-eye beans or Lima beans, manioc and corn. When the corn predominates in the stew the plate is called *Locro.*

On holidays or at feasts the *Locro* is quite an elaborate affair, because they add to it a number of vegetables, plus pork and chicken. As a matter of fact, the *Locro* prepared in this way is a delicious and nutritious dish. They usually eat also a cake made of corn or tapioca, prepared with milk and cheese and known by the name of *Chipa.* (See recipe for Paraguayan Chipa.) And a very important meal served on feast days by country people is *Chipá-guazu*, a large pudding made of corn, lard, onions and chopped meat.

Roast beef, roast lamb and roast poultry are important items in the countryside food list. But invariably every meal in Paraguay is accompanied by a portion of manioc or sweet potatoes. In the proper season corn on the cob is likewise served.

A CHILEAN–AMERICAN COOKBOOK

The influence of North America cooking on South America's cuisine has been very slight, although big cities such as Buenos Aires, Rio de Janeiro and Santiago de Chile have Yankee colonies numbering into the hundreds. North American women are always good missionaries for our national foods, however, and have carried Boston baked beans and apple pie recipes all the way from Panama to Patagonia, to return home with rules for making *carbonadas* and *empanaditas* picked up on the way.

We have seen cookbooks published by the ladies of American colonies in London, Paris and Tokyo, but the only South American contribution of this sort we've come across is a volume of *Recipes Collected and Edited by the Women's Auxiliary to the American Society of Chile*, dedicated "To the American women in Chile, far from home, and to their Chilean sisters." Many American engineers employed in Chile by the Braden Copper Company take their families along, so this bilingual book is a perfect primer for both Chilean cooks and North American mistresses. All of the recipes are printed in English on one page with the Spanish translation opposite, and since both Chilean and Yankee dishes are given it is also a fine text for furthering Chilean-American friendship and understanding.

An amusing and characteristically North American touch appears in the first two recipes which one also finds in the Ladies Aid Society cookbooks all the way from Portland, Maine, to Portland, Oregon:

HOW TO COOK HUSBANDS
Maridos: Como se Preparan

A good many husbands are spoilt by mismanagement in cooking, and so are not tender and good. Some women go about it as if their husbands were bladders, and blow them up. Others keep them constantly in hot water. Some keep them in a stew by irritating ways and words. Others roast them.

In selecting your husband, you should not be guided by his silvery appearance, as in buying a mackerel. Be sure to select him yourself, as tastes differ. By the way, do not go to the market for him. The best is always brought to the door.

INFALLIBLE RECIPE TO PRESERVE CHILDREN
Receta Infalible para Conservar Niños

Take one large grassy field, one half-dozen children, two or three small dogs, a pinch of brook and some pebbles. Mix the children and dogs well together and put them in a field, stirring constantly. Pour the brook over the pebbles. Sprinkle the field with flowers. Spread over all a deep blue sky and bake in the hot sun. When brown remove and set away to cool in a bathtub.

Such playful recipes translated into Spanish must please the Chilean ladies, for the cookbooks of South America are mostly limited to plain lists of ingredients and exact rules, without many such native, humorous touches.

We have tried out many of the recipes for fine Chilean dishes given in this collection, both on the spot, in Santiago and in our New York kitchen, and hereby extend our thanks to the "Women's Auxiliary to the American Society of Chile" for their valuable initiative.

TROPICAL AND BRAZILIAN GAME

Just as thousands of Americans have never tasted possum, muskrat, hedgehog or even marketed game such as venison, pheasant and rabbit, so great numbers of city-bred Brazilians have never eaten any of the wild creatures of their tropical jungles that appear so strange to Northern eyes. Big game in South America is not so plentiful as one might suppose from thrilling illustrations in school geography books. One must travel far into the interior to the haunts of the tapir and black leopard, and even then constant pursuit of food by native Indians has always depleted the supply. But small game of many sorts is plentiful everywhere. Wild hogs (*porco do matto*) and occasional pumas (*oncas*) roam through the dense undergrowths not far from the limits of Rio de Janeiro, attracting hunting parties from the city, but seldom reaching Rio markets.

Of all birds, the most prized by Brazilian gourmets is the macuca (*tinamou Braziliensis*), that grows as large as a wild turkey and has bluish flesh sweetened by the fruits and wild grain it lives on. There are a number of other big woodland birds of similar habits, almost resembling those of domestic fowls, all of which are prepared for the table in the same manner, namely the *jacutinga* ("white" guan), the *inhambú* and the *capoeira*. The domesticated guinea fowl, although it has dark flesh, is considered in the same class because of its wild way of life. In fact guinea fowl, originally native to Africa and adjacent islands, have escaped from plantations in some parts of the West Indies and South America to breed in the forest.

The following recipes serve for all of these birds:

MACUCO STUFFED WITH BRAZIL NUTS

Blanch and peel Brazil nuts. Fill bird with them and sew openings together. Brown bird nicely in 3 tablespoons butter or fat. Add 1 cup white wine, 1 garlic clove, 1 sliced onion, 4 whole peppers, 1 sprig basil, 2 sprigs parsley and salt. Cover closely and simmer 2 hours, turning occasionally. When tender take up on a hot platter. Slightly thicken gravy with flour. Add 2 tablespoons orange juice and 1 tablespoon lemon juice and serve in a gravy boat. Brazilians use the juice of the *laranja de terra* for such purposes, a flavorsome and sour orange which is excellent with all game and sea food, as is the bigarade orange of New Orleans fame.

Guinea hens done in this manner are something special.

MACUCA ROASTED ON THE GRILL
Macuca Assado

Lard the breast of the bird with ribbons of salt pork. Season with salt and pepper. Make a stuffing of finely chopped macuca liver, 4 slices bacon, chopped fine, 2 cups soft bread crumbs wet with milk and squeezed dry, 1 teaspoon sugar, ¼ teaspoon grated nutmeg and ¼ teaspoon salt. Stuff bird and sew up. Wrap in several thicknesses of banana leaves and roast on grill over live coals, turning frequently. When nearly done remove leaves and let brown.

This is an excellent method for preparing any wild birds, husks of green corn being used for wrapping when banana leaves cannot be obtained.

PARROTS, MACAWS AND PARAKEETS

If young, birds of the parrot family are seasoned, grilled before medium heat and basted from time to time with tablespoons of cream. The drippings are thinned with milk and thickened with cornstarch.

If old and talkative, as parrots usually are since some species live as long and get as garrulous as human beings, it sometimes takes as long as five hours to cook them tender. Here is one method:

STUFFED PARROT
Papagaio Recheado

Make a stuffing of chopped parrot's liver, 3 slices bacon finely minced, 2 chopped hard-cooked eggs, 1 minced onion, 1 teaspoon minced parsley, 1 dozen olives, 2 slices bread wet with *aguardiente* (white rum), salt and pepper. Mix thoroughly together. Stuff bird and sew up. Lard the breast with bacon strips. Wrap bacon slices around bird and tie securely. Place in pot-roast kettle with a little water or white wine. Bring rapidly to boiling point. Reduce heat and simmer until tender. Remove bacon wrapping and lay bird on hot platter. Skim gravy free of fat and pour over.

We had a blasphemous golden-headed parrot in Brazil who was always thieving and making a nuisance of himself, having the free run of the kitchen regions and patios. The cook who loved him and eventually inherited him when we were leaving usually laughed at his pranks, and he learned to laugh back at her in exact imitation. But once in a while she would turn on him, exasperated when he was caught tearing up something just for fun, or sneaking into the sugar bucket when her back was turned.

"I'll put you in the pot for that, Louro, you old scamp," she would threaten. "I'd cook you in a minute if you weren't ninety years old and tough as leather." She would make a pass at him with her butcher knife, and he would sidle away to his perch where he would sit and sulk until she brought him a banana as a peace offering. When a well-camouflaged bird appeared on the table it was our habit to go and make sure old Louro was still there before we started to carve.

DARK–FLESHED JUNGLE BIRDS

Most of the big birds from the depths of the jungle have dark flesh, and for that reason are cooked with spice and wine and are served with a tart salad—sometimes of borage leaves—or with a piquant sauce.

Chief among them from a culinary point of view is the fruit and seed-eating jacu (guan or Penelope) that grows to a length of thirty inches and resembles the curassow, with brilliantly colored naked throat, crested head and rather helpless wings which make it an easily tamed garden pet.

Then there is the true curassow, the *seriama* (of the curiamae family), the toucan, familiar in zoological gardens because it does well in captivity, the *aracari* which is similar to the toucan, the *guache* and numerous others that have no counterpart in temperate zones.

A familiar method of preparing all of these birds is as follows:

If birds are young, season and roast on grill before medium heat until nearly done. Remove and cut up at joints. Heat 2 tablespoons butter. Add 2 tablespoons flour. Stir and simmer 5 minutes. Add 1 cup orange juice, 1 cup white wine and drippings from grill pan. Stir and simmer until smooth. Add cut-up bird and simmer, closely covered, until completely tender.

STUFFED JACU

Make one of the stuffings described below. Fill bird and sew up. Cover bottom of saucepan with bacon slices and lay bird on top. Add 1 cup chopped salt pork, 2 sliced onions, 3 cloves, 3 parsley sprigs, 1 cup boiling water and 1 cup white wine. Bring quickly to boiling point. Reduce heat. Cover closely and cook gently until tender, turning bird over at least once. Take up bird on hot platter. Skim fat from gravy and thicken with a little cassava meal or with flour blended with a little cold water.

STUFFINGS FOR JUNGLE BIRDS

(1) Wet 1 generous cup soft bread crumbs with milk and squeeze dry. Add 1 cup chopped suet, 1 tablespoon sugar, 3 tablespoons seeded raisins that have been plumped in hot water, 4–5 crushed cardamom seeds, 1 cup chopped mushrooms, salt and pepper. Mix well and add 2 well-beaten egg yolks.

(2) Chop bird's liver. Mix with ½ cup minced bacon, ½ cup minced salt pork, 2 cups soft bread crumbs moistened with white wine, 1 chopped small onion, a very little salt, plenty of pepper and a tiny dash of ground ginger. Mix well together. A chopped carrot may be substituted for either bacon or salt pork.

These are excellent stuffings for Northern big-game birds such as pheasant.

BRAZILIAN SMALLER BIRDS

Brazil, in addition to her wealth of tropical feathered game, has many familiar birds besides—partridges, quails, doves and wild pigeons—which are either cooked after well-known French methods or in combination with native fruits and vegetables. Migratory song birds are also eaten, including larks and mocking birds (*cotovias* and *sabias*), a favorite accompaniment being fried red bananas.

Of water birds and the wader family there are snipe and woodcocks, water hens, "wood" ducks and geese (*pato silvestre* and *ganso silvestre*) and the famous Muscovy duck that has been domesticated in many countries. Brazilian cooks do a delectable job of roasting all of these with herbs, onion and garlic, basting them with a mixture of orange juice and Madeira.

EDIBLE REPTILES

The frog has long been the only reptile generally acceptable for food, among North Americans, relished by gourmets and many other folks who would shudder at snake meat. But since rattlesnake is now smoked and canned in Florida to appear at fancy prices in New York night clubs, snakes have joined the luxury class, and tolerance for them will no doubt grow after they have ceased to be a novelty, for there is no reason why their white clean meat should be taboo when frogs and eels are considered great treats. As for the huge gray lizards, or iguanas, that are piled in stacks in almost any Central American or Mexican market, each one alive with its jaws tied and feet tethered, every tourist who can work his courage to the tasting point finds them as fine as chicken. In fact he may have dined on fricaseed iguana unawares and never known the difference. Only the rough-skinned vegetarian lizards are eaten, never the smooth-skinned insect-eating species. They are often found in old hollow arbovitae trees. Mexican hunters cut a hole high up in the trunk and another low down, and if the beast cannot be stirred out with a stick thrust in from the top, a few hot coals dropped usually make him pop through the bottom hole, where he is seized and taken to be kept alive until wanted by the cook.

Although great numbers of the inhabitants of hot countries share Adam and Eve's repugnance to cold-blooded land animals, these grow to such size and meaty perfection that plenty of people proclaim their goodness, even their superiority to fish and many other kinds of game. And the same is true of the big brother alligator whose juicy tail is roasted in Colombia and makes as big a hit as baked kangaroo tail in Australia.

Gigantic frogs are found in the Argentine markets, and some

in Brazil are big enough to make their back and fore legs worth cooking, as well as their hind quarters. There is a giant land frog, too, similar to the crapauds of the West Indies, which makes excellent eating, a single frog (like an ostrich egg) making a meal for several persons.

Of the snakes the viviparous ones are claimed to be much better than those that lay eggs. Whether they are poisonous or not doesn't matter, since the poison lies only in pockets behind the jaws, and snakes are invariably beheaded for culinary purposes.

All three of these creatures, frogs, snakes and big lizards, are cooked according to the same methods, for their flesh is much the same in texture, if not in flavor.

FRIED FROGS, SNAKES OR LIZARDS

After skinning, dress and cut up the meat. Marinate 3 hours in sour orange juice (or in the juice of sweet oranges acidulated with lemon juice), adding a teaspoon of whole peppers and a dash of nutmeg to the marinade. Drain; wipe dry. Season with salt. Dip in beaten egg and fine crumbs and fry in deep fat, or butter, in a frying pan.

STEWED FROGS, SNAKES OR LIZARDS

Season pieces. Dredge with flour and brown in fat or butter along with 1 sliced onion. Add 1 cup boiling water, 1 teaspoon minced parsley and a dash of nutmeg. Cover closely and cook gently until tender. Beat 2 egg yolks with 1 cup white wine and add gradually, being careful not to let liquid come to boiling point and curdle egg yolks.

UMBRELLA ANT QUEENS

One might call this queer tropical food "ant roe," for it is classed as a sea food. When queen *tanajuras* and *sauvas*, which are enormous ants, want to form a new colony they go about it in much the same way as bees swarm, but first they grow wings and do not look like ants at all. In this condition they sally forth to make new ant hills, and the queens, extended with roe until their abdomens are big as Lima beans, are captured in quantities. These flying or "umbrella" ants are first scalded in hot water and drained. Then the abdomens are detached and fried in deep fat until well browned. Seasoned with salt and pepper, these little crisp tidbits taste something like shrimps.

Along the Amazon River they are esteemed, especially by Indians. And explorers become so accustomed to thinking of ants as food that they crush a new specimen between their teeth to determine by its lemony or other flavor to what species it belongs.

WILD PIGS

The most popular and commonly served of all wild animals in Brazil are the plentiful wild pigs that even appear on city restaurant menus. Three kinds are easily procurable, and all are *muito saboroso*, as the Brazilians say, "very flavorsome and succulent," being vastly superior to domestic pork because of their lean, fine-textured meat and gaminess.

There are three common kinds: (1) *porco do matto* or wild hog with especially white and tender flesh, (2) *queixado*, a black animal the size of a domestic pig and (3) *caititu*, or peccary, smaller and with reddish-brown bristly fur and very delicately flavored meat—a friendly creature in captivity that could easily be domesticated. All have unsavory glands that are removed as soon as possible after the animals are killed.

Cooking methods for all three are the same, and recipes are endless. They are cut into steaks and cutlets for grilling, and large cuts are baked, pot-roasted or stewed with prunes, with raisins, with pine nuts or with mushrooms. Less desirable parts are made into sausages. And the hind quarters, after being pickled in a spicy marinade of red wine, make wonderful smoked hams.

DEER

Next to wild pigs, venison is the most prized of Brazilian furred game. There are at least five species, from the big *cervo* (stag) to the tiny *vira*. Cooks follow European ways of preparing them, except when tropical fruits and vegetables are used in combination.

TAPIR (ANTA)

This long flexible-snooted woodland creature, of prehistoric mien, is frequently hunted in hinterland plantations because of its destruction of crops. But often the carcass is thrown away and only the tough hide is saved, from which the Portuguese conquistadores once made whips, more durable and cruel than any from bull's hide, with which they lashed their Indian slaves to work in the tobacco and sugar fields.

The meat makes excellent eating, however, after 24 hours of marinating in dry wine, lemon juice, oil, onion slices, garlic and herbs. (See Marinating Mixture for Rabbit.) It then becomes so tasty that it is preferred by some Brazilian epicures to all other game. The texture of an old animal is coarse and dry as horse meat, but a young one, a year old or less, is tender and succulent, and has a flavor between young beef and venison. The choice cut is the loin, which is larded with salt pork, marinated and grilled over coals. It is also cut into cabobs and grilled; wrapped in banana leaves and roasted barbecue-fashion in a heated pit covered with hot stones and earth; made into stews with yam wurzel or with okra; and cooked with sliced *sapucaias* (nuts resembling coconut) and flavored with ginger root and cloves. The most primitive dish of this gamy meat is made from a good-sized cut with the hide left on, just seasoned with salt and roasted in an outdoor mud oven. It is carved to include a strip of hide with each slice, and served with a little tart salad of borage leaves on the side and eaten with tiny dashes of a fiery sauce made of chili peppers mashed with lime juice.

SOUTH AMERICAN LEOPARDS AND ANTEATERS

Not much can be said for the eating qualities of leopards (*onças*) and anteaters (*tamenduas*), for the meat of both is tough and dry, and that of the *onça* is decidedly catty. They are eaten, however, by aborigines and by travelers into the interior if only for medicinal purposes. *Onça* flesh, once partaken of, is supposed to impart permanent strength, agility and courage to face anything. But several days of marinating and long slow cooking are necessary before either of these meats can be attacked by human teeth. (See Marinating Mixture for Rabbit.)

OTTER

Otter (*lontra*) tastes like rabbit, and any rabbit recipe can be used in its preparation.

For Brazilian rabbit recipes, see MEATS.

TROPICAL RODENTS

Wild rodents in the Torrid Zone have clean habits and are just as edible as are Northern squirrels and rabbits. They range in size from the big capybara to the tiny guinea pig that was domesticated for food purposes in prehistoric Peru. The three in highest culinary repute are capybara, paca and cotia.

CAPYBARA

The capybara (*capivara*), sometimes called water hog, which looks like a giant guinea pig with short front legs and brown fur, grows to the size of a year-old shoat. It is semiaquatic, living in burrows along streams and sallying forth at night to browse in sugar and rice fields. It is gentle and so easily tamed that specimens kept for sale often run about underfoot in country markets. Since it is supposed to eat fish as well as green stuffs the fat under the skin and in its insides has a rank taste. When this is removed the rest of the flesh is sweet and delicious. Its preparation illustrates the patience of the Brazilian cook, for it is marinated 24 hours (See Marinating Mixture for Rabbit.), soaked in water under a dripping tap another 24 hours, parboiled, drained, dried and then soaked in the juice of the wild orange 6–8 hours, when it is at last ready for cooking. Then it is browned in fat or butter, put into boiling water with a glass of white rum, seasonings, including herbs, onion, cloves and ginger, and cooked until done. The proper accompaniment is a wilted salad of wild greens.

PACA

This awkward-looking creature resembling the capybara, but having longitudinal stripes running down the back of its coarsely furred pelt, is so common that it is hunted in the outskirts of Rio de Janeiro with dogs which help dig it out of its burrows. Its food of fruits and tender green give its white flesh a sweetness resembling that of young pig. Undoubtedly it is best grilled before a moderate fire while being basted with a marinade mixture. Leftover meat is made into tasty balls with onion, garlic, herbs and a little ginger. Or it is simmered in clabbered milk and served with the cooking liquor made into a sauce with white wine and egg yolks.

COTIA

Common from Mexico southward, this little rodent about the size of a rabbit is daily fare in many parts. It breeds in captivity and is often seen in gardens, sitting up on its little tailless haunches like a prairie dog. The flavor of its flesh is something like rabbit, and methods of cooking are about the same, with lime or orange juice added to rabbit recipe. The cotia is also cooked with chayote, cassava root, squash, tomatoes and various other roots and vegetables—whatever is handy.

MONKEYS

Since most species of wild monkeys have no more intelligence than domestic animals we eat every day, there is no reason why they should be spared from our carnivorous appetites. Nevertheless Brazilians do not cook the heads of monkeys as they do of other animals destined for the table, and even sometimes take the meat from the bones after cooking, to remove all cannibalistic suggestions.

Monkey flesh is tender but dry, needing to be larded or cooked with fat pork. A favorite recipe is to stew it with whole unpeeled red bananas. When tender the meat is finished in a gravy made of its broth, to which is added a cup of white wine, a dash of lime juice and thickening. The bananas are peeled and used as a garnish at one end of the platter.

Roast monkey is a favorite in Eastern Peru.

COATI

This common tropical cousin of the raccoon, with an extra-long snout used for rooting up its food, is excellent and popular game. It is about the size of a big cat and is usually marinated and cooked whole, sometimes stuffed. It may be grilled, stewed or roasted.

GAMBA

Of all the small edible animals, the Brazilian gamba that looks like a miniature possum is most common. After its ill-flavored glands are removed it is prepared like possum, but when served up on the platter looks like a squirrel.

ARMADILLO

In Brazil the armadillo (*tatú*) has as many quaint legends and fancies woven around it as has the possum in our own South, for this curiously armored animal, with its comical head and rattling, plated tail, has the ability to roll into an impenetrable ball, dig itself into the earth so rapidly that no man with a shovel can keep up with it, and do other quaint tricks that no other animal is equipped to perform. The resemblance does not end here, for the armadillo when cooked tastes rich and porky, more like the possum than any other game. It is so easily captured and so universally liked that almost everybody from Mexico to the Argentine eats armadillo, and down in Texas during the Depression it was popularized under the apt name of "Hoover Hog."

Brazil has three varieties, and any cook will explain that it is not the rank-flavored kind which take up their abodes in abandoned cemeteries, nor the giant kind that are tough, but only the sweet, white-fleshed little *tatu mirim* which is fit for the table. After being dressed and the glands removed, the most frequent mode of preparation is to leave all the meat in the armored shell and bake it as is, merely with seasonings and a dash of minced parsley. Many delicatessen shops sell them already baked in this fashion, just as they do boiled lobsters.

But the *tatú* in home kitchens is also taken out of its shell and fried, stewed or pot-roasted.

FRIED TATÚ

Take meat from shell and cut into convenient pieces. Make a sauce with the juice of 1 lime, 1 chopped tomato, 1 sliced onion, 1 teaspoon minced parsley and 3–4 crushed whole peppers. Mash together. Mix thoroughly. Pour over meat in a close-fitting bowl and marinate 6 hours, turning meat over several times to season all evenly. Drain and dry. Season with salt.

Dredge with flour and fry in plenty of fat, as you would chicken.

STEWED TATÚ

Take *tatú* meat from shell. Wash well with soap and water, then wash in sour orange or lime juice. Cut up and wipe dry. Brown pieces in fat together with a sliced onion. Add 1 crushed garlic clove, seasonings and 1 scant pint of white wine. Cook gently until tender. Thicken gravy with flour, adding a little more white wine if gravy is insufficient.

The shells are often saved to polish and make into unusual little baskets lined with silk which you see in curio shops all over Latin America.

PROGRESSIVE LATIN-AMERICAN DINNER

"If a gourmet were gifted with ubiquity," says Dr William Lytle Schurz (the "Bill" to whom this book is dedicated, with his wife, Marie), "I should recommend to him the following menu of the best that Latin America offers. Were he of those who must have an apéritif before dining, his choice would probably be a daiquiri at Bacardi's own bar in Santiago de Cuba, and then":

Morro Crab Cocktail
(The Sevilla, Havana)

Canja Soup
(The Copacabana Hotel, Rio de Janeiro)

Artichokes
(The Bahia, Santiago)

Pollo a la Spiedo
(Villa's, Buenos Aires)

Chateaubriand
(The Trocadero, Buenos Aires)

Stuffed Tomato Salad
(The Maury, Lima)

Strawberries
(The Maury, Lima)

Palmyra Cheese
(Brazil)

Coffee
(São Paulo or Medellin)

Pour la Noblesse Cigarettes
(Rio de Janeiro)
or
Monte Carlo Cigarettes
(Mexico)

Cigars
(Havana or Bahia)

Wines
Benitez Rheinwein (Chile)
Venegas Derby (Argentine)

Liqueurs
Curaçao or Creme de Cacao

INDEX

INDEX

351

FOREIGN INDEX

A CATALOGUE OF
SELECTED DOVER BOOKS
IN ALL FIELDS OF INTEREST

A CATALOGUE OF SELECTED DOVER
BOOKS IN ALL FIELDS OF INTEREST

RACKHAM'S COLOR ILLUSTRATIONS FOR WAGNER'S RING. Rackham's finest mature work—all 64 full-color watercolors in a faithful and lush interpretation of the *Ring*. Full-sized plates on coated stock of the paintings used by opera companies for authentic staging of Wagner. Captions aid in following complete Ring cycle. Introduction. 64 illustrations plus vignettes. 72pp. 8⅝ x 11¼.   23779-6 Pa. $6.00

CONTEMPORARY POLISH POSTERS IN FULL COLOR, edited by Joseph Czestochowski. 46 full-color examples of brilliant school of Polish graphic design, selected from world's first museum (near Warsaw) dedicated to poster art. Posters on circuses, films, plays, concerts all show cosmopolitan influences, free imagination. Introduction. 48pp. 9⅜ x 12¼.
23780-X Pa. $6.00

GRAPHIC WORKS OF EDVARD MUNCH, Edvard Munch. 90 haunting, evocative prints by first major Expressionist artist and one of the greatest graphic artists of his time: *The Scream, Anxiety, Death Chamber, The Kiss, Madonna,* etc. Introduction by Alfred Werner. 90pp. 9 x 12.
23765-6 Pa. $5.00

THE GOLDEN AGE OF THE POSTER, Hayward and Blanche Cirker. 70 extraordinary posters in full colors, from Maitres de l'Affiche, Mucha, Lautrec, Bradley, Cheret, Beardsley, many others. Total of 78pp. 9⅜ x 12¼.   22753-7 Pa. $5.95

THE NOTEBOOKS OF LEONARDO DA VINCI, edited by J. P. Richter. Extracts from manuscripts reveal great genius; on painting, sculpture, anatomy, sciences, geography, etc. Both Italian and English. 186 ms. pages reproduced, plus 500 additional drawings, including studies for *Last Supper,* Sforza monument, etc. 860pp. 7⅞ x 10¾. (Available in U.S. only)
22572-0, 22573-9 Pa., Two-vol. set $15.90

THE CODEX NUTTALL, as first edited by Zelia Nuttall. Only inexpensive edition, in full color, of a pre-Columbian Mexican (Mixtec) book. 88 color plates show kings, gods, heroes, temples, sacrifices. New explanatory, historical introduction by Arthur G. Miller. 96pp. 11⅜ x 8½. (Available in U.S. only)   23168-2 Pa. $7.95

UNE SEMAINE DE BONTÉ, A SURREALISTIC NOVEL IN COLLAGE, Max Ernst. Masterpiece created out of 19th-century periodical illustrations, explores worlds of terror and surprise. Some consider this Ernst's greatest work. 208pp. 8⅛ x 11.   23252-2 Pa. $6.00

DRAWINGS OF WILLIAM BLAKE, William Blake. 92 plates from Book of Job, *Divine Comedy, Paradise Lost,* visionary heads, mythological figures, Laocoon, etc. Selection, introduction, commentary by Sir Geoffrey Keynes. 178pp. 8⅛ x 11. 22303-5 Pa. $4.00

ENGRAVINGS OF HOGARTH, William Hogarth. 101 of Hogarth's greatest works: *Rake's Progress, Harlot's Progress, Illustrations for Hudibras, Before and After, Beer Street and Gin Lane,* many more. Full commentary. 256pp. 11 x 13¾. 22479-1 Pa. $12.95

DAUMIER: 120 GREAT LITHOGRAPHS, Honore Daumier. Wide-ranging collection of lithographs by the greatest caricaturist of the 19th century. Concentrates on eternally popular series on lawyers, on married life, on liberated women, etc. Selection, introduction, and notes on plates by Charles F. Ramus. Total of 158pp. 9⅜ x 12¼. 23512-2 Pa. $6.00

DRAWINGS OF MUCHA, Alphonse Maria Mucha. Work reveals draftsman of highest caliber: studies for famous posters and paintings, renderings for book illustrations and ads, etc. 70 works, 9 in color; including 6 items not drawings. Introduction. List of illustrations. 72pp. 9⅜ x 12¼. (Available in U.S. only) 23672-2 Pa. $4.00

GIOVANNI BATTISTA PIRANESI: DRAWINGS IN THE PIERPONT MORGAN LIBRARY, Giovanni Battista Piranesi. For first time ever all of Morgan Library's collection, world's largest. 167 illustrations of rare Piranesi drawings—archeological, architectural, decorative and visionary. Essay, detailed list of drawings, chronology, captions. Edited by Felice Stampfle. 144pp. 9⅜ x 12¼. 23714-1 Pa. $7.50

NEW YORK ETCHINGS (1905-1949), John Sloan. All of important American artist's N.Y. life etchings. 67 works include some of his best art; also lively historical record—Greenwich Village, tenement scenes. Edited by Sloan's widow. Introduction and captions. 79pp. 8⅜ x 11¼. 23651-X Pa. $4.00

CHINESE PAINTING AND CALLIGRAPHY: A PICTORIAL SURVEY, Wan-go Weng. 69 fine examples from John M. Crawford's matchless private collection: landscapes, birds, flowers, human figures, etc., plus calligraphy. Every basic form included: hanging scrolls, handscrolls, album leaves, fans, etc. 109 illustrations. Introduction. Captions. 192pp. 8⅞ x 11¾. 23707-9 Pa. $7.95

DRAWINGS OF REMBRANDT, edited by Seymour Slive. Updated Lippmann, Hofstede de Groot edition, with definitive scholarly apparatus. All portraits, biblical sketches, landscapes, nudes, Oriental figures, classical studies, together with selection of work by followers. 550 illustrations. Total of 630pp. 9⅛ x 12¼. 21485-0, 21486-9 Pa., Two-vol. set $15.00

THE DISASTERS OF WAR, Francisco Goya. 83 etchings record horrors of Napoleonic wars in Spain and war in general. Reprint of 1st edition, plus 3 additional plates. Introduction by Philip Hofer. 97pp. 9⅜ x 8¼. 21872-4 Pa. $4.00

THE EARLY WORK OF AUBREY BEARDSLEY, Aubrey Beardsley. 157 plates, 2 in color: *Manon Lescaut, Madame Bovary, Morte Darthur, Salome,* other. Introduction by H. Marillier. 182pp. 8⅛ x 11. 21816-3 Pa. $4.50

THE LATER WORK OF AUBREY BEARDSLEY, Aubrey Beardsley. Exotic masterpieces of full maturity: *Venus and Tannhauser, Lysistrata, Rape of the Lock, Volpone,* Savoy material, etc. 174 plates, 2 in color. 186pp. 8⅛ x 11. 21817-1 Pa. $5.95

THOMAS NAST'S CHRISTMAS DRAWINGS, Thomas Nast. Almost all Christmas drawings by creator of image of Santa Claus as we know it, and one of America's foremost illustrators and political cartoonists. 66 illustrations. 3 illustrations in color on covers. 96pp. 8⅜ x 11¼. 23660-9 Pa. $3.50

THE DORÉ ILLUSTRATIONS FOR DANTE'S DIVINE COMEDY, Gustave Doré. All 135 plates from Inferno, Purgatory, Paradise; fantastic tortures, infernal landscapes, celestial wonders. Each plate with appropriate (translated) verses. 141pp. 9 x 12. 23231-X Pa. $4.50

DORÉ'S ILLUSTRATIONS FOR RABELAIS, Gustave Doré. 252 striking illustrations of *Gargantua and Pantagruel* books by foremost 19th-century illustrator. Including 60 plates, 192 delightful smaller illustrations. 153pp. 9 x 12. 23656-0 Pa. $5.00

LONDON: A PILGRIMAGE, Gustave Doré, Blanchard Jerrold. Squalor, riches, misery, beauty of mid-Victorian metropolis; 55 wonderful plates, 125 other illustrations, full social, cultural text by Jerrold. 191pp. of text. 9⅜ x 12¼. 22306-X Pa. $7.00

THE RIME OF THE ANCIENT MARINER, Gustave Doré, S. T. Coleridge. Dore's finest work, 34 plates capture moods, subtleties of poem. Full text. Introduction by Millicent Rose. 77pp. 9¼ x 12. 22305-1 Pa. $3.50

THE DORE BIBLE ILLUSTRATIONS, Gustave Doré. All wonderful, detailed plates: Adam and Eve, Flood, Babylon, Life of Jesus, etc. Brief King James text with each plate. Introduction by Millicent Rose. 241 plates. 241pp. 9 x 12. 23004-X Pa. $6.00

THE COMPLETE ENGRAVINGS, ETCHINGS AND DRYPOINTS OF ALBRECHT DURER. "Knight, Death and Devil"; "Melencolia," and more—all Dürer's known works in all three media, including 6 works formerly attributed to him. 120 plates. 235pp. 8⅜ x 11¼. 22851-7 Pa. $6.50

MECHANICK EXERCISES ON THE WHOLE ART OF PRINTING, Joseph Moxon. First complete book (1683-4) ever written about typography, a compendium of everything known about printing at the latter part of 17th century. Reprint of 2nd (1962) Oxford Univ. Press edition. 74 illustrations. Total of 550pp. 6⅛ x 9¼. 23617-X Pa. $7.95

THE COMPLETE WOODCUTS OF ALBRECHT DURER, edited by Dr. W. Kurth. 346 in all: "Old Testament," "St. Jerome," "Passion," "Life of Virgin," Apocalypse," many others. Introduction by Campbell Dodgson. 285pp. 8½ x 12¼.   21097-9 Pa. $7.50

DRAWINGS OF ALBRECHT DURER, edited by Heinrich Wolfflin. 81 plates show development from youth to full style. Many favorites; many new. Introduction by Alfred Werner. 96pp. 8⅛ x 11.   22352-3 Pa. $5.00

THE HUMAN FIGURE, Albrecht Dürer. Experiments in various techniques—stereometric, progressive proportional, and others. Also life studies that rank among finest ever done. Complete reprinting of *Dresden Sketchbook*. 170 plates. 355pp. 8⅜ x 11¼.   21042-1 Pa. $7.95

OF THE JUST SHAPING OF LETTERS, Albrecht Dürer. Renaissance artist explains design of Roman majuscules by geometry, also Gothic lower and capitals. Grolier Club edition. 43pp. 7⅞ x 10¾   21306-4 Pa. $3.00

TEN BOOKS ON ARCHITECTURE, Vitruvius. The most important book ever written on architecture. Early Roman aesthetics, technology, classical orders, site selection, all other aspects. Stands behind everything since. Morgan translation. 331pp. 5⅜ x 8½.   20645-9 Pa. $4.50

THE FOUR BOOKS OF ARCHITECTURE, Andrea Palladio. 16th-century classic responsible for Palladian movement and style. Covers classical architectural remains, Renaissance revivals, classical orders, etc. 1738 Ware English edition. Introduction by A. Placzek. 216 plates. 110pp. of text. 9½ x 12¾.   21308-0 Pa. $10.00

HORIZONS, Norman Bel Geddes. Great industrialist stage designer, "father of streamlining," on application of aesthetics to transportation, amusement, architecture, etc. 1932 prophetic account; function, theory, specific projects. 222 illustrations. 312pp. 7⅞ x 10¾.   23514-9 Pa. $6.95

FRANK LLOYD WRIGHT'S FALLINGWATER, Donald Hoffmann. Full, illustrated story of conception and building of Wright's masterwork at Bear Run, Pa. 100 photographs of site, construction, and details of completed structure. 112pp. 9¼ x 10.   23671-4 Pa. $5.50

THE ELEMENTS OF DRAWING, John Ruskin. Timeless classic by great Viltorian; starts with basic ideas, works through more difficult. Many practical exercises. 48 illustrations. Introduction by Lawrence Campbell. 228pp. 5⅜ x 8½.   22730-8 Pa. $3.75

GIST OF ART, John Sloan. Greatest modern American teacher, Art Students League, offers innumerable hints, instructions, guided comments to help you in painting. Not a formal course. 46 illustrations. Introduction by Helen Sloan. 200pp. 5⅜ x 8½.   23435-5 Pa. $4.00

THE ANATOMY OF THE HORSE, George Stubbs. Often considered the great masterpiece of animal anatomy. Full reproduction of 1766 edition, plus prospectus; original text and modernized text. 36 plates. Introduction by Eleanor Garvey. 121pp. 11 x 14¾.   23402-9 Pa. $6.00

BRIDGMAN'S LIFE DRAWING, George B. Bridgman. More than 500 illustrative drawings and text teach you to abstract the body into its major masses, use light and shade, proportion; as well as specific areas of anatomy, of which Bridgman is master. 192pp. 6½ x 9¼. (Available in U.S. only)
22710-3 Pa. $3.50

ART NOUVEAU DESIGNS IN COLOR, Alphonse Mucha, Maurice Verneuil, Georges Auriol. Full-color reproduction of *Combinaisons ornementales* (c. 1900) by Art Nouveau masters. Floral, animal, geometric, interlacings, swashes—borders, frames, spots—all incredibly beautiful. 60 plates, hundreds of designs. 9⅜ x 8-1/16.   22885-1 Pa. $4.00

FULL-COLOR FLORAL DESIGNS IN THE ART NOUVEAU STYLE, E. A. Seguy. 166 motifs, on 40 plates, from *Les fleurs et leurs applications decoratives* (1902): borders, circular designs, repeats, allovers, "spots." All in authentic Art Nouveau colors. 48pp. 9⅜ x 12¼.
23439-8 Pa. $5.00

A DIDEROT PICTORIAL ENCYCLOPEDIA OF TRADES AND IN-DUSTRY, edited by Charles C. Gillispie. 485 most interesting plates from the great French Encyclopedia of the 18th century show hundreds of working figures, artifacts, process, land and cityscapes; glassmaking, paper-making, metal extraction, construction, weaving, making furniture, clothing, wigs, dozens of other activities. Plates fully explained. 920pp. 9 x 12.
22284-5, 22285-3 Clothbd., Two-vol. set $40.00

HANDBOOK OF EARLY ADVERTISING ART, Clarence P. Hornung. Largest collection of copyright-free early and antique advertising art ever compiled. Over 6,000 illustrations, from Franklin's time to the 1890's for special effects, novelty. Valuable source, almost inexhaustible.
Pictorial Volume. Agriculture, the zodiac, animals, autos, birds, Christmas, fire engines, flowers, trees, musical instruments, ships, games and sports, much more. Arranged by subject matter and use. 237 plates. 288pp. 9 x 12.
20122-8 Clothbd. $14.50

Typographical Volume. Roman and Gothic faces ranging from 10 point to 300 point, "Barnum," German and Old English faces, script, logotypes, scrolls and flourishes, 1115 ornamental initials, 67 complete alphabets, more. 310 plates. 320pp. 9 x 12.   20123-6 Clothbd. $15.00

CALLIGRAPHY (CALLIGRAPHIA LATINA), J. G. Schwandner. High point of 18th-century ornamental calligraphy. Very ornate initials, scrolls, borders, cherubs, birds, lettered examples. 172pp. 9 x 13.
20475-8 Pa. $7.00

ART FORMS IN NATURE, Ernst Haeckel. Multitude of strangely beautiful natural forms: Radiolaria, Foraminifera, jellyfishes, fungi, turtles, bats, etc. All 100 plates of the 19th-century evolutionist's *Kunstformen der Natur* (1904). 100pp. 9⅜ x 12¼. 22987-4 Pa. $5.00

CHILDREN: A PICTORIAL ARCHIVE FROM NINETEENTH-CENTURY SOURCES, edited by Carol Belanger Grafton. 242 rare, copyright-free wood engravings for artists and designers. Widest such selection available. All illustrations in line. 119pp. 8⅜ x 11¼. 23694-3 Pa. $4.00

WOMEN: A PICTORIAL ARCHIVE FROM NINETEENTH-CENTURY SOURCES, edited by Jim Harter. 391 copyright-free wood engravings for artists and designers selected from rare periodicals. Most extensive such collection available. All illustrations in line. 128pp. 9 x 12. 23703-6 Pa. $4.50

ARABIC ART IN COLOR, Prisse d'Avennes. From the greatest ornamentalists of all time—50 plates in color, rarely seen outside the Near East, rich in suggestion and stimulus. Includes 4 plates on covers. 46pp. 9⅜ x 12¼. 23658-7 Pa. $6.00

AUTHENTIC ALGERIAN CARPET DESIGNS AND MOTIFS, edited by June Beveridge. Algerian carpets are world famous. Dozens of geometrical motifs are charted on grids, color-coded, for weavers, needleworkers, craftsmen, designers. 53 illustrations plus 4 in color. 48pp. 8¼ x 11. (Available in U.S. only) 23650-1 Pa. $1.75

DICTIONARY OF AMERICAN PORTRAITS, edited by Hayward and Blanche Cirker. 4000 important Americans, earliest times to 1905, mostly in clear line. Politicians, writers, soldiers, scientists, inventors, industrialists, Indians, Blacks, women, outlaws, etc. Identificatory information. 756pp. 9¼ x 12¾. 21823-6 Clothbd. $40.00

HOW THE OTHER HALF LIVES, Jacob A. Riis. Journalistic record of filth, degradation, upward drive in New York immigrant slums, shops, around 1900. New edition includes 100 original Riis photos, monuments of early photography. 233pp. 10 x 7⅞. 22012-5 Pa. $7.00

NEW YORK IN THE THIRTIES, Berenice Abbott. Noted photographer's fascinating study of city shows new buildings that have become famous and old sights that have disappeared forever. Insightful commentary. 97 photographs. 97pp. 11⅜ x 10. 22967-X Pa. $5.00

MEN AT WORK, Lewis W. Hine. Famous photographic studies of construction workers, railroad men, factory workers and coal miners. New supplement of 18 photos on Empire State building construction. New introduction by Jonathan L. Doherty. Total of 69 photos. 63pp. 8 x 10¾. 23475-4 Pa. $3.00

THE DEPRESSION YEARS AS PHOTOGRAPHED BY ARTHUR ROTH-STEIN, Arthur Rothstein. First collection devoted entirely to the work of outstanding 1930s photographer: famous dust storm photo, ragged children, unemployed, etc. 120 photographs. Captions. 119pp. 9¼ x 10¾.
23590-4 Pa. $5.00

CAMERA WORK: A PICTORIAL GUIDE, Alfred Stieglitz. All 559 illustrations and plates from the most important periodical in the history of art photography, *Camera Work* (1903-17). Presented four to a page, reduced in size but still clear, in strict chronological order, with complete captions. Three indexes. Glossary. Bibliography. 176pp. 8⅜ x 11¼.
23591-2 Pa. $6.95

ALVIN LANGDON COBURN, PHOTOGRAPHER, Alvin L. Coburn. Revealing autobiography by one of greatest photographers of 20th century gives insider's version of Photo-Secession, plus comments on his own work. 77 photographs by Coburn. Edited by Helmut and Alison Gernsheim. 160pp. 8⅛ x 11.
23685-4 Pa. $6.00

NEW YORK IN THE FORTIES, Andreas Feininger. 162 brilliant photographs by the well-known photographer, formerly with *Life* magazine, show commuters, shoppers, Times Square at night, Harlem nightclub, Lower East Side, etc. Introduction and full captions by John von Hartz. 181pp. 9¼ x 10¾.
23585-8 Pa. $6.95

GREAT NEWS PHOTOS AND THE STORIES BEHIND THEM, John Faber. Dramatic volume of 140 great news photos, 1855 through 1976, and revealing stories behind them, with both historical and technical information. Hindenburg disaster, shooting of Oswald, nomination of Jimmy Carter, etc. 160pp. 8¼ x 11.
23667-6 Pa. $5.00

THE ART OF THE CINEMATOGRAPHER, Leonard Maltin. Survey of American cinematography history and anecdotal interviews with 5 masters—Arthur Miller, Hal Mohr, Hal Rosson, Lucien Ballard, and Conrad Hall. Very large selection of behind-the-scenes production photos. 105 photographs. Filmographies. Index. Originally *Behind the Camera.* 144pp. 8¼ x 11.
23686-2 Pa. $5.00

DESIGNS FOR THE THREE-CORNERED HAT (LE TRICORNE), Pablo Picasso. 32 fabulously rare drawings—including 31 color illustrations of costumes and accessories—for 1919 production of famous ballet. Edited by Parmenia Migel, who has written new introduction. 48pp. 9⅜ x 12¼. (Available in U.S. only)
23709-5 Pa. $5.00

NOTES OF A FILM DIRECTOR, Sergei Eisenstein. Greatest Russian filmmaker explains montage, making of *Alexander Nevsky,* aesthetics; comments on self, associates, great rivals (Chaplin), similar material. 78 illustrations. 240pp. 5⅜ x 8½.
22392-2 Pa. $4.50

HOLLYWOOD GLAMOUR PORTRAITS, edited by John Kobal. 145 photos capture the stars from 1926-49, the high point in portrait photography. Gable, Harlow, Bogart, Bacall, Hedy Lamarr, Marlene Dietrich, Robert Montgomery, Marlon Brando, Veronica Lake; 94 stars in all. Full background on photographers, technical aspects, much more. Total of 160pp. 8⅜ x 11¼.   23352-9 Pa. $6.00

THE NEW YORK STAGE: FAMOUS PRODUCTIONS IN PHOTO-GRAPHS, edited by Stanley Appelbaum. 148 photographs from Museum of City of New York show 142 plays, 1883-1939. *Peter Pan, The Front Page, Dead End, Our Town,* O'Neill, hundreds of actors and actresses, etc. Full indexes. 154pp. 9½ x 10.   23241-7 Pa. $6.00

DIALOGUES CONCERNING TWO NEW SCIENCES, Galileo Galilei. Encompassing 30 years of experiment and thought, these dialogues deal with geometric demonstrations of fracture of solid bodies, cohesion, leverage, speed of light and sound, pendulums, falling bodies, accelerated motion, etc. 300pp. 5⅜ x 8½.   60099-8 Pa. $4.00

THE GREAT OPERA STARS IN HISTORIC PHOTOGRAPHS, edited by James Camner. 343 portraits from the 1850s to the 1940s: Tamburini, Mario, Caliapin, Jeritza, Melchior, Melba, Patti, Pinza, Schipa, Caruso, Farrar, Steber, Gobbi, and many more—270 performers in all. Index. 199pp. 8⅜ x 11¼.   23575-0 Pa. $7.50

J. S. BACH, Albert Schweitzer. Great full-length study of Bach, life, background to music, music, by foremost modern scholar. Ernest Newman translation. 650 musical examples. Total of 928pp. 5⅜ x 8½. (Available in U.S. only)   21631-4, 21632-2 Pa., Two-vol. set $11.00

COMPLETE PIANO SONATAS, Ludwig van Beethoven. All sonatas in the fine Schenker edition, with fingering, analytical material. One of best modern editions. Total of 615pp. 9 x 12. (Available in U.S. only)
                          23134-8, 23135-6 Pa., Two-vol. set $15.50

KEYBOARD MUSIC, J. S. Bach. Bach-Gesellschaft edition. For harpsichord, piano, other keyboard instruments. English Suites, French Suites, Six Partitas, Goldberg Variations, Two-Part Inventions, Three-Part Sinfonias. 312pp. 8⅛ x 11. (Available in U.S. only)   22360-4 Pa. $6.95

FOUR SYMPHONIES IN FULL SCORE, Franz Schubert. Schubert's four most popular symphonies: No. 4 in C Minor ("Tragic"); No. 5 in B-flat Major; No. 8 in B Minor ("Unfinished"); No. 9 in C Major ("Great"). Breitkopf & Hartel edition. Study score. 261pp. 9⅜ x 12¼.
                          23681-1 Pa. $6.50

THE AUTHENTIC GILBERT & SULLIVAN SONGBOOK, W. S. Gilbert, A. S. Sullivan. Largest selection available; 92 songs, uncut, original keys, in piano rendering approved by Sullivan. Favorites and lesser-known fine numbers. Edited with plot synopses by James Spero. 3 illustrations. 399pp. 9 x 12.   23482-7 Pa. $9.95

PRINCIPLES OF ORCHESTRATION, Nikolay Rimsky-Korsakov. Great classical orchestrator provides fundamentals of tonal resonance, progression of parts, voice and orchestra, tutti effects, much else in major document. 330pp. of musical excerpts. 489pp. 6½ x 9¼.   21266-1 Pa. $7.50

TRISTAN UND ISOLDE, Richard Wagner. Full orchestral score with complete instrumentation. Do not confuse with piano reduction. Commentary by Felix Mottl, great Wagnerian conductor and scholar. Study score. 655pp. 8⅛ x 11.   22915-7 Pa. $13.95

REQUIEM IN FULL SCORE, Giuseppe Verdi. Immensely popular with choral groups and music lovers. Republication of edition published by C. F. Peters, Leipzig, n. d. German frontmaker in English translation. Glossary. Text in Latin. Study score. 204pp. 9⅜ x 12¼.
23682-X Pa. $6.00

COMPLETE CHAMBER MUSIC FOR STRINGS, Felix Mendelssohn. All of Mendelssohn's chamber music: Octet, 2 Quintets, 6 Quartets, and Four Pieces for String Quartet. (Nothing with piano is included). Complete works edition (1874-7). Study score. 283 pp. 9⅜ x 12¼.
23679-X Pa. $7.50

POPULAR SONGS OF NINETEENTH-CENTURY AMERICA, edited by Richard Jackson. 64 most important songs: "Old Oaken Bucket," "Arkansas Traveler," "Yellow Rose of Texas," etc. Authentic original sheet music, full introduction and commentaries. 290pp. 9 x 12.   23270-0 Pa. $7.95

COLLECTED PIANO WORKS, Scott Joplin. Edited by Vera Brodsky Lawrence. Practically all of Joplin's piano works—rags, two-steps, marches, waltzes, etc., 51 works in all. Extensive introduction by Rudi Blesh. Total of 345pp. 9 x 12.   23106-2 Pa. $14.95

BASIC PRINCIPLES OF CLASSICAL BALLET, Agrippina Vaganova. Great Russian theoretician, teacher explains methods for teaching classical ballet; incorporates best from French, Italian, Russian schools. 118 illustrations. 175pp. 5⅜ x 8½.   22036-2 Pa. $2.50

CHINESE CHARACTERS, L. Wieger. Rich analysis of 2300 characters according to traditional systems into primitives. Historical-semantic analysis to phonetics (Classical Mandarin) and radicals. 820pp. 6⅛ x 9¼.
21321-8 Pa. $10.00

EGYPTIAN LANGUAGE: EASY LESSONS IN EGYPTIAN HIERO-GLYPHICS, E. A. Wallis Budge. Foremost Egyptologist offers Egyptian grammar, explanation of hieroglyphics, many reading texts, dictionary of symbols. 246pp. 5 x 7½. (Available in U.S. only)
21394-3 Clothbd. $7.50

AN ETYMOLOGICAL DICTIONARY OF MODERN ENGLISH, Ernest Weekley. Richest, fullest work, by foremost British lexicographer. Detailed word histories. Inexhaustible. Do not confuse this with *Concise Etymological Dictionary,* which is abridged. Total of 856pp. 6½ x 9¼.
21873-2, 21874-0 Pa., Two-vol. set $12.00

A MAYA GRAMMAR, Alfred M. Tozzer. Practical, useful English-language grammar by the Harvard anthropologist who was one of the three greatest American scholars in the area of Maya culture. Phonetics, grammatical processes, syntax, more. 301pp. 5⅜ x 8½.　　23465-7 Pa. $4.00

THE JOURNAL OF HENRY D. THOREAU, edited by Bradford Torrey, F. H. Allen. Complete reprinting of 14 volumes, 1837-61, over two million words; the sourcebooks for *Walden,* etc. Definitive. All original sketches, plus 75 photographs. Introduction by Walter Harding. Total of 1804pp. 8½ x 12¼.　　20312-3, 20313-1 Clothbd., Two-vol. set $70.00

CLASSIC GHOST STORIES, Charles Dickens and others. 18 wonderful stories you've wanted to reread: "The Monkey's Paw," "The House and the Brain," "The Upper Berth," "The Signalman," "Dracula's Guest," "The Tapestried Chamber," etc. Dickens, Scott, Mary Shelley, Stoker, etc. 330pp. 5⅜ x 8½.　　20735-8 Pa. $4.50

SEVEN SCIENCE FICTION NOVELS, H. G. Wells. Full novels. *First Men in the Moon, Island of Dr. Moreau, War of the Worlds, Food of the Gods, Invisible Man, Time Machine, In the Days of the Comet.* A basic science-fiction library. 1015pp. 5⅜ x 8½. (Available in U.S. only)
20264-X Clothbd. $8.95

ARMADALE, Wilkie Collins. Third great mystery novel by the author of *The Woman in White* and *The Moonstone.* Ingeniously plotted narrative shows an exceptional command of character, incident and mood. Original magazine version with 40 illustrations. 597pp. 5⅜ x 8½.
23429-0 Pa. $6.00

MASTERS OF MYSTERY, H. Douglas Thomson. The first book in English (1931) devoted to history and aesthetics of detective story. Poe, Doyle, LeFanu, Dickens, many others, up to 1930. New introduction and notes by E. F. Bleiler. 288pp. 5⅜ x 8½. (Available in U.S. only)
23606-4 Pa. $4.00

FLATLAND, E. A. Abbott. Science-fiction classic explores life of 2-D being in 3-D world. Read also as introduction to thought about hyperspace. Introduction by Banesh Hoffmann. 16 illustrations. 103pp. 5⅜ x 8½.
20001-9 Pa. $2.00

THREE SUPERNATURAL NOVELS OF THE VICTORIAN PERIOD, edited, with an introduction, by E. F. Bleiler. Reprinted complete and unabridged, three great classics of the supernatural: *The Haunted Hotel* by Wilkie Collins, *The Haunted House at Latchford* by Mrs. J. H. Riddell, and *The Lost Stradivarious* by J. Meade Falkner. 325pp. 5⅜ x 8½.
22571-2 Pa. $4.00

AYESHA: THE RETURN OF "SHE," H. Rider Haggard. Virtuoso sequel featuring the great mythic creation, Ayesha, in an adventure that is fully as good as the first book, *She.* Original magazine version, with 47 original illustrations by Maurice Greiffenhagen. 189pp. 6½ x 9¼.
23649-8 Pa. $3.50

UNCLE SILAS, J. Sheridan LeFanu. Victorian Gothic mystery novel, considered by many best of period, even better than Collins or Dickens. Wonderful psychological terror. Introduction by Frederick Shroyer. 436pp. 5⅜ x 8½.   21715-9 Pa. $6.00

JURGEN, James Branch Cabell. The great erotic fantasy of the 1920's that delighted thousands, shocked thousands more. Full final text, Lane edition with 13 plates by Frank Pape. 346pp. 5⅜ x 8½.
                                                          23507-6 Pa. $4.50

THE CLAVERINGS, Anthony Trollope. Major novel, chronicling aspects of British Victorian society, personalities. Reprint of Cornhill serialization, 16 plates by M. Edwards; first reprint of full text. Introduction by Norman Donaldson. 412pp. 5⅜ x 8½.   23464-9 Pa. $5.00

KEPT IN THE DARK, Anthony Trollope. Unusual short novel about Victorian morality and abnormal psychology by the great English author. Probably the first American publication. Frontispiece by Sir John Millais. 92pp. 6½ x 9¼.   23609-9 Pa. $2.50

RALPH THE HEIR, Anthony Trollope. Forgotten tale of illegitimacy, inheritance. Master novel of Trollope's later years. Victorian country estates, clubs, Parliament, fox hunting, world of fully realized characters. Reprint of 1871 edition. 12 illustrations by F. A. Faser. 434pp. of text. 5⅜ x 8½.   23642-0 Pa. $5.00

YEKL and THE IMPORTED BRIDEGROOM AND OTHER STORIES OF THE NEW YORK GHETTO, Abraham Cahan. Film *Hester Street* based on *Yekl* (1896). Novel, other stories among first about Jewish immigrants of N.Y.'s East Side. Highly praised by W. D. Howells—Cahan "a new star of realism." New introduction by Bernard G. Richards. 240pp. 5⅜ x 8½.   22427-9 Pa. $3.50

THE HIGH PLACE, James Branch Cabell. Great fantasy writer's enchanting comedy of disenchantment set in 18th-century France. Considered by some critics to be even better than his famous *Jurgen*. 10 illustrations and numerous vignettes by noted fantasy artist Frank C. Pape. 320pp. 5⅜ x 8½.   23670-6 Pa. $4.00

ALICE'S ADVENTURES UNDER GROUND, Lewis Carroll. Facsimile of ms. Carroll gave Alice Liddell in 1864. Different in many ways from final Alice. Handlettered, illustrated by Carroll. Introduction by Martin Gardner. 128pp. 5⅜ x 8½.   21482-6 Pa. $2.50

FAVORITE ANDREW LANG FAIRY TALE BOOKS IN MANY COLORS, Andrew Lang. The four Lang favorites in a boxed set—the complete *Red, Green, Yellow* and *Blue* Fairy Books. 164 stories; 439 illustrations by Lancelot Speed, Henry Ford and G. P. Jacomb Hood. Total of about 1500pp. 5⅜ x 8½.   23407-X Boxed set, Pa. $15.95

HOUSEHOLD STORIES BY THE BROTHERS GRIMM. All the great Grimm stories: "Rumpelstiltskin," "Snow White," "Hansel and Gretel," etc., with 114 illustrations by Walter Crane. 269pp. 5⅜ x 8½.
21080-4 Pa. $3.50

SLEEPING BEAUTY, illustrated by Arthur Rackham. Perhaps the fullest, most delightful version ever, told by C. S. Evans. Rackham's best work. 49 illustrations. 110pp. 7⅞ x 10¾.
22756-1 Pa. $2.50

AMERICAN FAIRY TALES, L. Frank Baum. Young cowboy lassoes Father Time; dummy in Mr. Floman's department store window comes to life; and 10 other fairy tales. 41 illustrations by N. P. Hall, Harry Kennedy, Ike Morgan, and Ralph Gardner. 209pp. 5⅜ x 8½.
23643-9 Pa. $3.00

THE WONDERFUL WIZARD OF OZ, L. Frank Baum. Facsimile in full color of America's finest children's classic. Introduction by Martin Gardner. 143 illustrations by W. W. Denslow. 267pp. 5⅜ x 8½.
20691-2 Pa. $3.50

THE TALE OF PETER RABBIT, Beatrix Potter. The inimitable Peter's terrifying adventure in Mr. McGregor's garden, with all 27 wonderful, full-color Potter illustrations. 55pp. 4¼ x 5½. (Available in U.S. only)
22827-4 Pa. $1.25

THE STORY OF KING ARTHUR AND HIS KNIGHTS, Howard Pyle. Finest children's version of life of King Arthur. 48 illustrations by Pyle. 131pp. 6⅛ x 9¼.
21445-1 Pa. $4.95

CARUSO'S CARICATURES, Enrico Caruso. Great tenor's remarkable caricatures of self, fellow musicians, composers, others. Toscanini, Puccini, Farrar, etc. Impish, cutting, insightful. 473 illustrations. Preface by M. Sisca. 217pp. 8⅜ x 11¼.
23528-9 Pa. $6.95

PERSONAL NARRATIVE OF A PILGRIMAGE TO ALMADINAH AND MECCAH, Richard Burton. Great travel classic by remarkably colorful personality. Burton, disguised as a Moroccan, visited sacred shrines of Islam, narrowly escaping death. Wonderful observations of Islamic life, customs, personalities. 47 illustrations. Total of 959pp. 5⅜ x 8½.
21217-3, 21218-1 Pa., Two-vol. set $12.00

INCIDENTS OF TRAVEL IN YUCATAN, John L. Stephens. Classic (1843) exploration of jungles of Yucatan, looking for evidences of Maya civilization. Travel adventures, Mexican and Indian culture, etc. Total of 669pp. 5⅜ x 8½. 20926-1, 20927-X Pa., Two-vol. set $7.90

AMERICAN LITERARY AUTOGRAPHS FROM WASHINGTON IRVING TO HENRY JAMES, Herbert Cahoon, et al. Letters, poems, manuscripts of Hawthorne, Thoreau, Twain, Alcott, Whitman, 67 other prominent American authors. Reproductions, full transcripts and commentary. Plus checklist of all American Literary Autographs in The Pierpont Morgan Library. Printed on exceptionally high-quality paper. 136 illustrations. 212pp. 9⅛ x 12¼.
23548-3 Pa. $12.50

AN AUTOBIOGRAPHY, Margaret Sanger. Exciting personal account of hard-fought battle for woman's right to birth control, against prejudice, church, law. Foremost feminist document. 504pp. 5⅜ x 8½.
20470-7 Pa. $5.50

MY BONDAGE AND MY FREEDOM, Frederick Douglass. Born as a slave, Douglass became outspoken force in antislavery movement. The best of Douglass's autobiographies. Graphic description of slave life. Introduction by P. Foner. 464pp. 5⅜ x 8½.
22457-0 Pa. $5.50

LIVING MY LIFE, Emma Goldman. Candid, no holds barred account by foremost American anarchist: her own life, anarchist movement, famous contemporaries, ideas and their impact. Struggles and confrontations in America, plus deportation to U.S.S.R. Shocking inside account of persecution of anarchists under Lenin. 13 plates. Total of 944pp. 5⅜ x 8½.
22543-7, 22544-5 Pa., Two-vol. set $12.00

LETTERS AND NOTES ON THE MANNERS, CUSTOMS AND CONDITIONS OF THE NORTH AMERICAN INDIANS, George Catlin. Classic account of life among Plains Indians: ceremonies, hunt, warfare, etc. Dover edition reproduces for first time all original paintings. 312 plates. 572pp. of text. 6⅛ x 9¼.
22118-0, 22119-9 Pa.. Two-vol. set $12.00

THE MAYA AND THEIR NEIGHBORS, edited by Clarence L. Hay, others. Synoptic view of Maya civilization in broadest sense, together with Northern, Southern neighbors. Integrates much background, valuable detail not elsewhere. Prepared by greatest scholars: Kroeber, Morley, Thompson, Spinden, Vaillant, many others. Sometimes called Tozzer Memorial Volume. 60 illustrations, linguistic map. 634pp. 5⅜ x 8½.
23510-6 Pa. $10.00

HANDBOOK OF THE INDIANS OF CALIFORNIA, A. L. Kroeber. Foremost American anthropologist offers complete ethnographic study of each group. Monumental classic. 459 illustrations, maps. 995pp. 5⅜ x 8½.
23368-5 Pa. $13.00

SHAKTI AND SHAKTA, Arthur Avalon. First book to give clear, cohesive analysis of Shakta doctrine, Shakta ritual and Kundalini Shakti (yoga). Important work by one of world's foremost students of Shaktic and Tantric thought. 732pp. 5⅜ x 8½. (Available in U.S. only)
23645-5 Pa. $7.95

AN INTRODUCTION TO THE STUDY OF THE MAYA HIEROGLYPHS, Syvanus Griswold Morley. Classic study by one of the truly great figures in hieroglyph research. Still the best introduction for the student for reading Maya hieroglyphs. New introduction by J. Eric S. Thompson. 117 illustrations. 284pp. 5⅜ x 8½.
23108-9 Pa. $4.00

A STUDY OF MAYA ART, Herbert J. Spinden. Landmark classic interprets Maya symbolism, estimates styles, covers ceramics, architecture, murals, stone carvings as artforms. Still a basic book in area. New introduction by J. Eric Thompson. Over 750 illustrations. 341pp. 8⅜ x 11¼.
21235-1 Pa. $6.95

GEOMETRY, RELATIVITY AND THE FOURTH DIMENSION, Rudolf Rucker. Exposition of fourth dimension, means of visualization, concepts of relativity as Flatland characters continue adventures. Popular, easily followed yet accurate, profound. 141 illustrations. 133pp. 5⅜ x 8½.
23400-2 Pa. $2.75

THE ORIGIN OF LIFE, A. I. Oparin. Modern classic in biochemistry, the first rigorous examination of possible evolution of life from nitrocarbon compounds. Non-technical, easily followed. Total of 295pp. 5⅜ x 8½.
60213-3 Pa. $4.00

PLANETS, STARS AND GALAXIES, A. E. Fanning. Comprehensive introductory survey: the sun, solar system, stars, galaxies, universe, cosmology; quasars, radio stars, etc. 24pp. of photographs. 189pp. 5⅜ x 8½. (Available in U.S. only)
21680-2 Pa. $3.75

THE THIRTEEN BOOKS OF EUCLID'S ELEMENTS, translated with introduction and commentary by Sir Thomas L. Heath. Definitive edition. Textual and linguistic notes, mathematical analysis, 2500 years of critical commentary. Do not confuse with abridged school editions. Total of 1414pp. 5⅜ x 8½.
60088-2, 60089-0, 60090-4 Pa., Three-vol. set $18.50

Prices subject to change without notice.

Available at your book dealer or write for free catalogue to Dept. GI, Dover Publications, Inc., 180 Varick St., N.Y., N.Y. 10014. Dover publishes more than 175 books each year on science, elementary and advanced mathematics, biology, music, art, literary history, social sciences and other areas.

641.598 Brown, Cora
BRO

      The South American
      cook book

DATE			